GREAT BOOKS:
100 Years,
100 Stories

GREAT BOOKS:
100 Years,
100 Stories

Great Books 1918-2018

The Great Books Colloquium
Pepperdine University 1986-present

Compiled by Michael Gose

The Center for the Study of the Great Ideas
and
Arete Publishing

©
2018

ISBN-13: 978-1-7926-5650-7

ACKNOWLEDGMENTS

Special thanks to Ken Dzugan and The Center for the Study of the Great Ideas for their sustenance of the Great Books legacy and their support of this project. Thanks to everyone in the Alumni Office and Hannah Dean for their help in finding alumni. Also to Sibel Akyol, Courtney Pereida, Mackie O'Malley, Brandon Oddo, and Sze Chai (Nicole) Wong for their work on compiling and publishing this book.

I rounded up the usual suspects and I am deeply appreciative to the 100 whose work is included herein. The reader will find them in this order:

Derek Sharp, McKeel Hagerty, Diana Keuss, Marisa Lackey, Scott Talcott, Kimberly Logan, Annemarie (Perez) Vanderwal, Pam Hasman Fox Kuhlken, Robert Miller, Andrew Washburn, Andrea Clemons, Curt Portzel, Michael Hotchkin, Bret Leece, Jason Pates, Betsy (Rose) Wilson, Kimberly Yee, Myrna Zakarian, Sarah Karman, Kelly Duncan Scott, Andi Kendrick Wang, Ana De Santiago, Ryan Falkner, Jessica Knapp, Christina Gustin, Charles Park, Ezra Plank, Joe Pohlot, Ben Postlethwaite, Melvin Sanchez, Clay Stockton, Marnie Sugden, John Swanson, Ed Wheeler, Paul Begin, John Carignan, Sarah Rockey, Creedance Kresch, Monira Parkinson-Cole, Will Johnson, Yuna Kim, Christina Littlefield, Jill Winquist Love, Michelle Liu Carriger, Kristine, Kimberley Kirksey, Paulo Rodriguez, Leighton Cowart, Shannon Corder, Justin Schneider, Amanda Tipton, Corrie Zacharia, Jonathan Bakewicz, Rachel Hofman, Matt Jewett, Kelly Pippin, Matt Duffy, Alison Jarbo, Jonathan Crabtree, Julie Jang, Matt Graves, Keith Cantu, Christiana Cha, Joe Hooker, Rebecca Hooker, Kanako Suzuki, Tricia Tompkins McKenzie, Nadia Despenza, Brendan Fereday, Alex Hakso, Travis Padgett, Megan Reel, Mary Stuzman Hinds, Jane Travis, Lauren Batterham, Klaire Korver, Alexis Allison, Luke Clardy, Mark Travis, Scott Woods, Makenzie Taylor, Dylan Shapiro, Hannah Ziegler, Scot Bommarito, Georgiana Gibson, Gathenji Njoroge, Marcel Rodriguez, Cassie Stephenson, Anna Walker, Elizabeth Waters, Ben Howard, Julia Howe, Sydney Jones, Lavin Lahiji, Sibel Akyol, Mackenzie (Mackie) O'Malley, Courtney Pereida, Brandon Oddo, Caroline Sharp, and Jason Cavnar.

CONTENTS

INTRODUCTION

On occasion I find myself indulging in the fantasy that especially as a Great Books professor I may have too much influence on some students. When a student thanks me for some effort on their behalf, I often think of the truism that students have the capacity to find what they need from us, often times when it is not clear that it is there. I often say that I accept credit I don't deserve because I get blamed for things I didn't do. I also realize that as I paraphrase Goethe that without your 3000 years of history, one is living hand to mouth, that any influence I might have is hardly mine alone. The cliché about standing on the shoulders of giants could not be more apt than it is for a Great Books professor.

Reflecting on the historical detail that John Erskine started the Great Books tradition in 1918 led me to the idea of <u>Great Books: 100 Years, 100 Stories.</u> Early on I made the decision only to contact students who had had me for at least one of our four course sequence in The Great Books Colloquium. One reason for this, I am the only person still on the faculty from our first year. Also, I have been our only professor who both met Mortimer Adler and participated in two of his seminars. I am also the professor most influenced by what I describe as the Adlerian method, emphasizing the great conversation about the 103 ideas.

Which of my former students did I ask to participate? In my career I have had a deep appreciation for the range of students I have had. I was limited in some regards to the students I could find. At least one of the missing has been something of a fugitive from the law, something about false identities and credit card fraud, and I remain convinced, ala Voltaire, that it was due more to boredom than any conventional notion of evil. I suspect another former student never cleared her tuition debt. I would love to know what they'd say about Great Books in retrospect. So I picked a diverse group, and one where I thought the individuals would especially have something to say. I also attempted to get a representative from as many of the past thirty-three years as possible. I have not been disappointed; in fact quite humbled, realizing how fortunate I have been to have known, and been blessed, by so many fine people. The great books and great people legacies necessarily overlap each other profoundly.

When I asked our Great Books alumni for their stories, I tried to be as vague as possible with regard to directions. I simply asked them to look back at their Great Books experience and to respond in writing in any way, format, and length that they wanted. I made an editorial decision. I recommend the interpretation that Gose wanted to honor the tv series, *The Good Place*, by referencing their scripts in a handful of selected places. Otherwise I did no editing, unless I caught a typo. (Split infinitives can be stylistic choices.) We kept the font type the same as submitted, because we thought that would suggest the differences in styles. In some instances we changed the font size and line spacing for convenience.

The stories start by identifying the author of the story, a title if they included one, and the year that person started the Great Books Colloquium. The basic Colloquium involves a four course sequence that counts towards the General Education requirements. Almost all students take Great Books I & II their first year. Some of our students finish III & IV their sophomore year, but many others head off to an International Program that year and finish the sequence their Junior, or sometimes Senior years. And while it is "expected" that the courses be taken in sequence, there have been the rare exceptions where, for example, I had two seniors finish Great Books II the last semester of their senior years. In a few instances I had essays written by the story tellers from when they were Great Books students. They are marked and included among the 100.

I also include 100 quotations. I very often gave students a page of quotations from their readings and asked them to identify the author. Most of the quotations were meant to help students recognize the kernel/core idea that the author added to the great conversation. Thus I added to the book 100 quotations I had used over the years. They are not linked to the stories that they precede. They are in a very rough chronological order meant to remind students of the authors and ideas and to reference "the great conversation".

I would also like to explain to the uninitiated about my fondness for Joseph Schwab's "polyfocal conspectus," which is referenced in several of the stories. My advisor at Stanford, Elliot Eisner, had been a student of Schwab at the University of Chicago, home to Mortimer Adler, Robert Hutchins and the start of The Great Books program. Among his many roles Schwab was the first director of the Great Books Extension Program. I suspect my having linked the great ideas to the polyfocal conspectus was not coincidental. Schwab describes:

Polyfocal conspectus is a pretentious name for what may appear at first glance to be a simple procedure. Its unit consists of alternation of mastery of a view-affording doctrine with thorough going involvement in bringing the doctrine to bear as a revealing lens on real, simulated, or reported instances of its subject matter...It is concerned with imparting to students a measure of inclination toward and competence for examining educational situations and problems in more than one set of terms...(It will) convey an ability (and its accompanying habit) to choose different instruments on different occasions, instruments appropriate to the practical situation they confront.

In my teaching experience I have found this an excellent way of describing the Great Books process. Both Erskine and Adler emphasized dialogue among the students, and dialogue with the texts. But they also recognized that the classics had been in conversation with each other. One can hardly talk about Augustine without referencing Plato, Aquinas without referencing Aristotle. The Great Books provide a series of perspectives by which to view reality. The key is in identifying the perspective that best allows insight into the "reality" that one is considering. Regardless of what one might think of Machiavelli, he offers perspectives that allow a deeper appreciation of the virtually daily international headlines.

If one undertakes studying the Great Books, one needs to bring a sense of humor and a share of big words. Polyfocal conspectus is both helpful and fun. Many or most of the stories

3

herein caused me to laugh; my own observation is that the two key characteristics of a great books discussion are a serious regard for the text, and laughter, another sign of high intelligence.

I referenced Elliot Eisner above. Elliot observed that with artists one generalized from the particular. I mention that here because I think that anyone who has read the classics will be able to find their own experience within these 100 stories. These stories not only bring back memories of having been in colloquia with the writers, but also of my first experience reading The Republic in John M. Daly's Honors History class at Mission Bay High School in San Diego. The first glimpse of the light casting shadows.

I have previously written something that I have not found that I can improve in terms of what it has meant to be a teacher of such students-teachers. It seems important to emphasize the potential the students have as our teachers as well. The teacher role is never truly independent from relationships with students. Teachers have a realization that we are guides to knowledge and examples of our own lived convictions. But an even deeper appreciation of what it means to be a teacher comes when our efforts have come full circle and it is the student who has blessed us as a guide, as an example, as someone who affirms us. Assembling this book has been that kind of affirmation.

P.S. With studied confidence I believe that the use of material available in the public domain is sanctioned by The Doctrine of Fair Use. That law recognizes the importance of critiquing public art. But if there are any questions about copyright, we will remove any contested image, story, or quotation. Best regards, m

DEDICATION & GENEALOGY

I dedicate this book to the Great Books legacy, but especially to the memory of Mortimer Adler, the pivotal figure in promoting Great Books and to the existence of a Great Books program at Pepperdine. Thus I had his name printed in bold in the following Great Books genealogy. But I do see it as a genealogy. John Erskine started the Great Conversation program at Columbia, where Adler was his student. The President of the University of Chicago, Robert Hutchins, brought Adler to Chicago to start a Great Books Program. While I, Michael Gose, was the professor who met with Adler at Pepperdine, there would not be a program without the campus influence, respect, and participation of Victoria Myers, Norman Hughes, and Royce Clark (as well as the support of Pepperdine President, Howard White).

While this book is intended to honor all the Great Books professors and students, past, present, and future and appreciate the 100 who took the time to look back and write for this volume, I draw special attention to three of my former students, who contributions are included. Thus far, Paul Begin is the only former student to return to the Pepperdine faculty and to have taught in our Great Books Colloquium. My only child, Creedance, took the four Great Books courses, and did take me for Great Books IV. Derek Sharp was in the very first section of Great Books in 1986, and his daughter, Caroline, is my first second generation Great Books student, currently enrolled in Great Books III. With a little luck, and if I can stay productive as long as Mortimer did, I will include my two grandchildren, Sia and Nolan Kresch, as additional lines to this genealogy. A "good" time had by all.

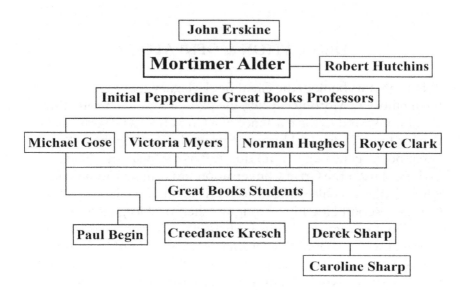

Genealogy of Great Books Tradition

THE CENTER FOR THE STUDY OF THE GREAT IDEAS

The Center was formed in 1990 by Mortimer Adler and Max Weismann in order to carry on the work of Dr. Adler. The best way to benefit from the Center is to become a member. A primary benefit of membership at all levels is receiving the weekly Journal, The Great Ideas Online, which typically is taken from work by Dr. Adler or others and focusses on an aspect of one or more Great Ideas. Some have referred to the Journal as a weekly dose of intelligent reading.

There are several levels of membership with a number of benefits. To learn more and to join please visit
http://www.thegreatideas.org/Membership.htm
Additional information about the Center is shown below.

Mission

The Center has two primary missions: One, to help awaken citizens from their moral and intellectual slumbers and to help them understand why philosophy is everybody's business: the possibility of finding sound and practical answers to questions about the good life and good society. And philosophy's ability to answer the most basic normative questions, what ought we seek in life? and how ought we seek it?

Two, to promulgate the insights and ideals embedded in Dr. Adler's lifelong intellectual work in the fields of Philosophy, Liberal Education, Ethics and Politics. To continue functioning as THE resource for, access to, and the on-going interpretation of his work.

Programs

The Center has and will continue to fulfill these missions through its tireless efforts to provide Dr. Adler's vision, guidance, and resource materials through both live and on-line seminars, educational consultation, international presence on the Internet, access to the Center's library collection of books, essays, articles, journals and audio/video programs. It should be noted that the Center's programs are unique in that they do not replicate other existing programs either started or developed by Dr. Adler, such as those offered by The Great Books Foundation, the Basic Program of Liberal Education for Adults at the University of Chicago, The Aspen Institute, The Paideia Group, or the Great Books curricula now found in some colleges and universities.

While we sanction and applaud the type of programs that these institutions offer as essential to a liberal education, the Center pushes the studies and inquiries further in following the lead of Aristotle who said in Nicomachean Ethics Book II, Chapter 2:

The purpose of the present study is not as it is in other inquiries, the attainment of knowledge, we are not conducting this inquiry in order to know what virtue is, but in order to become good, else there would be no advantage in studying it. For that reason, it becomes necessary to examine the problem of our actions and to ask how they are to be performed. For as we have said, the actions determine what kind of characteristics are developed.

Hence, the thrust and aim of the Center's efforts are not only to help students and citizens to develop a cogent understanding of practical philosophy, which is essential to understanding the good society and the extent that it bears on the conditions required for responsible citizenship and the pursuit of happiness, but rather to motivate them to engage in the kind of conduct in their personal and public lives necessary to make a really good life for themselves.

It is our conviction that this understanding can be uniquely facilitated through a process of liberal learning based on syntopical reading, thinking about, and discussing Socratically

The Great Ideas inherent in the great literature of our Western Tradition.
Manifesto
The only standard we have for judging all of our social economic, and political institutions and arrangements as just or unjust, as good or bad, as better or worse, derives from our conception of the good life for man on earth, and from our conviction that, given certain external conditions, it is possible for men to make good lives for themselves by their own efforts.

There must be sufficient truth in moral philosophy to provide a rational basis for the efforts at social reform and improvement in which all men, regardless of their religious beliefs or disbeliefs, can join. Such common action for a better society presupposes that the measure of a good society consists in the degree to which it promotes the general welfare and serves the happiness of its people — this happiness being their earthly and temporal happiness, for there is no other ultimate end that the secular state can serve.

A Planned Life
Plato's Socrates observed that the unexamined life is not worth living. Our understanding of what he means will lead us to conclude that an unplanned life cannot be lived well. Therefore we ought to seek — a sound and practical plan of life that will help us to make our whole life good.

A plan of that character consists of a small number of prescriptions about the goods to be sought and the manner and order of seeking them. These prescriptions, formulated with a universality that makes them applicable to all men without regard to their individual differences or the special circumstances of their individual lives, constitute what little wisdom is possible for the moral philosopher to attain with reasonable certitude, and that little is nothing but a distillation of the wisdom of common sense.

Categorial Prescriptives
That what is involved in making a good life for one's self can appeal to the truth of two basic propositions — both self-evidently true, both intuitively known.

9

(1) The good is the desirable.

(2) One ought to desire or seek that which is really good for oneself and only that which is really good.

Self-Evident Truths
The truth of the categorical prescription that underlies every piece of reasoning that leads to a true prescriptive conclusion is a self-evident truth. We acknowledge a truth as self-evident as soon as we acknowledge the impossibility of thinking the opposite.
GOOD vs. RIGHT

It is a mistake to give primacy to right over the good; it stems from ignorance of the distinction between real and apparent goods — goods needed and goods wanted.

It is impossible to know what is right and wrong in the conduct of one individual toward another until and unless one knows what is really good for each of them and for everyone else as well.

Real goods, based on natural needs, are convertible into natural rights based on those same needs.

To wrong another person is to violate his natural right to some real good, thereby depriving him of its possession and consequently impeding or interfering with his pursuit of happiness.

The only goods anyone has a natural right to are real, not apparent, goods. We do not have a natural right to the things we want; only to those we need.

To each according to his wants, far from being a maxim of justice, makes no practical sense at all; for, if put into practice, it would result in what Thomas Hobbes called "the war of each against all," a state of affairs he also described as "nasty, brutish, and short."

The denial of natural rights, the natural moral law, and natural justice leads not only to the positivist conclusion that man made law alone determines what is just and unjust. It also leads to a corollary that inexorably attaches itself to that conclusion — that might makes right. This is the very essence of absolute or despotic government.

Mind and Reality

The human mind differs only in superficial respects from one time or culture to another, therefore common sense persons concur in thinking

(a) that the human mind is the same the whole world over, not only in all times and places but also in spite of the diversity of languages and cultures;

(b) that there exists a reality that is independent of our minds;

(c) that we have minds that enable us to know and understand that reality which, being independent of our minds, is the same reality for all of us, and;

(d) that our human experience of that independent reality has enough in common for all of us that we are able to talk intelligibly about it to one another.

The Core of Common Experience

The definition of common experience . . . involves two points, one negative, and the other positive. The negative point is that it consists of all the experiences we have without asking a single question that calls for steps of observation especially contrived for the purpose. The positive point is that it includes experiences which are the same for all men everywhere at all times.

Philosophy – A Public Enterprise

A mode of inquiry aiming at knowledge has a public character:

(1) if the participants in the enterprise are willing and able to answer the same questions;

(2) if the questions or problems to be faced by the participants in the enterprise can be attacked piece meal, one by one, so that it is

not necessary to answer all the questions involved in order to answer any one or some of them;

(3) if it possible for the participants to disagree as well as to agree about the answers to be given to the questions that direct the inquiry

(4) if disagreements among the participants, when they arise, are adjudicable by reference to standards commonly accepted by participants in the enterprise;

(5) and if cooperation is possible among the participants; that is, if it is possible for a number of men working on the same problem or question to make partial contributions which are cumulative and which add up to a better solution than any one of them proposes.

Liberal Education, Free Men, and Democracy
Liberal education is absolutely necessary for human happiness, for living a good human life.

Adult liberal education is an indispensable part of the life of leisure, which is a life of learning.

The aim of education is to cultivate the individual's capacities for mental growth and moral development; to help him acquire the intellectual and moral virtues requisite for a good human life, spent publicly in political action or service and privately in a noble or honorable use of free time for the creative pursuits of leisure among which continued learning throughout life is preeminent.

Liberal education is education for leisure; it is general in character; it is for intrinsic and not an extrinsic end and, as compared with vocational training, which is the education of slaves or workers, liberal education is the education for free men.

If democratic citizens must be free men, they must have free minds, and minds cannot be made free except by being disciplined to recognize only one authority, the authority of reason.

Our schools are not turning out young people prepared for the high office and the duties of citizenship in a democratic republic. Our political institutions cannot thrive, they may not even survive, if we do not produce a greater number of thinking citizens, from whom some statesmen of the type we had in the eighteenth century might eventually emerge. We are, indeed, a nation at risk, and nothing but radical reform of our schools can save us from impending disaster. Whatever the price we must pay in money and effort to do this, the price we will pay for not doing it will be much greater.

The individual may be a good person in the sense of being virtuous. But a good person does not always succeed in the pursuit of happiness — in making a good life for himself or herself. Virtue by itself does not suffice for the attainment of the ultimate good. If it did, mankind would have little or no reason to carry on its age-old struggle for a good society, with liberty, equality, and justice for all.

If, in some way, the generations to come would learn what a good life is and how to achieve it and could be given the discipline, not only of mind but of character, that would make them willingly responsive to the categorical oughts of a teleological ethics, perhaps, then, the moral and educational revolution might begin and take hold.

To hope for this is to hope for no more than that the restoration of a sound and practical moral philosophy will enable enlightened common sense to prevail in human affairs.

The Center for the Study of The Great Ideas
Dr. Mortimer Adler and Max Weismann

THE HISTORICAL BACKGROUND OF THE
PEPPERDINE GREAT BOOKS COLLOQUIUM

"(Mortimer) Adler's reading of classic works of Western culture took firm root when he was accepted in a new course offered at Columbia in 1921. In 1918 John Erskine, professor of English, had developed a reading course of great books in an education program for the idle Army recruits who remained in Europe for some months at the war's end. He gained the faculty's approval to offer the course on a limited basis at Columbia during Adler's junior year. Called 'general honors,' the class was the most significant of all Adler's undergraduate classes. It presaged what would become the abiding theme of his educational ideas and programs for the rest of his life." Mary Ann Dzuback, Robert M. Hutchins: Portrait of an Educator

University of Chicago President, Robert Hutchins sought to "distinguish the undergraduate program at the University of Chicago in certain ways. He was intrigued with Adler's casual description of the Erskine general honors seminar at Columbia College...(Hutchins) decided he ought to begin reading some of the books in that seminar...he asked Adler if he would be willing to co-teach with him a seminar for freshmen in the college using those books. Adler agreed. According to his account, the news that the president planned to hold an honors seminar for freshmen created quite a stir on campus." Mary Ann Dzuback, Robert M. Hutchins: Portrait of an Educator

To the best of my recollection it was in December of 1984 when Mortimer Adler visited Pepperdine University. Adler had been asked to speak on campus at the request of the Dean of the School of Education, Bill Adrian. Adrian invited me (Michael

14

Gose) to attend Adler's speech, and then, unexpectedly invited me to have breakfast the next morning at the Pepperdine President's, Howard White, home on campus. President White, Adler, the Executive Vice President, and me, then still young and yet untenured.

The details of the breakfast were not memorable, but the occasion seemed momentous. Undoubtedly naively, I concluded that upper administration had invited me because they thought I might be able to make something happen with regard to a Great Books program. (I was not completely wrong in that assumption in that upper administration eventually played a key role in the eventual acceptance of a Great Books Program on campus.)

That same year I was the untenured member of the Rank, Tenure, and Promotion Committee. On that committee was the very popular and highly respected former Dean of Pepperdine's undergraduate college, Seaver College, Norman Hughes, and English Professor extraordinaire, Victoria Myers. I have often thought that if the Chair of that Committee, Norman Hatch, had been a punctual person, Pepperdine would not have a Great Books program. The committee met often, and because it often started late, and Hughes, Myers, and I were usually early, the three of us began discussing the possibilities of starting a Great Books program on our own campus.

To make the long story short, the first time our proposal went to Academic Council, it was defeated unanimously and tabled permanently. The interim Dean who told me the results reported them with some vehemence. As it had been for Adler and Hutchins, starting a Great Books program is not without its complications and perils. We managed to get the proposal untabled. The next time it came up before the Academic Council it was widely known that the proposal had the President's approval and support. The highly respected Norman Hughes and Victoria Myers were in attendance, and responded graciously and professionally to the questions. The greatest opposition came from the Humanities Division. In deference to them, the proposal was accepted only as an experiment to be re-considered in two years. Once the two-year, Great Books Colloquium began in the Fall of 1986, there was a surge in students wanting to major in the Humanities. The two-year review became unnecessary and Great Books, along with International Programs, became two of the signature programs for the school's "brand". While I am credited with having started The Great Books Colloquium, it would not have been possible except for President Howard White, Dean John Wilson, and Professors Victoria Myers, Norman Hughes, and Royce Clark.

The rest, as they say has been history. 100 years since Erskine's first iteration in Europe at the end of World War I. While the Pepperdine stories only go back to 1984, our heritage goes back a century.

100 STORIES

Note: I somewhat belatedly realized that I wanted to organize the stories chronologically, rather than when they arrived at my office. And I admittedly did not want to spend the time to ask 100 people what year they started the Great Books Colloquium at Pepperdine. So I consulted my files, records, and the Alumni Office, and guesstimated when each contributor probably started. I'm pretty sure I'm within a year of being correct, but the dates should be taken as suggestive rather than factual. And so it gose.

1986

I
DEREK SHARP

I was in Dr. Gose's first Great Books class 33 years ago, which makes me feel *very old*. Thinking back on that experience today, I can still remember how much the material excited and challenged me. Each week, we read incredible works from some of the western world's greatest thinkers. And then we had to go into class to discuss, debate and ultimately defend what we believed to be the key learnings from each text. It was a thrilling and, at times, terrifying experience.

I also recall the incredible scope of the material – Kant, Hume, Plato, Erasmus, Descartes, Dante, Newton, etc. We covered topics ranging from the nature of man to the concept of morality to the workings of the physical universe. The sheer breadth of subject matter was truly amazing.

To their credit though, Pepperdine's professors developed a cohesive course structure out of this collection of incredibly wide-ranging thoughts and concepts. And when all the ideas of these great writers came together, they created a spectacular educational mosaic.

I will admit it was often challenging to try and digest so much information so quickly and determine how best to apply the learnings to the issues we were studying at the time. There were many late nights and lots of coffee involved but, eventually, I got to the point where I could efficiently and effectively analyze all sorts of literature, grasp the key arguments and extract the most relevant points. Those critical thinking skills have proven invaluable throughout my academic and professional career.

Today, my family and I live in the U.K., where most university students go directly into their chosen field of study. The concept of liberal arts is foreign to most universities here. From day one, students are immersed in their major and, while I'm sure there are benefits to this system, I believe English kids are missing out on some of the fundamental building blocks of education which liberal arts courses like Great Books can provide. I think everyone should have the opportunity to build the kind of "mental muscles" we did through this program.

In closing, I suppose the greatest endorsement I could give Great Books is to tell you that our daughter, Caroline, is now taking the same course at Pepperdine. My wife and I encouraged her to do so for all the reasons I've outline above. And two years in, Caroline is loving it, which proves this program, just like the Great Books themselves, stands up to the test of time.

The Death of Socrates

"He who cannot draw on three thousand years is
living hand to mouth."
-Goethe

II
MCKEEL HAGERTY

Canon of a Lifetime

McKeel Hagerty comments on the founding the Great Books Colloquium at Pepperdine, Fall of 1986

It's August of 1986 and the entire freshman class at Seaver College is jammed into the Smothers Theater to register for classes. The process is extremely tedious. The required Freshman classes have to get scheduled, and the rest of our schedule, the electives, are up to us – our token of independence. For some, it is very clear which classes we need for our pre-destined majors. Some of us are far more tentative. Regardless, we have just minutes to make these monumental decisions. Scratching them onto a piece of paper, we queue up so a staff member can punch our choices into a mainframe computer terminal. With anticipation, we step forward, hoping our top choices will still be available by the time we make it to the front of the line. Many of us have to go through that line several times to fill out our schedule. Each time through the line our options become more and more limited. These choices and ever-dwindling lack of options will either make or dash every idea we have held about our college careers. Lives will be forever changed by this capricious administrative system. But sometimes these strange turns in life yield the most amazing results.

I walk into Smothers Theater with a good idea of what I would study for the next four years. I would be a business administration major, eventually earn a BS, and then maybe go on to an MBA. I never imagined that in fact, I would be walking out of that long line and into the bright sunshine in Malibu taking my first steps toward becoming an English literature major—soon to be a double major in English and philosophy. Not only that but it barely registered with me that I had signed up for the very first session EVER of the Great Books Colloquium at Pepperdine. Great Books was one of the few open classes left. It sounded like literature to me. I liked reading books. So, why not?

In the coming days and weeks, I would come to learn how different this program would be. There was a cool vibe in the first sessions. Under scrutiny, observers watched us and other professors asked us what we thought about the program. Some of the more technical fields on campus seemed skeptical about whether one could learn anything truly valuable about science and math from studying original sources, but we soldiered on, one book and one discussion at a time.

In the first week of the program we were invited to the president's house for a reception on the front lawn and it was here that a wise older professor gave a talk to us about how to read books. "Read a bit every day," he said. He told us to keep a dictionary within arm's reach and admonished us to "Look up every word you cannot define precisely from memory" (It was a tip I immediately employed.) No one else in my dorm had gotten the coveted invitation to the president's house. Maybe I wasn't such a geek, after all!

Unlike other classes, Great Books had distinct ground rules. This class was to employ the "shared inquiry method." All references and discussions about the books we read had to be about the books themselves. No other references or discussions were allowed. No other books or movies or funny stories could creep into our thinking. We would construct our shared knowledge and perspectives together -- and not just for one semester but four. Great Books became a sort of mini-major, and, for many of us, regardless of our other majors, the program changed us forever. It wasn't really "mini" at all. It rewired our entire way of thinking about the world and about ourselves.

Great Books isn't just a reference to the Western canon and the work of Mortimer Adler, it's a sort of calling to something, well, greater. It's a calling to a life of mind. It's a notion that we build our knowledge of the world up brick-by-brick. It's foundational thinking. Shared inquiry, for sure. But more importantly it levels the playing field for those brave enough to play along with the best thinking and writers ever to live. It took me years and even decades to realize that those two years of the Great Books Colloquium at Pepperdine truly started the development of the internal canon of my lifetime. Even in this tech-forward world we now live in, those foundational two years set me up for successes I never imagined. But the connection between the Great Books and my current life took nearly a 20-year hiatus. What the heck happened? How could I love something so much and just walk away from it?

Here's how the journey became my own Hero's Journey, a la Joseph Campbell.

After my undergraduate studies at Pepperdine, I craved learning. I earned an MA in Russian Orthodox theology in New York then pursued an MA in classics and doctoral studies in ancient Greek philosophy in Boston. I devoured reading and all forms of study like someone starving since birth. I knew I would translate my love of learning into becoming a teacher and hopefully a college professor someday. But other duties started to call. I was married and my family's insurance business desperately needed help. I dropped out of my last degree programs and moved back to Michigan to take over the business. It seemed like a surrender or even a failure. The deep thinking and incredible intellectual foundation I had built now seemed antiquated in the fast-paced world of a busy executive. As I started to raise a family and travel a great deal for work, my memory of the Great Books and even my core studies began to fade. Dust was gathering on my bookshelves full of classics. I became the business person I dreamed of becoming on my first day at Pepperdine. I thought I was living the dream. I was seeing the world, earning business respect, making money. I started growing our little family business a great deal. Everything had come full circle, so I thought.

But something was missing. And I knew the answer was somewhere in those dusty books. I was still a reader, more than the average CEO, but I could not give myself the permission to pave a middle path. Business is business and all my fellow business peers were reading Jim Collins and Jack Welch.

Then I joined YPO. Originally dubbed the Young President's Organization (now simply YPO), the group was founded back in 1950 to give company presidents and CEOs a group of peers from whom to learn and a safe and confidential environment in which to grow. As they say, it's lonely at the top and CEOs need to learn, too. Without having anything like a business education, I needed something like YPO, and I threw myself in. Much of the business growth I was subsequently able to create came from experiences and mentorship from other YPO members. We had chapter events in Michigan and beyond. Then I started attending events across the U.S. and around the world. I discovered other, broader-thinking leaders like me. I started reading serious books again. I started to integrate my old world and my business world together. My questions and leadership went from worrying about the bottom line and growth figures to larger matters of human interest. I realized that to be a true leader is to be able to frame the largest questions of life into context and meaning. The best leaders bring their leadership from very deep places. I needed and was again using Great Books in my everyday life.

With this, my business started really to grow (from 5x to 10x to 30x) and so, too, did my leadership. In YPO, I went from a participant to a leader. I soon chaired our chapter and regional boards. I then was elected to the global board of directors and, in 2016, was elected global chairman of the entire organization. The last three years involved over 160 days of travel for YPO. Because of it, I have traveled to more than 70 countries and have met and had personal meetings with countless heads of state and business leaders. Just in the last month, I have had meetings and one-on-one visits with the Prime Minster of Singapore, Queen Rania of Jordan, and President Bush and former CIA head James Woolsey. I learned important lessons from all of them because I was able to talk about truly significant themes like justice, the basis for moral choice, sovereignty, property rights, citizenship, etc. Later this month I am attending May Day festivities in Moscow where I will meet and interview Sophie Shevardnadze and many other Russian thinkers. Boy, do I have some questions for them!

I think I had the hero's Journey all wrong. It wasn't about going from business back to business, it was about going from the Great Books back to the Great Books, and to combine the treasures of both.

Just this week, I gave a speech on leadership to a group of CEOs in Philadelphia that started with an exposition of Aristotle's transitive notion of living a life of excellence (Arete) and ended with a reference to Locke and to the changing notions of citizenship happening in the world today. To that roomful of MBAs, I must have seemed like an alien being. But the standing ovation at the end told me that I continue to be on the right track. I always give books away to such leaders when I meet them. Recently, I gave a little copy of Seneca's "On the Shortness of Life." The Stoics, I have come to believe, offer the perfect operating system for the modern leader. Go figure.

The Great Books Colloquium might be better titled "Great Thoughts You Will Need for the Rest of Your Life." For those two years of the Great Books Colloquium back at Seaver College in Malibu, I am most grateful.

Now...what to read next?

"Fight for you country — that is the best."
-Homer, *The Iliad*

III
DIANA KEUSS

Personal Reflection on Studying with the Great Books Colloquium at
Pepperdine University

Am I glad I had a Great Books undergraduate education?
Wholeheartedly. In 1986 we were the inaugural class of Great Books
students at Pepperdine. In my remembrance of things past (and here
we go – madeleine anyone?), the presentation of a Great Books
education was geared toward preparing us to digest the pivotal ideas
that have shaped our culture, our political sphere and the way we
search for meaning. Yes, we certainly received that education. Perhaps
even more significantly, however, is the way I was encouraged to think
about ideas, listen to classmates bring to light areas of insight I missed,
and realize that the well of thinking and generating ideas is indeed
deep. The Great Books approach to ideas has introduced me to the
value of source-based learning, the freedom in asking hard questions
and the integrity of applying knowledge and wisdom toward living well
with others. And yet, as the conversation surrounding the Western
male-centric collection even in the 80's revealed, we ought not read this
particular canon with blinders on and in that vein not be afraid to
expand our vantage point with perhaps a more worldwide great
collection as some have suggested.

Read the primary source material! I credit the Great Books attitude of
delving directly into primary texts along with my English Lit background
for helping me craft college courses in which source material always has
a place somewhere in the syllabus. I begin one course with a poetic,
question-riddled Vedic creation hymn in which the text raises as many

unanswerable questions about the source and original creator of the universe as it purports to answer. This seems to me an apt analogy for the way poets and philosophers often try to move us from our certainties to more humble stances of awe and wonder so that we are able to see more clearly, with discernment. I have benefited from a Great Books approach to study by being less concerned with disciplinary demarcation and more inclined to embrace growth, as scholars and students engage with each other through the wisdom of approaching questions from different research emphases. The theology student, visual arts student, biotech student, political science student all reading Kant or Jung together and sharing from a variety of perspectives is an unparalleled learning opportunity.

Are the Great Books of the West a false category altogether? I introduce my religion students to the philosophical conversations of the Greek King Milinda (Menander I) and Buddhist monk Nāgasena in the *Milindapañha*. These conversations are apologetics for, among others, the Buddhist no-self argument taken up and greatly expanded a couple hundred years later by the Indian Buddhist philosopher Nagarjuna, a deconstructionist before it was vogue. Greek forays into the Indic peninsula were at that time already 'historic' with Alexander the Great's conquests and remnant Greek communities. Reaching further back, orthodox schools of Indian philosophy contemplate, much in line with the pre-Socratic Greeks, the atomic organization of matter, a search for causation, and whether or not the world was created or uncreated. What was East and what was West? And who vetted the ideas and great works along the way? Much later in the course I teach, students read selections of Al-Ghazali, the great Reviver of Islamic faith in the 11th century who wrestled with the Greek philosophers Plato and Aristotle to craft an argument for the proper place of reason within faith. Al-Ghazali's writings, along with other Arabic writings, are included in the inspiration St. Thomas Aquinas credits for his own work with the Greek philosophical tradition. Suppressed works of Greek philosophy in Europe, analyzed and critiqued by Islamic and Jewish theologians reenter the ideascape of the Christian world as medieval-era great books burning gives way to the Renaissance. Although we enjoy thinking of our current age as the 'global' one – and we have increased the speed at which this globalization happens – it is erroneous to ignore the way ideas and practices, politics and economic fortune flowed along the trade routes and through conquered territories. The orthodox canon of great Western writings is both indebted to and an influencer of the greater world community of ideas. I do not suggest that tracts of thought have not taken unique shape and expression in specific cultural and social contexts, and yet Western culture is not an isolated expression; it is part of an ancient dialogue and rich exchange of ideas and theorems. Perhaps the canon itself should reflect the admission of such exchange?

Women historically often accepted the role of doer rather than recorder (although that was certainly not the case with the world's first novelist, Lady Murusaki, whose *Tale of Genji* artistically records Heian Japan's court life which was not a reputable man's job). Recently, the academy has come under some criticism for over-emphasizing written texts and giving too little attention to the practices that also shape a community. When the text reigns supreme and practices are subsumed as orthodox or unorthodox enactments of its dictums, the understanding of community formation is flattened. Great Books always pushed us to see great movements and significant works of art in deeper relief. Asking questions is more important than laying out set answers and yet, great ideas eventually ought to move us toward great action. Once we have immersed ourselves in the great ideas and questions that emerge from discussing the tri-partite nature of the human, we must necessarily apply that reflection to living into better patterns and constructing relationships of integrity; it takes the courage of a leap of faith.

Participating in the Great Books Colloquium at Pepperdine was a privilege that I appreciate and in certain ways continue in the way I approach learning and teaching. We ought to recognize that our Western canon is a series of voices in the greater chorale straining to articulate the transcendent while living the present.

"Those words stirred within Achilles a deep desire to grieve for his own father. Taking the old man's hand he gently moved him back...then when brilliant Achilles had had his fill of tears...filled with pity..."
-Homer, *The Iliad*

IV
MARISA LACKEY

(Written circa 1987)

I have always believed that higher education has a personal purpose: self-cultivation. On entering college, the goals I had in mind had nothing to do with insuring that I made six figures when I got out. I hoped that the whole experience would instill in me a certain epistemology, an approach to knowing that would continue to help me grow and find meaning for the rest of my life. Sounds pretty ivory tower, I know. But as I approach graduation in ten short passes of the sun, I still believe this.

I was born with a natural curiosity, a desire for complete awareness, which has helped me be a successful student. I have found that truth is a thing that must be actively sought. Like an object which is seen most clearly when light hits it from multiple directions, great ideas gain dimension when they are examined from the perspectives of as many great thinkers as possible. Questions lead to answers and yet more questions, connections are made, and a network of thought emerges. This process is more than a means to an end, it is a rewarding end in itself, for it teaches one to seize life with the unique powers of the human mind. This is fundamentally enriching; this is intellectual food. And most of all, this is what I wanted from higher education. Naturally, not every class fulfilled these expectations. The digestion and regurgitation of information was all that some classes had to offer, and the monotony of this process was often frustrating, leaving me uninspired, unfulfilled. I could not argue that I didn't "learn" from these classes, but the information by itself was somehow flat, one-dimensional, static. Much of it left me wondering if I would ever connect it with anything else in my life, if it would ever become part of the meaningful network of thought I was seeking. But this was not the case with my experience in Great Books IV. It is typically a difficult task to acclimate oneself to a new system, especially when that system requires your participation. I had never been a part of the Great Books method of learning before this class. On my first introduction to it, I was delightfully disarmed and even a little intimidated. I thought I had this college thing wired, but here it was not enough to be an astute sponge. At last, a welcome challenge.

One of my most monstrous peeves with the system of higher education has been its affinity for busywork. I am not against putting knowledge to work in hands-on practice, but I often wondered if the sole purpose of some of these senseless drills was to give the teacher some basis for evaluating me. If I didn't turn in assignments x, y, and z, I was obviously either indolent or asleep, as this was all the persuasion a teacher needed that I was NOT learning. In Great Books IV, this burden was happily lifted, and I finally felt like I was trusted enough to find my own approach to grasping the material outside of the classroom. This gave me the time to read carefully, critically and analytically, and the freedom to form my own thoughts and ideas on the subject. I no longer felt the pressure to submit written "proof" that I was an awake, thin kin g being. The fact that I was an intelligent, autonomous individual was a given assumption in Great Books. It was my responsibility as such an individual to bring to the group effort in class my singular understanding, and my reward to benefit from the unique understanding of my peers. Allow me to elaborate on the significance of the " group effort." Unfortunately, the sources of understanding in most classes are limited to two: the professor and the text. The student is isolated in most cases from the rich variety of intellectual response that is going on silently around him in the heads of his comrades. If he does not gain a full and satisfying understanding from the two available sources, he has reached an infuriating dead end. He has no basis for comparison in his learning experience, as he is for the most part cut off from his equals. Some may argue that this separation sets up a healthy competition where the student asks himself "Do I know this stuff as well as John Doe to my right or Jane Doe to my left?", therefore he tries harder to be sure he will "make the grade." I disagree. As I stated before, a plurality of perspective contributes to greater understanding, and a student's peers are a priceless source for adding depth and meaning to a subject.

This is not to say that all discussion courses, as opposed to lecture courses, work better. It is an intrinsic fact about the nature of studenthood that a student doesn't know what he knows. That is to say, he must be shown what he knows; he must be drawn out by a delicate process of questioning and probing. The student must be gently (or even aggressively, at times) pushed in the right direction or any direction for that matter, just as long as his mind keeps on moving. With this method, the static quality of the learning process is removed, replaced by a fluid progression of ideas. This is what I encountered in Great Books that made such an awesome difference. There was never a time when the discussion stopped moving. If it reached "nowhere" end, it shifted direction immediately. If it reached a confusion end, it was opened up to incorporate other, already discussed ideas with which we could compare the confused idea for clarification. We were never told what to think, so the discussion was free to go in any direction, yet support from the text was encouraged to keep the discussion from dissolving into abstraction. The atmosphere was casual enough to prevent anyone from feeling inhibited, and yet not so casual that it became counter-productive. Again I stress that this is a delicate balance that is seldom achieved in a learning environment. Of course the success of such a system depends largely on the participants, which in the case of this class was a lucky mixture.

My experience in Great Books has given me faith that what I sought in college is not a nebulous impossibility. The exchange of ideas that took place left me excited and interested enough to continue my own examination of the ideas on my own. The symptoms of this particular enthusiasm showed in the fact that I would think about things brought up in discussion off and on all day or even several days, bringing up points to those around me who are not in the class. I would actually explain some of the ideas that particularly intrigued me to my close friends and generate discussions with them to gain even more perspectives on the to pic. That is when I knew I was understanding, actively understanding the works I read. I felt confident enough to explain things to them, all the while exploring and probing the ideas more deeply. I was delighted to find that through conversational exchange, the heart of an idea can become almost tangible. And the feeling of comprehension was made even more meaningful by sharing it with other students who sought the same thing. The ideas came alive in the mouths of my peers and in my own mouth.

At first I was a bit in awe of it all. When ideas got flowing quickly, I was not used to having to verbalize my train of thought and sometimes retreated back into my old familiar astute sponge state. I would sit there and watch the ping-pong game and listen meticulously to the flow, paralyzed by the intensity of it all. I fear that I was guilty of this too frequently, but I suppose that was all part of being new to the game.

Probably the concept that was the newest to me, and the one I most thankfully take with me from this class is the connecting of great ideas. I was accustomed to learning one author and his or her work, then dropping it completely and going on to the next like bounding over a set of hurdles. At most, one aspect of a new work would echo or contradict that of a previous one, and the connection would be recognized in passing. But in Great Books for the first time I was forced to see the relationships between the ideas I was learning, putting them in an altogether new light with each new comparison. This taught me how to gain even more perspectives on an idea, and showed me what can be accomplished by putting on the spectacles of a great thinker and looking at another great thought. The network of meaningful ideas just keeps growing and multiplying, and the beauty of it is I believe I have not only learned through this process, I have learned the process itself, so that I may carry this wonderful set of tools with me and work my way around any new idea like a professional thinker.

"And you made free to overstep my law?"
"Because it was not Zeus who ordered it, nor justice...nor did I deem your ordinance of so much binding force, as that a mortal man could overbear the unchangeable unwritten code of Heaven; this is not of today and yesterday."
-Sophocles, *Antigone*

V
SCOTT TALCOTT

Great Books was vital to my college experience at Pepperdine. Without the intimacy of the small class sizes and opportunity to engage every week in meaningful discussion with Dr. Gose and my classmates, I would not have graduated from Pepperdine.

It's that simple. It's not hyperbole.

Great Books embodies the ideal academic environment. It's not multiple choice. It's not notes taken from an overhead projector on a path of mindless memorization. It's stepping forward into your own mind and finding out what you have – and what you don't.

Great Books was more than just reading and talking. It wasn't a book club. It was a challenge … a worthy challenge. A circle of equals based only upon the merits of your expression and understanding. You cast your ideas into the arena. They are thrashed about amongst your fellow travelers on the journey through some of the most illuminating voices in human history.

You learn from the thrashing. You learn from your mistakes. You enjoy the sense of accomplishment when an idea reaches into a new frontier of your understanding.

For a moment to stand on the shoulders of giants. A glimpse into the minds of the millennia.

Sadly, the glimpse passes quickly. Leaving behind a few precious remnants of an unforgettable awakening.

By the way, the older I get, the more I see the wisdom in Erasmus' *The Praise of Folly*. Even though he may have meant it to be satire, I find myself wishing for the life of a simple mind. Give me the Blue Pill of folly, a blissful absence of awareness and idle dreams of Beatrice. The Red Pill is too brutal. A plunge into the Inferno. With the passage of time, I seek the banality of a summer blockbuster movie. No more Machiavelli. Whisper in my ear a happy ending, so I may be at ease. I no longer possess the power to withstand the searing intellectual flames of the Great Books.

Long may they live in my memory.

"I can do no other thing."
"Of women you will be most unhappy."
"So it must be."
-Euripides, *Medea*

1987

VI

KIMBERLY LOGAN

The Influence of the Great Books
(Written December 4, 1987)

I can't read the classics without analyzing my own beliefs and applying what each author says to my life. When Aristotle states that happiness is a result of perfect virtue, I can't help but reflect upon the many unvirtuous acts in my life. When I read how Antigone disobeys the King and dies for her beliefs, I wonder if I would have possessed half as much honor as she. In the Bible I see Abraham willing to kill his own son for God, as a result I question my own faith and obedience. The great books are very personal to me; and that's why I find the class difficult but rewarding. With each book I learn more about myself and humans in general. We've been studying universal truths. Questions present since the beginning of time. Truths like: Is there a God? If so, does he intervene? Is reason more important than faith? Is there a supreme principle of life? Is truth more important than one's friends? How do we achieve ultimate happiness? Through wisdom; through honor?

Of course, there are no easy answers to these questions; and therefore, I don't really enjoy talking about them. Of course, I do draw my own conclusions; and the great philosophers have helped me to realize the many possible answers.

Each classic teaches me something new and helps me understand the different aspects of life better. One idea that touched me and that I could really relate to was Aristotle's divisions of friendships. His divisions of utility, pleasure, and true friendships made me examine the relationships in my life. I discovered that I possess many utility and pleasure friendships, and that true friendships are rare. This realization made me treasure my true friends all the more. Aristotle also talks about young people possessing mostly pleasure based friendships; that's why the friendships come and go so quickly. I could relate to that statement and especially when he talks about friendships of love and how they are based on emotion and pleasure in one's youth. That's why the young can fall in and out of love three times in one day. The "love" isn't based on anything solid. Perfect friendships are based on similar virtues. Several times during this trimester, I caught myself falling into the patterns Aristotle talks about. One morning I would be in "love" with "Jim"; and by the afternoon, Jim was forgotten but "Steve" was perfect for me. I would catch myself doing this and think "what a bright man Aristotle was."

I've been able to learn a lot about myself from the philosophers; and I enjoy this new knowledge. I like reading what Augustine has to say about God, creation, time, evil, peace, and judgment because these are issues I contemplate about all the time. St. Augustine's conclusions help me to form my own.

What I have learned from the classics is that I have much to learn; this learning will continue throughout my life. The great books help me to find answers to some very difficult questions and that's why I want to stay in the course. I feel "enlightened"; and it's a good feeling.

2018 Update

When asked to contribute to this anthology, I wondered if I could find any of the essays I had written for my Great Books courses in college. I found one of my course folders (now thirty years old) in a storage bin in my basement. As I read through some of my writing, I noticed the comments from my professor written in the margins. He mostly responded with questions and challenges like: "How? You haven't shown this yet. Evidence?" My professor required me to test and defend my conclusions and introduced me to epistemology; it was the first time a teacher asked me, "How do you know what you know?"

I found a list of objectives for one of the Great Books courses I took in 1988. Some of the goals included helping students "install a bullet proof, shock resistant, water proof, crap detector" and have an "improved 'tolerance of ambiguity' and enjoy a 'polyfocal conspectus." The Great Books courses helped accomplish this for me. One of the papers I found addressed how Great Books had changed my thinking. My nineteen-year-old self wrote, "No one can tell me what the theme of *Hamlet* is now; they can support their point and perhaps I'll come to agree with them. But no longer will I passively write down a teacher's omniscient quote in the analysis of great literature....I'm just angry that for all this time I've been <u>told</u> the truth instead of encouraged to <u>seek</u> the truth. What a major flaw in education."

The Great Books courses introduced me to the power of Socratic seminars, and it was the first time I was taught *how* to think, not *what* to think. I will forever be grateful for those experiences that shaped my academic trajectory. Those courses, those enlightening and frustrating discussions with my peers and professors, still serve as model for what I believe education can and should be.

"Hecuba: Though fortune change, endure thy lost;
sail with the stream, and follow fortune's tack,
steer not thy barque of life against the tide,
since change must guide the course."
-Euripides, *The Trojan Women*

VII
ANNEMARIE (PEREZ) VANDERWAL

Experiences of the Great Books
(Written circa 1991)

To be used in reply to "What are the Great Books and why did you spend two years reading them?"

In 1986 The Great Books Colloquium was initiated at Pepperdine University. The Colloquium was to consist of four classes. Professors of Religion, English, Education, and even Natural Science were to lead the classes. The subject matter was to be "the very best, the most powerful, the most profound, the grandest of man's intellectual works." (Elliot Eisner's The Educational Imagination, p.68) Books would range from Plato's Republic, to Darwin's The Origin of Species, to Dostoyevsky's The Brothers Karmazov. Each class had a "core" curriculum, and each was conducted in essentially the same way: the "great books" were analyzed, scrutinized, and actively discussed by the group. Instructors were not to "teach" the books; they were instead to lead discussions. Genuine conversations were to take place.

In 1990 a fifth class was added to the Colloquium. This past semester I had the opportunity to participate in this fifth class - Great Books V. The course began with a review; excerpts from Plato, Aristotle, and the Bible were again read. But for the remainder of the course, "tradition" was left behind. With only a few exceptions, works chosen were not those considered part of the Great Books Canon. Yet the reading and discussion of these books led to important discoveries, for they helped answer a vital question any Great Books student must consider: What is a Great Book?

38

Mortimer Adler, editor/founder of the most (in)famous Great Books List, would have a definite answer. According to Adler, great books must meet three criteria: pertinence to contemporary life, worth rereading, and containment of "great ideas." What overwhelmingly fits this list have been works of Anglo-Saxon males. Some critics have disputed the relevance of today's diverse students reading works by dead white men. In the Los Angeles Times (December 3, 1990) Adler responded to such critics with, "They're all ignorant. They have no background, they have no depth of knowledge, no memory. I would not be so impatient if they were relevant." What is relevant to Adler is that our society is a result of Western ideas. The works of Western males have shaped our background, our depth of knowledge, and our very world. Thus there seems to be a fourth method of criteria for Adler: a Great Book must have influenced and still be influencing our beliefs and ideas. Great Books are those that have stood the test of time. Although they may have been written hundreds of years ago, the ideas in them have shaped civilization and continue to shape civilization today.

As for the Great Books classroom, Adler has definite views towards this as well. In 1982 he published the Paideia Proposal - a proposal to change our approach to education. According to Adler, schooling should do two things - prepare students for further learning and be of equal quality for all. What will do both is didactic instruction. This instruction is characterized by the telling and explanation of problems to be solved, difficulties to be overcome, and connections to be found. More importantly, "the telling should be tempered with questioning." (52) A true discussion is to take place. These beliefs did not originate with Adler. In Plato's Republic, we see some of the most profound discussions ever to take place. Socrates challenges his students to question, clarify, and expand on their beliefs. The Great Books classroom is to do the same.

As a participant in the Great Books classroom, it is easy to attest to the high levels of discussion that can take place. But a unique form of discussion takes place in Great Books V. For it is in a seminar environment that the discussions can cover the most important aspect of Great Books: what constitutes a great work? I have now had the opportunity, in the context of the Great Books Colloquium, to read Virginia Woolf, Martin Luther King, Mao, Paul Tillich, J.D. Salinger, Flannery O'Connor, Solzhenitsyn, and various poets. With the exception of Woolf, none of these were considered part of the Great Books Colloquium Canon. But I have found each to be instrumental in the determination of what a Great Book should be.

" 'This great book,' 'this worthless book,' the same book is called by both names ... so long as you write what you wish to write, that is all that matters; and whether it matters for ages or only for hours, nobody can say. But to sacrifice a hair of the head of your vision, a shade of its colour, in deference to some Headmaster ... is the most abject treachery." (106) What Virginia Woolf says in A Room of One's Own is relevant for many other great books. What would our world be like if Martin Luther had given in to his "headmasters?" What if Ibsen had allowed his plays to be influenced by society's standards? And what if Emerson had been a conformist? Great thoughts are not a result of blindly and absolutely following the rules of the headmaster. Virginia Woolf was determined to walk on whichever side of the grass she chose. She paved the way for Judith Shakespeare's and the acceptance of such Judiths. A Room of One's Own should most certainly be considered a Great Book. It may not be as technically perfect as her fiction, but it is still vital to civilization. What she said in 1929 shaped our world and still has the potential to continue shaping. For what she says regarding female writers can be said for all writers/thinkers. One must have a room of one's own and, to quote another Shakespeare, to shine own self be true.

What could Martin Luther King, Mao, and Tillich possibly have to say towards great books? Through the reading of their works, I feel able to make educated guesses as to what each would respond to the question, "What is a Great Book?" Mao would believe a Great Book should help the group as a whole in some way. He would never choose Emerson's Self Reliance, but he would especially enjoy the writings of Marx. Other writers have also chosen to write about "the group." Mill's On Liberty, Swift's Gulliver's Travels, and works by Hobbes and Locke all describe how a group should function in a society. This is most certainly a great idea and these works in particular are pertinent today and worth rereading. As for King, he would also see great importance in the purposes of a group, but in a different manner. Whereas Mao is mainly concerned with preserving the group at all costs, King is concerned with when and how the group should be changed. "Injustice anywhere is a threat everywhere. We are caught in an inescapable network of mutuality, tied in a single garment of destiny. Whatever affects one directly, affects all indirectly." (Letter from a Birmingham Jail, p. 76) King sees the unity a society has as a reason all should be involved in correcting injustices. He would believe Great Books are those that address the responsibilities of the individual to society and vice versa. Emerson, Thoreau, and Woolf would be great thinkers. I also believe King would have found Machiavelli and Marx's works valid as Great Books, although I don't feel he would have agreed with their beliefs.

(Agreement with the author is not a necessary component of a Great Book) I also believe King's own "Letter" will be added to the Great Books List. It is masterfully written; it merits being read several times. The ideas of justice, responsibilities of a society, responsibilities of the individual, and nature of disobedience are all great ideas, and unfortunately, the oppression of people is likely to be an issue that will always be dealt with.

Lastly, how does Tillich's Courage to Be help one choose a great book? Throughout his work Tillich speaks of the courage one must have in a life that can seemingly have no meaning. "Most important is the creative individual, the genius in whom, as Kant later formulated it, the unconscious creativity of nature breaks into the consciousness of man ... their courage was both the courage to be as oneself and the courage to be as a part." (105) Thus a great writer can be loyal to the group as well as to himself (or herself). Tillich recognizes the strength all writers must have if they are to faithfully address great ideas. For this reason, I believe Tillich would admire all the authors of the Great Books simply because they dared to be creative in societies that were not always receptive to such courage.

In Salinger's The Catcher in the Rye Holden Caufield asks "How would you know you weren't being a phony? The trouble is you wouldn't." (172) Thus two important issues are raised: what is truth and how do we know it? This seems to be a basic question all the Great Books address. Each has vastly different "truths" ranging from aspects in art, to matters of religion, to types of government. But what each writer must do is convince his or her audience that s/he has found some way to determine truth. Be it John's convincing us of Christ's existence, Wordsworth's concepts of nature, or Freud's ideas about human nature, each author must illustrate how s/he came to find the truth as well as prove its existence. Holden Caufield seems unable to do this; does this make Catcher in the Rye incapable of being considered a Great Book? A distinction must now be made between a work that should be part of the canon and a work that may be used to study the canon. I believe Salinger's work to be the latter. It is truly too early to tell if Catcher in the Rye will be relevant 100 years from now or if it is merely a work illustrative of its time. My "hunch" is that it will be considered a "period piece." Yet Salinger's novel is relevant in that it brings up this concept of truth. All Great Books are judged by how much "truth" they contain. Holden challenges us to examine this in our lives; Great Books writers do the same.

Solzhenitsyn's <u>One Day in the Life of Ivan Denisovich</u>, as well as the various poems we examined, have one trait in common: the examination of the human spirit. Langston Hughes addresses what happens to the spirit when one's "dreams are deferred" once too often. A.E. Houseman shows us the fleeting nature of man in "To An Athlete Dying Young." Tennyson's "Lady of Shalott" illustrates the artistic spirit. Jose Garcia Villa chose to address man and his relationship with God and "the way my ideas think me." Coelridge's "Rime of the Ancient Mariner" is an example of the imperfect nature of man, the mistakes humans make, and how we must live with these mistakes. Wallace Steven's "The Emperor of Ice Cream" clearly illustrates the potential obscurity of man's artistic side. Dylan Thomas argues for the strength in the human spirit as he pleads with his father to "not go gentle into that good night." Solzhenitsyn's work does the same. It examines the effect the most damaging physical surroundings can have on an individual. All of these works are important when studying the canon, for we must never forget the importance of our own human nature. What use are Mill's ideas of government or Smith's theories of economics if one does not remember these theories must be applied to human life?

The stories of Flannery O' Conner also illustrate the many aspects of the human spirit as well as challenge how we determine truth. In "A Good Man Is Hard to Find" it is very difficult to determine who exactly the good people are. How do we measure a good man? How do we measure any aspect of man? In her preface to the novel <u>Wise Blood</u> O'Connor asks, "Does one's integrity ever lie in what he is not able to do? I think that it usually does, for free will does not mean one will, but many wills conflicting in one man. Freedom can not be conceived simply. It is a mystery and one which a novel, even a comic novel, can only be asked to deepen." (<u>Wise Blood</u>, 3) The human spirit is a complex matter that great works may not explain, but can most definitely illustrate.

Will Flannery O'Connor ever join the ranks of the Great Books? I believe so. Her works are worth rereading. One must read simply to determine meaning, but one will also find oneself rereading for pure enjoyment's sake. I believe her works will be being reread by the 23rd century, for they do contain many "great ideas:" the nature of justice, of God, of society, and most importantly, of man. O'Connor most definitely illustrates all aspects of individuals, and she does it in a unique, humorous, and sometimes overwhelmingly powerful manner.

Thus a Great Book is a work that should have the following characteristics. It should be relevant to contemporary life, no matter if it was written in 300BC or 1948. It should be worth reading and rereading. It should contain certain great ideas. (see Adler's Synopticon for 102 ideas) And it should have made some sort of impression and/or change in civilization. These four are Adler's criteria. I have added one more: it must never forget the complexity of the human spirit. What has possibly given me the gall to add a measurement criteria. The Great Books Colloquium. Through two plus years of active, sometimes passionate, conversation, I have learned to discuss, analyze, question, conclude, and even judge. This is the legacy of the Great Books: individuals who never forget they are students and who are determined to pursue truth. "For we are inquiring not in order to know what virtue is, but in order to become good." (Aristotle)

The Civility of Great Books Colloquium
(Written 2018)

Thirty years ago, I finished my first year of Great Books. So many names and so many ideas to remember – Plato vs. Aristotle, Erasmus vs. Machiavelli, the faith of Aquinas, Augustine and Luther, and the angst of Kierkegaard and Sartre. I remember the lively class discussions, the gentle (and sometimes not so gentle) prodding of gifted professors, and the papers – I most certainly remember the papers.

What I don't remember is our discussions leading to on-line arguing – of course there was no social media and well, there wasn't an internet. There were healthy discussions, but I honestly don't remember any one personally attacking another class mate – there were no below the belt hits.

And to be honest, no one will have any memories of my vehemently arguing my point or pointing out what I deemed as inaccuracies in someone else's point of view. I preferred to listen, take in, silently agree or disagree, and then express my ideas in a written format. I needed the time to discern, re-read (or at times rapidly catch up on what I should have read the night before), decide my viewpoint and by the time class met again, change that viewpoint. I wanted time. I did not impulsively blurt out an idea simply to be contrary, nor did I hold tight to a point that I *felt* had to be absolute truth.

As a former high school educator and as a parent, I am continually in awe of how much our world has changed in 30 years. It's amazing.

Brilliant even. Our access to ideas and resources and people is incredible. We are truly a global society –I can speak to a friend in India and see her face to face on my phone. I can get on Twitter and find out what is happening to people all over the world. I receive alerts daily on breaking news, my phone buzzing away to let me know that something "important" has occurred. And every day on social media, I see falsehoods being spread like wildfire. I see how one tweet can create hundreds of reactions in less than five minutes. I see an absolute lack of civility in how we state our opinion, argue our point, and react to others. It's an ugly, ugly place.

I haven't been in a Great Books course in decades, but I hold fast to the image of what the classes were to me. A place where one's opinion had better be supported textually. A place where one was treated in a respectful manner, even if no one agreed with you. A place where common courtesy was a given.

Great Books taught me to listen. Great Books taught me to hold my tongue. Great Books taught me to find proof – textual, historical, and in a pinch, anecdotal – but proof nonetheless, before stating whatever popped into my head.

Perhaps civility isn't the best word for my title. One learns *humility* when one "does" Great Books. Having the shared experience of reading thousands of pages in one course, as well as the experience of not being sure exactly what it was you just read, bonds a group of people together. And when you have that shared humility, you treat others with respect. It is very hard to lash out a person you disagree with, once you remember how long we have all been disagreeing with one another. And that may be the greatest gift Great Books Colloquium gave me.

"The most successful people are those who stand up to their equals, behave properly to their superiors, and treat their inferiors fairly."
-Thucydides

1988

VIII
PAM HASMAN FOX KUHLKEN

Down the Rabbit hole chasing the elusive "A":
    an excellent mark for a superlative idea.
Dante guides my pilgrimage.
Flying with wax wings towards an ideal
    with other aesthetes
Craving more than mere excellence,
Onward toward the pagan trinity
    the true, the good, and the beautiful!
Wading through a swampland three millennia old
Back to the deliciously dialectical OG symposia of the pre-Socratics
    bearing tomes from the future.
We recline and drink Dionysian wine.
Echoes of Diotima and Athena!

All Michael's Gose-lings aspired to earn that scarlet letter on dialogues,
but he could be as unyielding as Kafka's gatekeeper in "Before the Law":
proceed to the gate marked "mortal," unless you're a demigod or deity
and dare inquire further.

Those were cherished Great Books seminars at Pepperdine in the
1990's. As a university professor for the past 20 years, I start every class
describing that ideal—the pedagogy of my favorite class…the
cornerstone of my undergraduate thinking.

My wax wings still harnessed to my scapula, I offer this way of life:
questioning answers themselves and refining certitudes (and cursing
Hegel for charting our course on a treadmill—thesis > antithesis >

synthesis > rinse and repeat--always escalating levels on us, that bastard!).

My humanities courses this semester, as in semesters past, were infused with Great Books DNA: sucking the marrow out of life unafraid of contradiction and never succumbing to conformity with Whitman; rising with Nietzsche's Ubermensch and Dostoyevsky's Holy Fool towards unprecedented horizons in this world or the next; the existential anguish in Kieslowski's *Dekalog* film series of subjectively applying 4,000 year old moral absolutes with the promise of a guaranteed blessing.

This is a fortunate path less taken, but at a state school with over-committed, under-motivated students, it can get lonely, even discouraging. My patron saint is often Emily Dickinson in her room with a garden view, writing terse verse, or Montaigne in his study imagining conversations with his dead best friend in archetypal essays. (How many lectures are imagined with ideal—dead—conversationalists...but professors are, after all, present to mentor students. My wax wings retract.)

I want to read, think, and write when I can hope beyond an "A," leaving behind Dante in Paradiso. Shakespeare deeply taught me to relish English for its *joie de vivre* (and how he lampooned the French!) and demonstrated his wisdom in perfecting the five-act format and iambic pentameter to unleash such rising phoenixes as Lear, Prospero, and Hamlet! Aristotle's rhetorical appeals and poetics of tragedy...oh to be Aristotle to a student's *Oedipus*! (And yet there are true masterpieces from my students, annually, if not every semester, and I feel like Siddhartha under my SoCal Bodhi tree with the inner scream—*Eureka!)* (Then why does that epiphany lead to Munch's *Skrik/Der Schrei/The Scream* and Conrad's Kurtz "The horror! The horror!" Mere reminders that my wings are wax and there is no guide beyond Paradiso?)

I trust the Great Books keep us company from horrors. I'm grateful for the rite of passage to the other shore, and for my current role as a ferryman. Gose-ings are free to take a raft--or swim--but we have a better chance of staying afloat and offering guidance out of Plato's cave.

"The unexamined life is not worth living."
-Socrates

IX
ROBERT MILLER

An Unlikely Matchmaker

Who would've thought that a now 100-year-old curriculum, dreamed up by an old white guy and intended to revere even older, dead, white guys, would lead to young love?

Decades ago, while I was in high school, my parents decided I needed access to the broadest wealth of wisdom available to us: the Encyclopaedia Britannica. For those in the internet generation, imagine someone printing out the entirety of Wikipedia and putting it in a fancy binding. Leather, no less, and with gilded edges. In an effort, no doubt, to emphasize to their impressionable son the value of education and knowledge, they selected an add-on purchase: the Great Works of the Western World. I was both in awe and in fear. I knew I needed to delve into those riches, but knew that I was wholly inadequate to the task of understanding them. Those wonderful books sat idle for a few years, collecting dust. Then, when planning my first semester at Pepperdine University, I read about a program called The Great Books Colloquium. I had no idea what a "colloquium" was, but if it would help me understand those fancy books written by fancy philosophers, I was in!

While the series of courses was intended to run four consecutive semesters, I was hooked from the beginning. Three years later and I had taken not only the required four semesters but had participated in a pilot program to add a fifth semester. Twice. The classes taught not only what the great thinkers of years gone by had to say, but also a respect for conflicting conclusions, and even a "tolerance for ambiguity," something I hadn't even known existed, let alone was something to be cultivated.

Now as a senior, I had taken three years worth of classes studying the classics of philosophy and literature that I had admired so much but been afraid of five years before. Over the Christmas holiday, I decided to attend a missions conference with some friends. I didn't know many of the people who would be going but looked forward to spending time with the close friends who'd signed up. I arrived at the airport early, as did a freshman girl I recognized as a member of the group but had never met. We chatted briefly prior to boarding, and our seats were next to each other on the flight.

I pulled out a book to pass time, and the girl, whom I'll call "Amy" since I've called her that in the years since, was curious. I was kicking myself because the book was what I admitted to her was a "cheesy spy novel;" why couldn't I have brought one of the Great Books to overawe her with my profundity? As it turned out, this freshman had just completed her first semester of The Great Books. Interesting. We talked about what she'd read, what she'd liked and what had made her go "hmm." I was smitten. Cute and smart. Better than smart - thoughtful. Ultimately, what I would come to appreciate as one of her most charming traits was her ability to put up with me for long stretches at a time.

We spent as much time as we could together over the week of the conference, including taking communion together at midnight on New Year's Eve. I took up as much of her time as I could over the ensuing semester - my last at Pepperdine - and vowed to keep in touch while I was traveling for the summer and she spent the following school year abroad. We did keep in touch, and perhaps the greatest pull between us was a love of the Ideas, and wrestling with them. Because that was something we could do by letter (again, youngsters, we weren't using email at the time), we grew more and more fond of each others' mind and heart.

When she returned from her year overseas, we made the romantic aspect of our relationship official and were married shortly after. A love of the Ideas, and of discussing them, had formed the foundation of our relationship and has kept us coming back to each other, seeking each others' perspective on both abstract and imminently practical issues, for

25 years. Without that mutual hunger for participating in the Great Conversation, I'm confident we'd not have taken the time in the beginning to pursue a relationship, and without a respect for others' ideas even when we disagreed - surprisingly she and I have not always agreed on everything - I don't believe we'd have had the wisdom to make room for each other's. Consequently, we have always looked on The Great Books Colloquium as our matchmaker, however unlikely that may seem.

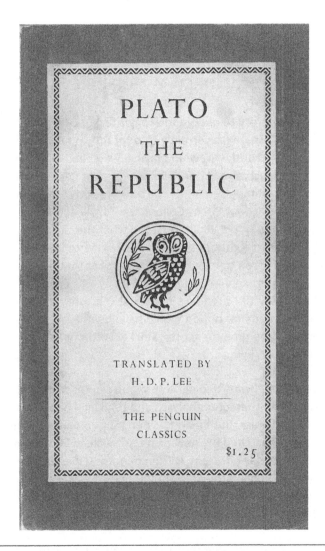

"Justice is simply the interest of the stronger."
-Thrasymachus in Plato's *Republic*

X
ANDREW WASHBURN

A great contemporary thinker (and songwriter) once wrote, "I was born in a small town." That was certainly true for me. In my case, small town also meant small world. I grew up playing, watching, and thinking about sports and not much else. After I was accepted at Pepperdine, I had a choice for my freshman seminar: "Me and My Body" (paraphrasing) or something called "Great Books Colloquium." I will admit I had to look up the word *colloquium* to even understand what the class was. The course requirements: read eight books per semester, write four papers per semester ... and agree to take four semesters. At that point in my life I am not sure I had read eight books *total.* Why was I considering doubling my entire life's reading in my first semester of college? The other freshman seminar option would have been easy, stress free, and leave plenty of free time for sports. Still I was **compelled** to sign up for Great Books.

Two semesters in, I was reading Homer and Dante, writing about symbolism, doing character analysis, and thinking I had a pretty good handle on the classics. But I didn't. When I sat down for the first Great Books III class, I watched my new professor walk in and immediately knew something was different. Within minutes, I was exposed to a phrase that I have been thinking about and using ever since—*polyfocal conspectus*. Even as Dr. Gose defined the term, my small world thought was, "What is this pretentious, made-up phrase?"

After two weeks it was time for the first exam. I had read all the books, participated in class, and was ready for the test. (Pride goeth.) It was one question, something like: *Using polyfocal conspectus, compare and contrast Nietzche's "Beyond Good and Evil" with Kant's moral imperative.* I read the question fifty times. I started writing fifty times. After two hours of angst and frustration I turned in a blank piece of paper and walked out of the room. The next class, Dr. Gose handed back my test with three handwritten words: *So it Gose.*

I had missed a larger point. Great Books were not just great works of literature; they were books filled with Great Ideas to be recognized, pondered, and understood. By reading the Great Books I could consider and discuss the same ideas conceived by the greatest thinkers, poets, and philosophers. Using polyfocal conspectus I could even use one great thinker's lens to understand another great thinker's idea. Being able to recognize the ideas was satisfying enough, but being able to understand them changed how I saw the world and how I moved through it. These great ideas still affect us—me—now.

It has been 25 years since I graduated from Pepperdine. And I still watch a movie and trace the plot to an idea from Aristotle, or read a book and identify the Platonic themes, or see an art gallery's depiction of "hell" and recognize it as Dante, or read about the founding fathers and evaluate Washington's ideas based on Jefferson's writings.

The decision to take Great Books was pivotal. It taught me to love reading. It taught me to be open to new ideas. And it taught me to learn from other people even if, especially if, they see the world differently. Great Books—filled with great ideas, led by great teachers, surrounded by great classmates—expanded my world forever.

"Justice belongs to the highest class of good…"
-Plato

1989

XI
ANDREA CLEMONS

Dear future Great Books student,
I don't know you or anything about you. And you don't know me. But I hope that the Great Books Colloquium is the beginning of a great learning experience for you. I, on the other hand, didn't learn a damn thing.

When I was asked to write about the Great Books experience, I had a serious Winnie the Pooh moment: "Think, think, think." What do I think about the Great Books Colloquium? All those books, plays and poems. All those hours of reading and writing and thinking…. And still, I got nothing for you.

So, if you want to move on to another chapter now, I completely understand.

Faced with this huge blank that I am drawing to say anything meaningful about the GBC, maybe I can tell you what Great Books didn't do for me. I don't think that the Great Books course made me the learner and the teacher that I am today. It was the start, but I was too young, too inexperienced. I was too afraid to get it "wrong" in front of my classmates.

Today, I have two Masters degrees, a PhD. I am a Fulbright scholar. So, in case you were worried, you see, it kinda worked out in the end. I like to think of myself as a deep thinker, but not necessarily a quick thinker, although I am probably wrong about this, too. The GBC readings and the discussions made me think, of course. But with the volume of reading

and writing, I didn't feel that there was a lot of time for deeper, critical reflection. At least not enough for a snail's-pace thinker like me.
I was consumed with understanding what great ideas the author (he, for the vast majority of writers!) was trying to communicate, and I thought this was what was expected of me. Although this made me a good "student," someone who studies well, I don't know that it made me a good thinker. Certainly not a critical thinker, which is what the GBC aims to foster. I didn't think out loud in class and rarely threw out ideas that I hadn't thoroughly thought through.

I wanted to be the one who got it "right." I mean, who doesn't want to be that person, right? Especially in college!

And, I think occasionally I did get it "right." But, it is only in hindsight that I realize that I got Great Books all wrong. So, this is probably where you should stop reading and move on to another chapter...

Still reading? Well, here goes: What I've come to understand after many more years of learning and, finally, teaching, is that this tension, this silence after a question was posed, those moments that I hated most in my Great Books classes, they weren't moments that I (or me peers) got it "wrong." They were a green light to keep going, keep reading, keep listening and sharing. But, at the time, in class, I could only try to look like I knew the answer but was holding back for some mysterious reason, all the while hoping that the sweat stain under my armpits wasn't showing.

The pedagogy of the GBC was sound. Questions. Interaction. Questions. Scaffolding. And more questions: What do you think? Why do you think that? What does it mean? Still, I think that it was this last question that we could have taken further. What does it mean? For whom? For whom does it have meaning? Could this mean something different from a different perspective? A non-Western perspective? A woman's perspective? A slave's perspective? A queer perspective?

Almost the entire syllabus consisted of books written by European and North American men. I think that Jane Austen was in there and George Eliot, maybe. Those questions above most certainly would have caused more tension, but I think that they also would have generated discussions that would have filled some of the silences!

Now, I'm really sorry that you read all the way through this letter. I really wanted to impress you with quotes from Aristotle, Descartes, Nietzsche... but in the end, all I can tell you is that reading the Great Books taught me nothing, except to embrace what I don't know. And that, I only understood much later.

In the end, whatever course of study you choose and wherever your life leads you, I hope that you will ask and answer the hard questions, even if they make you sweat. I also hope that you will follow Rilke's advice, "Be patient toward all that is unsolved in your heart and try to love the questions themselves... Live the questions now. Perhaps you will then, gradually, without noticing it, live along some distant day into the answer"

Sincerely,
Andrea Clemons

The soul includes: the reasoning part, appetite or desire, and the spirited.
-Plato, *The Republic*

XII
CURT PORTZEL

(Adapted from remarks at the Pepperdine Great Books 25th Anniversary Conference)

Steve Jobs, Greek Philosopher

In January of 2000, Steve Jobs was asked by Fortune magazine: Design aesthetic has always distinguished the products of the companies you've led. Is your obsession with design an inborn instinct or what?

"We don't have good language to talk about this kind of thing," Jobs replied. "In most people's vocabularies, design means veneer. It's interior decorating. It's the fabric of the curtains and the sofa. But to me, nothing could be further from the meaning of design. Design is the fundamental soul of a man-made creation that ends up expressing itself in successive outer layers of the product or service. The iMac is not just the color or translucence or the shape of the shell. The essence of the iMac is to be the finest possible consumer computer in which each element plays together. ... That is the furthest thing from veneer. It was at the core of the product the day we started."

Is it true, as Jobs said, that we lack the language to talk about these deep and hidden things?

The Jobs' quote reminds me of a conversation in an old book:

"Since the beautiful is opposite of the ugly, they are two."

"Of course."

"And since they are two, each is one?"

"I grant that also."

"And the same account is true of the just and unjust, the good and the bad, and all the forms. Each of them is itself one, but because they manifest themselves everywhere in association with actions, bodies, and one another, each of them appears to be many."

"That's right."

"So, I draw this distinction: On one side are those you just now called lovers of sights, lovers of crafts, and practical people; on the other side are those we are now arguing about and whom one would alone call philosophers."

"How do you mean?"

"The lovers of sights and sounds like beautiful sounds, colors, shapes, and everything fashioned out of them, but their thought is unable to see and embrace the nature of the beautiful itself."

"That's for sure."

"In fact, there are very few people who would be able to reach the beautiful itself and see it by itself. Isn't that so?"

"Certainly."

"What about someone who believes in beautiful things, but doesn't believe in the beautiful itself and isn't able to follow anyone who could lead him to the knowledge of it? Don't you think he is living in a dream rather than a wakened state? Isn't this dreaming: whether asleep or awake, to think that a likeness is not a likeness but rather the thing itself that it is like?"

"I certainly think that someone who does that is dreaming."

"But someone who, to take the opposite case, believes in the beautiful itself, can see both it and the things that participate in it and doesn't believe that the participants are it or that it itself is the participants--is he living in a dream or is he awake?"

"He's very much awake."

This dialogue is between Socrates and Glaucon in Plato's Republic. My copy was already dog-eared and well worn when I acquired it for my Great Books freshman seminar in 1988. Over the next 30 years it would criss-cross the country many times. I'd like to say I read it regularly, but mostly it just sat in a box or on a shelf until a quote or idea brought it to mind. Like now.

Language. Fundamental Soul. Creation. Essence. Core.

Jobs was not just an entrepreneur or a CEO. He was also a philosopher. A Greek philosopher. A Platonist, whether he knew it or not. Jobs understood that there is more to life than the shadows on the cave wall and that for each object or idea we perceive, there is an ultimate form of that object that represented the Good. Where consumers saw a personal computer or a portable music player, Jobs saw an imperfect reflection of a higher reality. He became an evangelist, spreading the gospel of design perfection. Is it any wonder people talk about Jobs' "reality distortion field?"

Jobs sought virtue in the classical sense. Arete. Excellence. The soul of things. The essence of tangible objects as commonplace as a personal computer. In doing so, he revolutionized multiple industries and created the most valuable brand and company in the world.

When Jobs says "we don't have good language to talk about this kind of thing," he was wrong.

We DO have good language to talk about this kind of thing. We get this language from Socrates, Plato and Aristotle. From the Persians, the Greeks, and the Romans. We get this language from ancient Christians and Jews. From Buddhists and Muslims. From Augustine, Aquinas, Luther, Calvin. We get this language from ancient Arabs, Indians, Chinese, Africans, and native peoples around the globe. We get this language from Milton, Shakespeare and Spencer. From poets, theologians, scientists, and philosophers.

Civilization is built on these ancient words. Ancient words transcribed in dusty books. Great Books that have stood the test of time. The Great Books are filled with this language, but without the Great Books we risk losing that language. And when we lose that language, we lose the core of what it means to be human. We risk losing human civilization.

Robert Hutchins with one of the very first Great Books classes

"The city is greater than the man"
-Plato, The Republic

1991

XIII
ANONYMOUS

IRINA

by Anonymous

Los Angeles. Tom, a divorced dad in his 40s, swipes through an endless series of women's profile photos on Tinder—the world's most popular dating app.

Swipe left... Swipe left... Swipe left... Swipe left... Swipe right... Swipe left... Swipe left... Swipe left... Swipe left... Swipe right... Swipe right... Swipe right...

Tom stops on a photo of a striking blond woman. Irina. Age: 38. Education: British Higher School of Design Moscow. Miles away: 5,967.

Sitting up, Tom taps the screen of his iPhone, clicking through each of Irina's profile pictures. Irina in a fancy dress... driving an ATV... walking on the beach... posing with friends...

More than a little intrigued, Tom swipes right on Irina's picture.

Ding! A message appears on Tom's phone: It's a Match!

A little rush of adrenaline. Tom wastes no time sending the first message, sticking with his customary non-offensive opening compliment.

TOM: Hi, Irina. Cute pics :)

A long pause, then three little bubbles appear below his message, signaling an incoming text. Tom stares intently at his phone for what feels like an eternity.

IRINA: Privet, John. I like your fotos too.

Tom smiles, typing a quick response.

TOM: This is going well so far.

IRINA: Haha.

TOM: So... tell me a fun fact about you.

IRINA: Hmmm. I live in Moscow. And I have dog named Mia Chocolate Amore. And I don't speak good English)))

TOM: Those are fun facts. And your English is perfect. Much better than my Russian :)

IRINA:))) And what is your funny fact?

TOM: I can put my entire fist in my mouth. Which either means I have a really big mouth or tiny baby hands.

IRINA: [Crying with Laughter Emoji x 3]

TOM: What are you doing now?

IRINA: In my bed, reading... Was very busy day, tired! How are you? Is it morning there?

TOM: I'm good. Working from home. But getting distracted by this cute

Russian girl... What book are you reading?

IRINA: I am reading Dostoevsky))) Do you know him?

TOM: Of course you are. You are so Russian :)

IRINA: I like different books – not only Russian) but classic always is classic) Did you read Tolstoy or Dostoevsky?

TOM: I think I read The Brothers Karamazov in college.[1] But it's been a long time.

IRINA: I am reading now exactly Brothers Karamazovu)))

TOM: Ah, good. You can give me the summary. Haha.

IRINA: Why did you read it in college? Was it in colleges program?

TOM: Yes, I took a course called "Great Books." It lasted 2 years and we read many, many classic works.

IRINA: Ooo, nice!

TOM: It was very interesting. But to be honest, I have now forgotten most of what I read. I need to go back and re-read them. Or I can just watch Netflix... Do you watch any American television shows?

IRINA: No! They are much more interesting to read. Absolutely different understanding and perception of the book... Be honest, I don't watch tv. Strange I understand)))

TOM: I've never had a sip of coffee. We are both strange.

IRINA: [Crying with Laughter Emoji x 3]

[1] Tom has not read The Brothers Karamazov. However, he did read Dostoevsky's Notes from the Underground.

TOM: I should let you go. The Karamazov Brothers must be getting lonely.

IRINA: Ok, I was glad to talk to you... it's time to sleep)

Tom googles how to spell "good night" in Russian.

TOM: доброй ночи (Did I get that right?)

IRINA: Yes! Very good! Good night! [Face Blowing a Kiss Emoji]

The End / конец[2]

[2] Tom is still single.

"This unity is what we call a form, something that really is."
-Plato, *The Republic*

XIV
MICHAEL HOTCHKIN

Remembrances of Great Books

I came to the Colloquium accidentally—a passing comment from an incoming admissions counselor—and later became an adherent, fascinated by the evolution of my thinking as we consumed each of the works. At its core—my remembrance now softened by some twenty years—it seems simply a survey of the development of Western intellectual thought. But, it was so much more. For me the fun and the fascination were in the journey, the cross-connections and critiques from one thinker to the next, all guided by an experienced master of engaging dialogue. Indeed, it takes an experienced provocateur to guide successful Socratic dialogue, plus a blend of empathy and intuition to foster evolving student understanding as connections are fostered and concepts elucidated. I was quite fortunate to have had an extraordinary guide adept at the balance of bombastic engagement and critical thought as we disassembled each of the works in class. This, I would submit, dear reader, is the secret to the delight of the Great Books—it is one's teacher that makes the experience resonate and live. Despite the name's implication, these works aren't all necessarily 'great' and many seem a bit of a struggle when looking back. But, they do provide, per Joseph Schwab's conceptual frame work of the polyfocal conspectus, a kaleidoscope of analytical and ethical approaches to thinking about reality. This 'view affording doctrine' has stuck with me over the years and continually lurks in the recesses of my thought. With transparency I remain continually uncertain regarding epistemology and unclear regarding the appropriate foundations of ethics—what is 'right'. I can still recall a simplistic confident certainty in my views as an incoming college freshman, which as we explored the canon in greater detail slowly yielded to something broader, deeper, and more malleable. This journey—this kaleidoscope of different thought, concepts, values, ethics, critiques, knowledge—continues to resonate with me despite my many years removed from study. Indeed, Great Books, remains the only college course that I continue to reflect on.

A few summary thoughts for students considering the Colloquium:

- Find a great teacher: don't accept someone who has the 'answers' and certainly don't accept someone who isn't an engaging instigator
- It's a beautiful journey; respect the growth that will unfold over time
- Cherish uncertainty
- It's a lot of reading but definitely do the reading
- It's a shared conversation—your participation is essential to the dialogue
- Integrate your ideas; it's hard to live an ethical life without foundation

In the end, an essential thought that remains with me over these many years is Candide's exhortation that,

"…we must take care of our garden." "You are in the right," said Pangloss; "for when man was put into the garden of Eden, it was with an intent to dress it…"

Have fun and build your own garden.

Regarding the dialectic: "…seeking understanding solely by means of rational discourse. He strives to know each thing in its essence and does not desist until he is led by pure intelligence to know goodness itself."
-Plato

XV
BRET LEECE

Life is dangerous.
Our bodies are programmed to survive.
Organizing the world around us is critical to survival.
Value systems like religions and philosophies help people survive.
Great Books is called great because it is bigger than any one religion or philosophy.
It spans them all.

And what we learned in Great Books was how to extract simple ideas often buried in complex rationalities. And we learned how to test them, compare them, rate them and sometimes live them. In an ideologically polarizing world, these skills are essential for bringing people together and communicating. Perhaps more importantly, always having a few quotes handy when asking oneself "how then should we decide?" followed by ... "Homer's hero would never!" is a well grounded way to think about life.

And so, Great Books, has helped me thrive in a complex and messy world. And for that I thank the most esteemed Dr. Michael Gose and my [forking] awesome classmates. Jerry Garcias. No, I won't regret this later #Camus

---

"Justice belongs to that highest class of good things which not only produce good effects but which are, above all, valuable in themselves."
-Plato

64

XVI
JASON PATES

In secondary school, literature study was primarily a one-way interaction, author to reader. We read famous works to grasp high-level concepts and supposed meaning. We memorized the ideas of others for a grade. There was a bit of patronage built into the process: learn this and recite it back so that your knowledge may be measured. No pain, no gain.

Great Books at Pepperdine transformed that paradigm by introducing – mandating – dynamic student-led group deliberation. College students of ranging backgrounds and experiences contemplated preeminent works of Western culture and fashioned a point of view.

This was a didactic revolution. Who were we to debate the world's greatest thinkers? We were just fledgling undergrads — no degrees or career accomplishments yet to speak of. But our observations, interpretations, and opinions, mattered. More than that, we drove the dialogue.

The opportunity to challenge modern thinking with our own genius was uniquely empowering, especially at the moment in our lives when the world began looking to our generation for ideas. We gained agency to take ourselves seriously and fight our internal naysayer with new, albeit untested, theories of our own. But these introspections remained valid, all the same. Not just valid – worth examining.

It is our duty to humanity to advance great ideas by inserting ourselves into the discussion. Ask questions. Listen to answers. Live in the moment. Tend our own gardens. Believe in our ideas. And praise God!

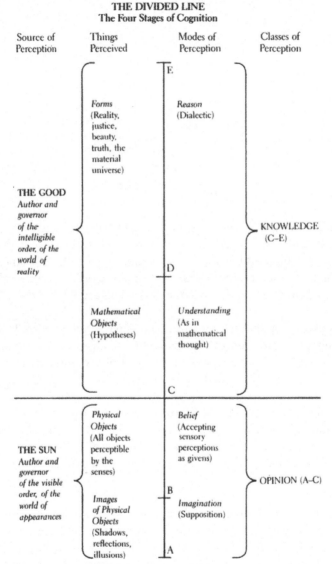

THE DIVIDED LINE
The Four Stages of Cognition

Source of Perception	Things Perceived	Modes of Perception	Classes of Perception
		E	
	Forms (Reality, justice, beauty, truth, the material universe)	Reason (Dialectic)	
THE GOOD Author and governor of the intelligible order, of the world of reality			KNOWLEDGE (C–E)
		D	
	Mathematical Objects (Hypotheses)	Understanding (As in mathematical thought)	
		C	
	Physical Objects (All objects perceptible by the senses)	Belief (Accepting sensory perceptions as givens)	
THE SUN Author and governor of the visible order, of the world of appearances			OPINION (A–C)
		B	
	Images of Physical Objects (Shadows, reflections, illusions)	Imagination (Supposition)	
		A	

Note: Plato prescribes the lengths of the line's segments at 509d–e and 511d–e.

A diagram of Plato's "Line" from the Norton & Company
publication of Plato's *The Republic*

"All the capabilities with which nature endows us are distributed among
men and women alike."
-Plato

XVII
BETSY (ROSE) WILSON

Fall of my senior year, while first applying for college, I mentioned Pepperdine as an option. My mom was concerned that Pepperdine's academic year was too short, so I didn't apply. Fast forward a few months. Our local paper ran an article about an intriguing program called Great Books that encouraged students to delve into the writings of instrumental thinkers and to engage in meaningful dialogue with their peers – a program that happened to be part of Pepperdine University. My college applications had been submitted, I was in the midst of deciding between a couple of top choices, and my mom (yes, the same mom from the beginning of this paragraph) shared the article with me and, having completely forgotten her previous sentiments, asked if I'd be interested in applying to Pepperdine. So, you could say, because of Great Books, I went to Pepperdine.

My freshman year, I entered a classroom of about 20 students and was immediately intrigued by the engaging structure of the class. Most of my classmates were about the same age - an age of independence, when we were questioning thoughts and beliefs that had been formulated through our early years. This class was a place to explore those thoughts – discover where they came from, hear how others think, and question those thoughts from various angles. This by far became my favorite class. The dialogue was stimulating, and I was challenged in my ideology as I began to learn how differently we all think. I learned to truly hear the thoughts of others and try to understand where they were coming from, as well as finding the right words to formulate and express the thoughts I had tumbling around in my head. It was also interesting to discover how great thinkers of the past shaped our culture and way of thinking.

Not only did I enjoy the students in my class, but our professor was incredibly gifted at facilitating these discussions and challenging us to think in different ways. It just so happened that my professor was going to London the following year as the host professor for the Pepperdine London program. Now, most college freshmen I knew at the time couldn't stop talking about going to Europe, especially participating in one of the amazing programs our school had to offer. I on the other hand, had not traveled much with my family, wasn't sure what was so exciting about going to Europe and frankly was a little uneasy about living abroad for an entire school year. However, I really enjoyed this professor! And if going to London meant another year of Great Books with him, well, maybe I'd consider it.

I applied to the program, got more excited about the idea, and then went and had one of the most amazing years of my life. While in London, our Great Books class had a few outings, but one in particular stands out. We spent our class time climbing a sprawling tree in Hyde Park and reading poetry together. These were the people that were willing to open themselves up to each other, listen to one another, and grow together. Each person, hanging out on a different branch of the same huge tree, sharing a bit of something that was special to them. This image reflects what these people had become to me – each of us on our various branches, sharing where we're coming from and learning from one another. They each had a part in deepening my desire to explore how my own beliefs had been formulated, to discover and respect the rich diversity of thoughts of people around me, and to practice having productive dialogue that leads to deeper understanding and growth.

When I reflect on my college years - what I learned, how I was shaped, and how I grew - Great Books is truly the anchor that represents that time. It was the most influential course of my college education. How great it would be to find a place like that today – a group of people to think with, to explore with, to growth with, to be challenged by. Life has so many questions to explore, and the people around me have so many thoughts to discover. Conversations with people that think differently than me are stimulating and necessary – not for the sake of throwing my ideas at them, but to hear their story and their thoughts and to not be stagnant, but continually growing. It's just as important to question my own thoughts and hold them up to "the light" to see if something needs to shift. Great Books has inspired me to listen, to question, to be open minded, to share my thoughts, to shift when needed, and to think deeply.

Great Books has been a catalyst for so many amazing things for me. I truly wish I could be a part of something like this again, particularly in a day and age when we as a society need to be more open minded, more willing to listen to those who think differently than us, more capable of sharing our thoughts graciously, and more willing to shift when needed.

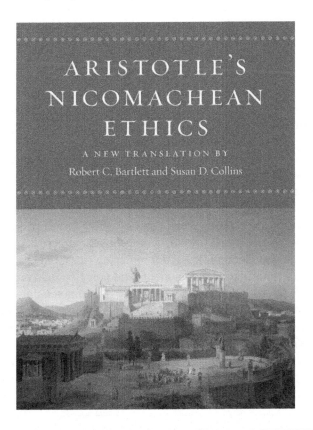

"There is some one End which we desire for its own sake—Happiness."
"For we are inquiring not in order to know what virtue is, but in order to become good."
-Aristotle, *Nicomachean Ethics*

XVIII
KIMBERLY YEE

As a student of Pepperdine University's Great Books Colloquium, I experienced a wide ranging spectrum of historical literature from Aristotle to Dante and from philosophical to political contexts. As a young 18 year old freshman studying the "good" of the city-state in Aristotelian ethics and politics, who would have known that twenty years later I would be serving as an elected State Senator in my home state of Arizona and dealing with the everyday reality of ethics and politics in the halls of the State Capitol? Spending all of those hours in the Great Books so many years ago allowed me to experience the foundation of Western civilization through the texts of literary giants. The experience was not just about reading these great works, it was about analyzing and writing about them. Even though I now have staff members and consultants who are hired to write what my office or campaign releases, I still prefer to write the text myself. In recent years, there have been discussions in education policy about replacing treasured classical literature with informational documents and non-fiction. As a policymaker, I have publicly opposed these recommendations citing the enormous intellectual growth students receive when they are able to experience even just a few of the classics from a Great Books Colloquium, just as I had the wonderful opportunity to experience firsthand. I am confident that for many years to come, students who will be studying these great literary classics will not only become more well-rounded, they will grow in their character.

"What is the work of man?"
"...the work of Man is a working of the soul in accordance with reason...in the way of perfect virtue." "Happiness is a kind of working of the soul in the way of perfect Excellence."
-Aristotle

XIX
MYRNA ZAKARIAN

A Personal Perspective of the Great Books Colloquium Experience
At Pepperdine University, Seaver College

Great authors are great teachers and mentors. Their works not only impart wisdom from experience but they also challenge us to see the world for what *it can be* and reach our potential.

The Great Books Colloquium is a journey into the hearts and minds of brilliant authors whose lessons have inspired generations and continue to do so. For me, the Great Books experience was so much more than an academic exercise thanks to a professor who embodies the spirit of those authors; sharing the lessons of history and empowering his students to forge their own path. Dr. Michael Gose. I am thankful I was fortunate to be one of his students.

I met Dr. Gose when I enrolled in his Great Books class freshman year, and I quickly deduced his class was to be like no other I had before. He organized the class so that students sat in a circle facing each other. He employed the Socratic method to lead our discussions. Dr. Gose never lectured. Instead, he engaged us and pressed us to share our thoughts and opinions on the great works we were reading. This was initially a bit terrifying, but Dr. Gose persevered and with a guiding hand encouraged even the shyest students to find the confidence to speak their mind. Steven Spielberg once said, "The delicate balance of mentoring someone is not creating them in your own image, but giving them the opportunity to create themselves." Dr. Gose executed this balancing act to perfection.

As luck would have it, Dr. Gose was slated to be the visiting faculty member of Pepperdine's London Program my sophomore year and he invited me and a handful of other Great Books students to participate in the program. It was an amazing semester abroad! The Great Books experience became surreal as we read, for example, works by Sir Thomas More and then visited the plaque in the middle of the floor of Westminster Hall commemorating More's trial.

After my fall semester abroad, I returned to Pepperdine and finished my fourth and final semester of the Great Books Colloquium. But I never stopped being a student of Dr. Gose - - or, should I say, he never stopped being a mentor. My senior year, unsure of what the future had in store for me, I sat down with Dr. Gose for a one-on-one conference. He encouraged me to consider attending law school after graduation. The thought had never even crossed my mind. Twenty-three years after that fruitful conversation with Dr. Gose, I find myself celebrating 20 years of practicing law.

In a letter to his rival Robert Hooke dated February 5, 1676, Sir Isaac Newton remarked, "If I have seen further it is by standing on the shoulders of giants." My giant was Dr. Gose and the Great Books Colloquium experience.

"Law is the highest reason, implanted in Nature. "
-Cicero

1992

XX
SARAH KARMAN

Class starts like any other. Have you done the reading? Everyone knows the drill. Each is looked straight in the eye by the professor and responds accordingly, one by one we are checked off his list. No one is late today, no cookies-in-place-of-apologies. Up for discussion is Martin Buber, "I and Thou". I read it. I'm ready. Class has begun.

Dr. Gose turns to me and says he was glad to have attended the second half of my recital over the weekend. He says that he was teaching a class during the first half but he stopped by afterward and caught part of my singing and really enjoyed it. And he thanks me for inviting him. Wait... What?

I guess it's a pretty normal thing to say, this is the first time we've seen each other since the event and so I smile and say "I'm glad you made it!"...while my brain goes down two tracks, one thinking about the second half of the recital, a distracting ringing in my right ear the entire second half that didn't stop until after the reception. I wonder to myself what the second half sounded like, the part that he caught. The other train of thought is wondering why he is talking about this in class...

...but it seems that's not all.

He continues to engage in conversation about the recital, my song choice, the passionate poetry set to music, the paper program full of the translations of these songs in other languages. He is really into it, what we might call "geeking out" over the details of the event and peppering me with questions that draw me away from my self-conscious pondering about the odd timing of this discussion and into the conversation itself until I'm sort of "geeking out" too.

I feel a sense of pride in my accomplishment and more importantly that the music I'd worked so hard to select matters to someone. The feelings override my self-consciousness of discussing this publicly. While I'm thinking I was pretty pleased with my song choice -- having researched unusual songs that aren't part of the usual repertoire -- I am also beginning to notice an uncomfortable shift in the room. Students move in their seats, someone lets out a sigh; the atmosphere has turned slightly hostile.

Dear professor, he probably has no idea about the lifetime of teachers who've made me their pet. Flashes of memories, stumbling through the social awkwardness of being singled out float to the surface of my consciousness...this is not something new to me and as the conversation about my recital continues on, and on... a little too long now, I start to grow uncomfortable. Not because there is anything inappropriate in the conversation itself, it's just the timing, after the proverbial bell has rung, all are assembled, roll has been called. It is the growing sense of the crowd of eager students around us trying to glean any wisdom from what is being said, their demeanor more and more frustrated and confused as to the relevance of this part of class, and the emotional and social toll this will take on me. I can already feel it.

On the other hand, this is sort of unexpected from this professor, unusual that he would take class time to discuss anything other than the literature. Needless to say, by this time my radar is up on high alert: What is going on?

It becomes too much for someone. Possibly as much as 5 minutes or more has passed and he just can't take it anymore. Not only is he having his valuable time consumed with a conversation that doesn't seem relevant to anything resembling why he signed up for this class, nothing to do with his GPA, but probably more important: this discussion doesn't include him. "Um, what does this have to do with anything?" he asks impatiently.

Finally the wheels in my head slam into gear. All the self-consciousness drops away as the situation slides into focus, and the topic for today rolls back into view... I start to speak, realizing my eyes are locked on Professor Gose for confirmation, which he gives me with a glint of his eye. It's hard to pull my gaze from where they have been subconsciously locked on Dr. Gose up to this point, having tried to sort out the situation with every fiber of my emotion and intellect.

"It's like in the book, 'I and Thou'," I say, addressing the class, and at some additional signal of assent from Dr. Gose, at long last I withdraw my eyes from him to look at my classmates. "He's SHOWing you an example of what we've read, rather than just talking about it. My recital is a shared experience that Dr. Gose can talk about with me, a connection, if you will, that wouldn't make sense to anyone outside of that experience. I can feel it, and I imagine Dr. Gose feels it too, but you all are not experiencing the connection because we are talking about something that you didn't experience. It's the 'craning of the neck' when a cat looks at you as if for a moment it understands. It can only be understood by experience which is likely why Buber talks about a cat, because most people have experience with cats. What he writes about is not actually about cats at all, though, it is about our connection with God which can only really be understood through experience."

Flash forward a year. I've been driving long distance after graduation, from my home town on the east side, all the way back to Pepperdine to study Voice with another college professor, a very talented opera singer and Classical Voice instructor. I run into Dr. Gose on the track as he is going for a walk and so I start walking with him. I tell him what I've been doing since graduation and he says to me "I always thought you would sing something more like Celine Dion. Your singing is so passionate." It is a different way of looking at what I've always known. It is a profound statement, not that I'd ever seek a career like Celine Dion specifically, but rather, to sing my own music with passion, to sing something more accessible to the modern ear... and that one sentence sets me on a different path because I know what he is saying. So I start on writing songs again, throwing myself into it full force, and singing out of who I am.

That was the last time I saw Dr. Gose but the effects have gone on well beyond that moment.

Today I seek to hear God's voice speak to me directly in quiet moments... heart to heart. However, there were many moments throughout my life when God has put someone in my path, often someone who didn't know me very well, and God spoke through them. He has met me, heart to heart, in places like the track at Pepperdine, and changed my path. I think it is actually thru the people we don't know really well that God can speak best. If they hit on something they couldn't possibly know about you, it changes you... we call that a "Word" in the Pentacostal tradition. Someone speaks the unknowable to you and you know God is in it for how it lands, how it impacts you. Like the world around is less random for a moment and rather uniquely orchestrated, and we all play our part.

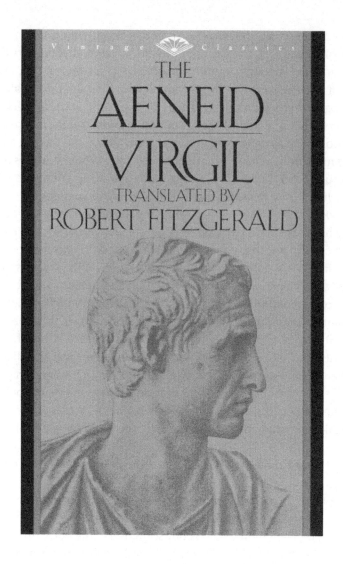

"But you, Roman, remember, rule with all your power
The peoples of the earth — these will be your arts:
To put your stamp on the works and ways of peace,
To spare the defeated, break the proud in war."
-Virgil, *The Aeneid*

XXI
KELLY DUNCAN SCOTT

The Great Books Colloquium had a profound impact on me, and it is still a series of classes that I remember from my time at Pepperdine, nearly 25 years ago. As an incoming college freshman, I had some familiarity with the ancient works of Plato, Virgil, Aristotle and others, but I am certain I had no actual plan as to why I wanted to embark on these courses. As it turned out, the Great Books Colloquium was a remarkable open forum for sharing ideas, intellectual growth and academic rigor.

The format of the Great Books classes taught in the Socratic Method was the ideal preparation for law school, which focuses primarily on teaching students how to think critically. The Great Books tradition readied me for law school study and serious thinking about not only the rule of law but the philosophy of law.

Today I am a prosecutor representing the People of the State of California. A prosecutor holds a great deal of power in the criminal justice system. He or she decides which cases will be filed, what charges will be brought, who will be punished, and how will they be punished for a crime. It is often said that a prosecutor's job is to seek justice. But what is justice and what is "doing the right thing" in the criminal justice system? I think about these philosophical questions often when deciding whether to file charges - how will the community be affected by this case, how can we bring restitution to this victim, and how should a defendant be punished? It is not just a matter of applying the law, but a decision about what is just and equitable for the victims, defendants and the community. The great thinkers considered these same issues of

77

justice, the law and morality, and I know that my early training at Pepperdine in the Great Books tradition taught me how to think deeply about these important questions.

"Justice in the life and conduct of the State is possible only as it first resides in the hearts and souls of the citizens." - Plato

---

"Be not perturbed, for all things are according to the nature of the universal..."
-Marcus Aurelius

XXII
ANDI KENDRICK WANG

GBC *circa* 1993 – La Guernica.

So, through four semesters of the Great Books Colloquium at Pepperdine in the early nineties, the most influential subject of study for me was, no, not a book, but a painting. When we entered class that day, the chairs were moved so that they were arranged in a circle as usual, but this day there was a projector which displayed a large mural copy of a painting of horses and people, dark, gray muddled colors. Today we would be reviewing the painting, not a book.

The GBC was unique. I recognized that because while my friends were taking English 101 in an amphitheater with hundreds of students, I was subjecting myself to Socratic attention, one row of circular seats, maybe 15 students. There was no hiding in this class. You either did your homework, or you didn't; but if you didn't, there was no hiding it. You were going to get skewered by the teacher. I didn't like to read back then. And yes, I was challenged. I was challenged because the professor cared; more than the literature, it was a life lesson in responsibility. I failed in a lot of ways in that regard at the time, but the message sunk in and I attribute a lot of my success in life today to Professor Gose and the other professors who were not ok with a student shirking that responsibility.

The profoundness of this painting still hits me today. It was political no doubt. It was emotional. It is an art object. Books, they are art objects. Maybe not so much non-fiction. But certainly fiction. Historical fiction, well that's what La Guernica was to me. It was a political statement in 1937, and some say led to the end of the Spanish civil war. I was able to view La Guernica years after we studied it in that class. I was in law school, doing a semester abroad in London. I went to Madrid and I remember the grandness of the painting at Museo Reina Sofia. In person, it's an impactful art object. It's huge. It's dark. It's sad. It's motivating. It immediately triggered memories of spending an hour studying it almost eight years earlier. And we really studied it. We studied the symbolism of the horse and the bull. The horse was the people, the bull a destroyer. Or something like that. Whatever the symbolism, the anguish was palpable.

This painting is as relevant today as it was when it was painted in 1937 by Mr. Picasso. Bombs falling from the sky on civilians in Spain in 1937. Bombs falling from the sky on civilians in Ghouta, Syria in 2018 (or just fill in the City and Year of your choice). You read CNN and it seems like bombs fall on civilians every day. Civil war. Foreign invaders dropping bombs. Guerilla groups bombing civilians. All are present now. Has anything really changed? I don't think so. And, just like in Picasso's time, art is present now for those who are open to its meanings; present to interpret, symbolize, analyze, to provoke emotion or outrage, whether it be Ai Weiei, or Banksy. Art for many people, including myself, strikes the emotional strings that books or other forms of communication do not, and in many ways that one day in GBC class solidified that for me.

GBC taught me that boxes are meant to be broken down, borders breached, limits expanded, and ultimately was the most influential class I've taken in my life. I know that.

Vanity of vanities, saith the Preacher, vanity of vanities; all is vanity.
-*Ecclesiastes*

1994

XXIII
ANA DE SANTIAGO

"The Joy of Recognition Surpasses the Joy of Surprise." This phrase often repeated during Great Books class by Dr. Michael Gose has stuck with me for over 24 years. The Great Books Colloquium was the most formative and thought changing course of my college experience. It opened a parallel universe for me, where everything I thought I knew was exposed to deeper exploration, analysis and understanding. The seminar discussions helped me to be receptive to ideas and concepts that were foreign to me. These ideas and concept variations kept coming up time and time again in different books and discussions. What at first was foreign, slowly and sometimes painfully, became familiar ideas that propelled me to seek out a broader understanding of the world around me. Almost a quarter century later, the joy in recognizing these great ideas in current politics, social movements, work or in my everyday life, bring me the same great joy and satisfaction as in greeting an old friend.

Professionally, I can think of no better preparation or training to a legal career than by having taken the Great Books Colloquium. The analytical skills I learned proved invaluable in Law School and greatly prepared me for a legal career as a criminal prosecutor. I can think of no better training than becoming comfortable with the Socratic method in a classroom setting, the demanding reading load, and the critical writing component expected of Great Books students. Losing the fear of expressing a critical thought, backed up by literary references, to make my point during class was my first experience into oral advocacy. Being able to express my thoughts and arguments in a concise, critical and persuasive way, was truly a great introduction to what I later learned in law school to be as the "IRAC" method of legal writing. (Issue, Rule, Application, Conclusion.)

Personally, I remain immensely grateful for the opportunity to be part of the Great Books experience. I still chuckle every time I have an "aha!" moment and continue find immense joy in recognizing the great ideas that keep popping up in everyday life. I just wish I had a better memory to remember all those wonderful quotes! But maybe, I just don't know what I think I know. Then again, I am not old enough yet to be the Philosopher King.

How beautiful you are my love.
Solomon, *Song of Songs*

XXIV
RYAN FALKNER

Dear Dr. Gose,

I'm writing you this letter about the process of writing my submission for what taking part in a Great Books curriculum has meant for me as a way of writing my submission. My hope is that in doing so this way I will make for a more authentic and honest assessment of my experience.

You see, my first thought was to use a quote from a luminary past to begin my message because what better way to sound erudite and set a tone of intellectual reverence than by connecting my message to a great historical mind? This way, I could prove in a concrete sense, just how impactful the curriculum was to the formation of my intellect and how it has built a foundation of knowledge from which I constantly draw for understanding the world. Either that, or at least I could prove that I am a lot of fun at dinner parties.

Thinking more upon it, however, I imagine that you're going to get a lot of impressive quotes to start off astute and well crafted messages of support for the curriculum. And frankly, I must admit that no great literary or philosophical expression of yore comes to mind and I refuse to turn to Google for help in the matter. Does this mean that Great Books has failed me? If I can't remember any of Pythagoras' great dictums off the top of my head or the cleverest quips of Mark Twain's, what has the curriculum really accomplished?

The answer to that question is much more than a surface glance would reveal. Far more important than rote memory of important passages and who wrote them is the ability to think critically. It has been over twenty years since I graduated from college and as sad as it may sound much of the learning that took place has faded from my memory. However, what has remained is a framework for being able to apply context to raw information, understand multiple viewpoints and a conditioning to search for deeper meaning. The ability to contextualize information, to have reference points for where certain ideas have originated has given me an incredible sense of confidence as I have navigated my way through life. That which the curriculum taught me stays with me as I read the news, helping me discern between fake and real, relevant and irrelevant. It helps me think "big picture" or step back from hot button issues in order to see them more clearly and it helps me to frame complex ideas and human behavior in ways that make them easier to digest and explain. Most important of all, the curriculum has helped foster a love of learning.

I remember you stating in your class that to understand much of what separates the ideologies of the Right and the Left in our country is to know the philosophy of Burke versus that of Mill. This bit of perspective has come in handy many times as I have sought to explain the motives of segments of the population to others. Recalling Buber, I am reminded of how revelatory it was to be given the tools to reframe primitive tribalism so common still into the idea of oneness.

Being blessed with the knowledge afforded to me from reading all of those great minds has in some ways helped give me a sense of purpose. It is both humbling and encouraging to read from the canon of master works of literature and thought. To do so, while I haven't thought about it all that much until now, has perhaps contributed to a feeling of responsibility. On one hand, I feel a certain responsibility to impart what I have learned to others. On the other hand, I struggle with how best to do so and whether I am capable of being a good vessel for educating or enlightening. Perhaps, the message contained in this letter is my best opportunity to impart just how important and useful the Great Books tradition was for me and must continue to be for the next student. With that, I hope that this letter serves you and your goal well.

Sincerely,
Ryan Falkner

"But let justice roll down like waters, and righteousness like an ever-flowing stream."
-Amos

XXV
JESSICA KNAPP

I fell in love with Humpback whales when I was in fourth grade and PBS aired *The Voyage of the Mimi*. I was fascinated by these amazing creatures. Since then I have traveled around the world dragging my husband whale watching; hoping to catch a glimpse of these magnificent creatures leaping out of the water. I have spent countless hours listening to humpback whale songs. They are beautifully haunting.

In studying humpback whale songs biologists have learned that there are some songs which are shared throughout the population of humpback whales in a particular area. Although different individuals join in the singing, they all share in the same song. Each whale participates in the song not as an individual but as a member of the community acknowledging the melody that was established before.

Like the humpback whales, humans have underlying melodies in our language and communication. In college I lived in Italy for three semesters. While studying Italian, I began to realize native Italian speakers knew this lyrical song and if I could just hear the song in my ears I would be able to know the correct rhythm and intonation as I spoke. I learned a lot of Italian vocabulary, but I had to be immersed in the language listening to native speakers and hearing their conversations to hear the song.

Although the languages are different around the world, the themes we wrestle with and the ideas we explore are universal. Kibbe suggests that when academics write we are joining a conversation that has been taking place for centuries. This metaphor then guides his instruction for writing. One must first seek to understand the conversation, by listening/reading what has been written on the topic. Great Books teaches us that this metaphor is valid not just for academics, but the conversations we wrestle with are part of a larger dialog. Like the humpback whales, each individual adds to the conversation in their own way, but the song is communal. How we come to understand justice, truth, honor, shame, God, purpose, peace, and love is shaped by how our culture before us understood these giant themes. Western or eastern, rational or passionate, elements of truth based on rules of logic all influence the views we hold. We can choose to be ignorant of those forces which shape our ideas, or we can read, write and discuss the great books and come to a deeper understanding of our cultural milieu.

My great books reading has deeply affected my perspective on life. It is not uncommon for me to encounter a situation where is seems totally appropriate to reference Plato's Cave Allegory. I left Pepperdine and headed for graduate school for a PhD in Mathematics. Graduate school was a good place to have deep conversations about truth. I kept my great books on my office shelf. I often referred to Descartes, Locke, Plato, Aristotle, and Euclid. My interests in truth, what is true, how we know, find, or prove truth became the foundation for my dissertation. I studied the development of proof writing among undergraduate mathematics majors.

I continued to use my great books experiences as a professor, asking students to write about historical ideas in mathematics as part of their coursework. In my experience as an educator, when Calculus students read Newton and Leibnitz, when they understand the politics which led Newton to be considered the father of calculus even though we use Leibnitz's ideas, they have a better appreciation for their development and experiences over the course of the semester. These students can now have an informed dialogue on the contributions of mathematicians to the field. More importantly, they begin to see themselves as students of mathematics rather than identifying as a student who happens to be taking a mathematics course.

In 2012 I left the academic world on a journey to find my calling and purpose. Although I was no longer steeped in the common academic dialogue, I still found my great books reading to be helpful. In today's climate it is difficult to avoid discussions on the political divide of our country. Understanding how we arrived at our form of government requires a discussion of Rousseau, Kant, Locke as well as the writings of the founding fathers. Realizing that although we may not like the current government, we could do much worse as evidenced by Machiavelli's

Prince or reading the recent history of China through *Wild Swans: Three Daughters of China.*

Beyond politics, the lens with which we read scripture is painted with the strokes from the great books. In the first century the early church fought the Gnostics who denied the deity of Jesus and believed that fleshly things (of the earth) were bad and only spiritual things were Godly. Today, the modern evangelical movement typically espouses a perspective of scripture and heaven that is consistent with Gnostics. We read Paul and are convinced that he means flesh is bad in Romans 8. But it is not Paul who provided our understanding of the afterlife this way. It was Plato. When we begin to look at scripture with more critical eyes, seeking to understand culture and context, then we read that God created man in his own image, in the flesh and saw that it was good. We don't have to look to Romans to untangle our culture from the reading of scripture.

Interestingly, my great books reading helped me see something else with regards to scripture. There is likely Hellenistic influence on the writers of the bible. The author of Ecclesiastes most certainly wrote his work after having read works from Plato. These Hellenistic writings influenced the authors of scripture during this time.

Today, I work as a part-time campus minister and spend the majority of my days at home with my kids. While parenting, my great books discussions often come flooding back into my mind. How I view Justice, Honor, Shame, Forgiveness, Mercy, and Grace all impact how I parent my children. These topics are an integral part of the readings and discussions of Great Books.

This summer I read Stephen King's *On Writing*, a well written semi-autobiography in which King tells readers the only way to be a great writer is to read voraciously. I think fondly of the many books I read prior to entering the great books program, but I smile when I consider that my great books semesters didn't just give us a taste of great works, we were baptized in them. Since I have left school, I read a wider range of books than those assigned, but I think King's call to read and be well read is an important one for our society. It is not just "knowing" all the "facts" in the great books; after all one could find those on Wikipedia. The act of reading and discussing broadens one's horizons, builds one's vocabulary, and challenges one to think deeply about a particular topic.

Great Books allows us to engage in the conversation which has been ongoing for centuries. More importantly it gives perspective on the depth and direction of the conversation as it has changed over the years. It allows one to approach a conversation as a non-anxious presence. Regardless of the choices and decisions made in this single conversation, by this generation, or even in this country, the dialogue will continue. There is no reason to approach life in crisis mode: civilizations rise and fall, yet these great books themes continue. I approach each day with the hope to make the world a better place, but my Great Books curriculum allows me to see a long term trajectory and seek a bigger picture of justice, truth, peace, purpose, and love.

My generation will not come to definitive answers on the many questions we explore. Those who follow us will have to learn for themselves the purpose of life. They will investigate the relationship between humanity and nature. They will have to determine which way the pendulum will swing between rational and emotional argumentation. Will logic or passion win out in the next generation? If we have done our job well, we will have contributed our own voices to the dialogue. We will have first read the great books and digested the ideas from the many generations before us. Then our voices can chime into the beautiful dialogue woven through history. This is the lasting legacy of the great books curriculum; our voices are more than a clanging cymbal, they have become a part of the dialogue. Like humpback whales we each add our own input, but the conversation belongs to the society not the individual.

Bibliography

Chang, J. (2003). *Wild swans: Three daughters of China*. Simon and Schuster.

Kibbe, Michael. *From Topic to Thesis: A Guide to Theological Research*: InterVarsity Press, 2016.

Machiavelli, N. (1961). *The Prince; Transl. from the Italian*. Penguin.

Wilson, Kathleen S. *The Voyage of the Mimi, Interactive Video Prototype: Development of an Exploratory Learning Environment for Children*: Bank Street College of Education, Center for Children and Technology, 1987.

"I'm giving you a new commandment to love one another. Just as I have loved you, you also should love one another."
-Jesus, *Gospel of John*

XXVI
CHRISTINA GUSTIN

Twenty-two years and ten moves later, the book still sits on my shelf. *The* Book. "Classics of Western Though, Volume III, The Modern World," fourth edition, edited by Edgar E. Knoebel. By now the pages have faded to an attractive sepia, and the passages I highlighted so many years ago have faded to a dusty yellow. Occasionally I will actually crack it open looking for a quote or refreshing a concept, but it's really there to represent the foundation of ideas. Logic. Philosophy. Beliefs. And seeing it on the bookshelf reminds me that amidst the noise of everyday life, there are some things that are constant and true. Like Plato's "Forms". I find comfort in that.

I was a member of Dr. Gose's "Great Books Colloquium" class during my Freshman and Sophomore years at Pepperdine, back in the mid-90's. I have vivid memories of sitting in class, debating the latest grand idea we were studying, and as our voices escalated Dr. Gose would calmly stop everything and demand, "You must define your terms." Often we uncover mis-understandings. Or interpretations that were incompatible with the text. Or preconceived notions that we weren't even aware were influencing our absorption of the new idea. This simple discipline of breaking ideas down to their simplest form, and agreeing on fundamentals before building on them, is the single most valuable thing I learn from Great Books. I believe it's a method of conflict resolution, and it's a practice I use all the time, from the dinner table to the board room.

After obtaining a B.A. in Art History with my right brain, my left brain promptly embarked on a career in Finance. Over the years it has surprised me to discover that so much of Finance and Economics is really just the study of human behavior. Adam Smith's *Wealth of Nations* may have been the most literal influence on my work today, but as I pass through life I am often faced with one Great Book idea or another, and it always feels like seeing an old friend.

More than any other college class, Great Books was a turning point for me. A catapult. A sling-shot from one level of awareness to another. It created a synthesis of ideas that made me a better communicator. And of all the skills I learned in college, the ability to communicate is the one I value and enjoy the most. Even in Finance, I believe that my writing skills set me apart from my peers. The ability to communicate complex ideas in a clear and simple way is a competitive advantage. This web of ideas, known as Great Books, has enriched my life, and will always be one of my fondest college memories.

Rainer Maria Rilke, Letters to a young poet, M.D. Herter Norton (trans.), New York: Norton, 1993, p. 35

"Meanwhile these three remain: faith, hope, and love; and the greatest of these is love."
-Paul, *I Corinthians*

XXVII
CHARLES PARK

College was Great Books for me. When Dr. Gose wrote to me, over the summer, saying that I needed to have read the Iliad before the first Great Books class, I thought he was kidding. "Really, I have homework before I even start Pepperdine?" I thought. So the first Great Books class rolls up in the fall of 1994 and I was a bright-eyed, bushy-tailed, ready-to-go freshman (who hadn't read all of the Iliad; I was like halfway done with the Latimore translation) who walked and sat in a room on the third floor in CAC and waited for the class to start. Dr. Gose walks in, sits down and asks each person one at a time if they had read The Iliad. 90% of the class had not, including me. What happened next is something I will never forget. Dr. Gose, stood from his chair, threw down The Iliad onto the floor in dramatic fashion and then looked away from us and pointed at the door. At first, us 14 students all looked at each other and in unison stood up and quietly left. As I was leaving the classroom at the door frame of passing through the doors, I had the courage to look at Dr. Gose and I swear, from the corner of my eyes, I saw him smirking, trying to contain a quivering laugh underneath his downward posture. "Now that's great teaching," I thought to myself because all of us read the Iliad that night and 100% of the students had read the book before the next class and we had a riveting Socratic dialogue. From that point on, I made sure to read each book before a Great Books class. I remember, I had taken a friends trip to SF and they had an outing planned to go visit Ghirardelli's. I stayed behind to finish reading St. Thomas Aquinas so I can have it read over the weekend before the Monday class. More than Great Books, this type of discipline helped me work efficiently and helped me to develop a good work ethic and it has helped me even into my professional career as a school administrator. Who knew?

As a Pepperdine freshman, I lived in Dorm 4; the best dorm. One evening, I was confused about the reading about Plato's Republic. So I invited a few colleagues in the dorm who had Great Books up to the roof of the dorm to discuss the work. It was simply an amazing Socratic discussion. We challenged each other's thoughts and ideas and in the midst of it, a grandiose sunset occurred over the ocean and we paused for a second to admire it, then went right back to bickering about Plato's "good" and "ideals" vs ideas. I will never forget that moment and it all happened because of Great Books.

If anything, Great Books has been the spark of my intellectual thoughts, and my times at Pepperdine in the Honors Program were the most intellectually challenging years of my life. Great Books was the vehicle for challenging thoughts and ideas and helped me develop an ability to have mutual discourse with peers without making it personal. For this reason, I am grateful and more grateful for Dr. Gose who brought me into the Great Books light.

"Yet we know that a person is put right with God only through faith in Jesus Christ, never by doing what the Law requires."
-*Galatians*

XXVIII
EZRA PLANK

Goodness and Truth: A Reconsideration of the Good Life

My years as an undergraduate were consumed with anxiety and questions about the future. Would I discover a life that would be meaningful: a partner to provide companionship, adventure to provide excitement, and, of course, a job to provide income and security? Perhaps one of the greatest gifts the faculty of the Great Books Colloquium gave to me was the opportunity to question my own desires – what was this "Good Life" I was pursuing? By tracing influential Western thinkers over the past two millennia, I was exposed to historical conceptions of virtue and vice, stories which analyzed people's decisions, and competing notions of what "good" was. These courses pushed me to consider my identity, the orienting principles of my life, and my process of becoming, all while I was crossing the threshold to adulthood.

The questions raised by these courses still echo in my life nearly twenty years later, during which time the world has changed dramatically. The dawning of the Digital Age with the internet, personal smart devices, and social media have all fundamentally transformed the context in which these questions are asked. This is true especially with regards to information. While in the past one had to seek out the few experts who knew the answers to certain questions, now humanity's collective knowledge is available with a few taps of a finger. Information is more accessible than ever, and therefore this (understandably) brings the value of a liberal arts education into question.

I have remained within the field of higher education at a religious (Christian) institution – as an administrator, student care professional, and professor in a study abroad program in Switzerland – and I often wonder how the changing cultural landscape has impacted how the Good Life is understood by young adults. As I see students struggle to define the Good Life – specifically, to understand the role of their education in light of their future goals – the Great Books Colloquium seems more relevant than ever.

I have noticed that the majority of my students tend to approach their liberal arts education with an obsession of leveraging it into something else. It appears that they are striving to attain the Good Life (get a job, buy a house, go on vacations, buy things, and so forth), and their education is understood as a utilitarian vehicle to get them there. Because the goal is thus defined for many students, their education seems to them to hold little value apart from the doors it will open in the future. Grades matter more than learning. In this economy, students do not care what the answer is to any particular question (which would demonstrate critical thinking and moral development), as long as they know what it is for the exam. On multiple occasions I have had students turn in a draft of a paper to me and ask "What do I need to do to make this an A paper?" They usually don't say, "Do you have tips for strengthening my writing?", or, "Is my argument cogent and compelling?" – it is simply about getting through the university experience to achieve something else. In the most skeptical recesses of my mind, I worry if students were offered a choice – the opportunity to pay for a university diploma without doing the course work – that many would eagerly accept.

At this point, the *information* that my university provides in its curriculum is simply a neutral commodity. Even more concerning to me is that this information, pursuit of understanding, truth (whatever you want to call it) is perceived as being disconnected from and having little relevance to "real life."

This is not a new problem, and really, many would lay the responsibility for this shift at the feet of the Enlightenment. In one of the books I studied in the Great Books Colloquium, René Descartes' 1637 publication "Discourse on the method for conducting reason well and for seeking truth in the sciences," he contends that whatever can be doubted should be rejected. He was convinced of the logic and objectivity of mathematics, and as Elizabeth Adams St. Pierre claims, he advocated a method of determining the truth that "mathematize[d] science [and] privilege[d] individual reason as a source of justification (rationalism)." Only scientific knowledge could be true. This was a huge shift from previous understanding of the ancient Greeks who maintained that "goodness was the price of truth... a [person] had to be ethical to know the truth." Three and a half centuries later Michel Foucault critiqued Descartes, asserting that Descartes, broke with this [tradition] when he said, 'To accede to truth, it suffices that I be any subject that can see what is evident.' ... The relationship to the self no longer needs to be ascetic to get into relation to the truth. It suffices that the relationship to the self reveals to me the obvious truth of what I see for me to apprehend the truth definitively. Thus, I can be immoral and know the truth. I believe this is an idea that, more or less explicitly, was rejected by all previous culture. Before Descartes, one could not be impure, immoral, and know the truth. With Descartes, direct evidence is enough.

According to Foucault, Descartes eradicated the accepted relation between living a good life and knowing the truth. This epistemological shift was a watershed moment, and many other Western thinkers built on this worldview. Individuals like the nineteenth century philosopher Auguste Comte asserted that former stages of human intellectual life – namely the theological and metaphysical – were misguided and untrustworthy; knowledge about both the natural world and the social world should be scientific, measurable, quantifiable, certain, and precise. Eventually this approach would be applied to most realms of human understanding. It seems to me that this understanding of knowledge is now a ubiquitous and normalized part of our society today: real knowledge is context-free, value-free, and un-incarnated. Our students, who only demand the right Answer (essentially, Truth without living it) are indeed descendants of Descartes and the Enlightenment tradition.

In this context, I ponder Jesus' statements in the third chapter of the Gospel of John. This chapter tells the story of Nicodemus, a religious leader who visits Jesus under the cover of night and starts his conversation with Jesus with "Rabbi, we know..." Knowledge. He *knows* who Jesus is. Jesus refutes his claim, and says that he cannot *know* the truth of Jesus' identity, because he has not experienced it (being born again of water and spirit). Christians are drawn to John 3:16 ("For God so loved the world..."), and they often fail to read the following verses. Jesus states, "This is the verdict: Light has come into the world, but people loved darkness instead of light because their *deeds* were evil. Everyone who *does* evil hates the light, and will not come into the light for fear that their *deeds* will be exposed. But whoever *lives by the truth* comes into the light, so that it may be seen plainly that what they have done has been done in the sight of God" (3:19-21). Living by the truth, knowing the truth, walking in the light, doing good deeds – for Jesus, these are all the same thing.

The way my students approach academics – viewing education (knowledge, truth) as disconnected from living – is symptomatic of the way they approach life. I often witness the way they live their lives is inconsistent with what they *know*. If my university is going to live up to its religious ideals - is going to be engaged in the business of redemption and transformation – it will have to reimagine a world in which Truth cannot be estranged from Experience and Action. In this way, I would argue that I cannot believe *in* truth, I find beliefs to be True through living them. In my Introduction to the New Testament course, my students frequently ask of the Bible, "Is it True?" But I wonder if this the wrong category of a question to ask of this sacred text, and is akin to asking "Is Tuesday red?" or "Is your marriage delicious?" Because they are adopting Descartes' method, they believe that they can apply some scientific rubric to the Bible and label it as "True." They do not feel compelled to live its truths to determine if it is true; as Foucault asserts, they believe they can be both immoral and know the truth. While human history contains many stories of individuals whose religious beliefs have propelled them toward incredible acts of kindness and service, it also is littered with those who proclaimed the truth of the Bible and destroyed others' lives and cultures.

In the academic world of a liberal arts college, my students are striving for the Good Life. But courses in Great Books interrogate them, What is the Good Life? Or even more basically, What is Good? and what is Life? Can people know the truth of the Good Life from a distance, like Descartes claimed? Or, like the ancients held, is goodness the price of truth: do you have to live Good, live rightly, live justly, live ethically, to experience the Good Life?

In the Middle Ages monasticism spread from the Syrian and Egyptian deserts and flourished in Europe and around the globe. Monasteries and nunneries could be mixed experiences: some who were there were pious and sought intimacy with God, others were sent there by their families, and still others went because they had no place to go. And my sense is that, while we may like to romanticize them, these sacred places would have been difficult places to live. Men and women were crammed into small spaces and surrounded by people with different personalities, work ethics, and hygiene practices. They may or may not like the work assigned to them. They may or may not like the disposition of the abbot/ess. From letters and petitions that come out of these religious communities, many felt it was like a road trip that went one week too long – it was miserable. And that is why I think it is instructive that monasteries were referred to as "schools of *caritas*" (*caritas* as in love, not charity). These schools of love were where you lived out your beliefs, your spiritual ideals, as you rubbed shoulders with the annoying, and perhaps smelly, uber-spiritual brother or sister next to you. Life in these communities was not about affirming the idea of love – it was about living the truth of love.

I think this is why I am drawn to Jesus' way of living among people. He did not say, "Believe this context-free, value-free, and un-incarnated Truth." He invited, "Eat with me." "Touch my wounds." "Let me smear this mud on your eyes." "Pull in your nets of fish." Breathe the Truth, feel the Truth, taste the Truth, live the Truth, know the Truth. If Jesus' claims to be incarnated divinity were true, how could it be that the human experience of the divine (Truth) would be body-less? Perhaps that is why I find Jesus call to "Follow me" compelling: Come, let us live out this truth together and you can experience (know) it. Do you want to know if it is better to love your enemies? Follow me and find out if that is true and why it is true. Do you want to know if serving others is part of the Good life? Follow me. Do you want to know why it is better to give than to receive? Follow me. Follow me. Follow me.

Even if others do not find the Christian narrative compelling, maybe it is time to reconsider Descartes' thesis. And while I would never advocate that life was better in a pre-scientific era – and for that I am grateful to Descartes! – I think there is too much Truth to be lived in life that cannot be reduced to numbers. This is particularly true of the field of education, which is often valued solely for the access it provides to a secure life. I am grateful for the Great Book Colloquium faculty who questioned this narrative and instead challenged me to consider the hazards of a Cartesian epistemology. In honor of their investment, I redirect my students' desire to capture the truth – like an object to be owned. I problematize their belief that truth can be fully understood apart from the living out their moral code. And I invite them into my study abroad community in the Swiss Alps – a school of *caritas* – where they practice living a good life and, in doing so, discover the Good Life.

Art by Ezra Plank circa 1996

"Faith without works is dead."
-James

XXIX
JOE POHLOT

Almost 25 years ago I stepped into my first Great Books classroom as a college freshman. I was five minutes early, as it is poor form to arrive late for one's first class of the semester. It was a relatively small gathering of students, somewhere between 12 and 20 sitting in a circle, all freshmen waiting with apprehensive excitement to discuss Homer's *Iliad*. Now, "to discuss" for a college freshman really means "to express one's own opinion in the most words possible in order that one may appear more intelligent than one's peers." So, there's a good chance that the eagerness to discuss was more about determining the classroom hierarchy than it was to talk about the book.

Although I didn't recognize it at the time, Fortune smiled upon myself and my classmates that day as the self-proclaimed "Pumpkin King" deftly wrested control of the classroom. By that I mean he checked each one of our books for underlining, highlighting and margin comments. As I hazily recollect, not one of us had underlined, highlighted or commented enough to his satisfaction. The hierarchy had been established and each freshman in that room was on equal footing at the bottom. It did make for a more productive discussion over the next two semesters as we all treated each other as equals, equals in the same way that peasants are all equals before their feudal lord. We quickly understood that we were each responsible for one another's learning.

The "Pumpkin King," to our early frustration, relied upon the Socratic/dialectic method of teaching. It is a brilliant and irritating means of instruction which engages the students by asking them questions so that they either come to discover the author's meaning or are led to more questions. For a professor, I imagine it takes a fair bit of work to stay on top of the conversation. For an incoming student, it took every last ounce of energy to get up for an 8:00 AM class, pay attention to the discussion instead of the opposite sex and then answer questions when called upon. Luckily, we could either bring food or a drink into the classroom to keep our energy levels high, but not both as the warning sign only prohibited "Food and Drink." Our early mastery of critical thinking (and arguing) skills seemed to work in our favor here. This method of instruction not only honed our critical thinking skills (especially for our own self-interest) but also firmly established the Great Ideas from these Great Books in our minds. I've found that a dialectic-generated thought lasts with me a lot longer than a principle taught from a textbook. Does anyone remember how sines, cosines and tangents work? Me neither.

My recollection on classroom details for the remainder of my two-and-a-half semesters of Great Books with the "Pumpkin King" consists of tidbits of memories, fading more as time passes. However, the ideas proffered by the Great Books I read during that time have remained ingrained in my mind and heart since. From Honor in the *Iliad*, to Duty in the *Aeneid*, to the "teleological suspension of the ethical" in *Fear and Trembling*, to the roles of faith and reason in *The Divine Comedy*, to "faith alone" described by Luther contrasted with James' description that faith without works is dead, to Machiavelli's statement that it is "better to be feared than loved, if one cannot be both." All of these ideas and my time spent reading and discussing these books over a ten-month period in the mid-1990s have led me to reread them multiple times over the past 20-odd years. I can't imagine ever re-reading these books if not for the ideas described in each as well as the teaching method employed in the instruction.

Now that I am a father, I find myself asking my sons questions instead of providing the quick and easy answer when they ask questions. Regardless of their ages, it has been tremendously effective in boosting their critical thinking skills. Seeing their faces light up when they make a connection between something they've learned and something new fills me with joy as their dad. Each time, it brings me back to a quote that the "Pumpkin King" told us in class, probably as half of us were drinking and the other half were eating: "The joy of recognition surpasses the joy of discovery." It's true.

"The corollary of your perfection is that the imperfection of created things is displeasing."
-Augustine

XXX

BEN POSTLETHWAITE

THE QUESTIONS OF THE CANON
(written 1996)

I enquire now as to the genesis of the philologist and
assert the following:
1. A young man cannot possibly know what Greeks
and Romans are.
2. He does not know whether he is suited for finding
out about them.

- Friedrich Nietzche,
Unzeitgemasse Betrachtungen

Come then, and let us pass a leisure hour in storytelling, and
our story shall be the education of our heroes.

- Plato,
T'he Republic, Book II

Most contemporary Great Books students and discussants are so
involved in discussing the works of the canon that they fail to ever
consider the nature of the canon itself. However, an evaluation of the
concept of canon raises many significant questions. What is the canon? Is
the canon in fact necessary? What is the purpose of the canon? What is
the criteria for inclusion of works into the canon? Finally, is the Canon
open or closed?

Towards Reaching a Definition of "The Canon"
The word canon automatically brings about religious connotations.
One often pictures a "sacred" collection of infallible, unquestionable

101

works, but is unable to precisely define the term within the Great Books Colloquium. Like other religious words such as 'sanctification' and 'omniscience', the 'canon' is often bantered about without being fully understood. However, in order to attempt to answer the relevant questions concerning the canon, it is first necessary to reach at least a preliminary definition.

According to Mortimer Adler, one of the co-founders of the current Great Books tradition, the canon could best be described as the collection of those books which are "essential to a liberal education." Adler's definition implies that the canon's constituents are, for the most part, books; however, several shorter works and treatises are included in his canon. What these particular works in specific is the subject of this paper. Some scholars argue that the definition of canon should be expanded to include works of popular culture including art, music, and film. For example, Jane Tompkins, a radical feminist English professor at Duke University, advocates the inclusion of George Lucas' *Star Wars* and Steven Spielberg's *ET*. While the inclusion of such items is certainly open for debate, currently the use of the term canon refers to books and "third person dispassionate prose." Furthermore, the term canon implies some sense of unchangeable structure. The current use of the term suggests both to discussants and participants that the majority of works comprising the canon are classics which have, in fact, maintained there position over the centuries.

On the Necessity and Function of the Canon

University catalogues are amazing documents. Anytime students, faculty, and administrators can all be held to a binding agreement, something remarkable has been accomplished. The Great Books canon functions in much the same manner: it holds discussants and participants together, measuring new and old ideas against a given standard. Because the concept of canon implies such an immovable standard, many radicals protest the very concept. But one need not agree with the canon's standard, or frame of reference, to make good use of it.

What is true of the canon is true of rules in general. Rules and standards of conduct are necessary for the functioning of society. The absence of rules in society leads to anarchy and chaos, a world where individuals cannot safely function on their own. The absence of rules of conduct in religious and family spheres leads to the breakdown of the respected institutions. In the academic sphere an absence of all standards would be none but disastrous: on the rare occasion that new knowledge was actually gained, it could neither be measured nor reported, for there would be no frames of reference.

Accordingly, the canon serves the purpose of providing an unchangeable frame of reference, a collection of shared knowledge of what society has come to know as sacred. For example, the canon allows a current university student in California to have a meaningful discussion with a grandparent born sixty years ago and two thousand miles away. Although they may be separated by decades of technological and societal differences, the canon allows them to become contemporaries in terms of the Great Ideas. With regards to the Great Ideas, the canon eliminates or greatly retards the effects of time. If anything, it would be only be the canon that would allow a contemporary discussant to enter into a significant dialogue with Plato, Aquinas, or Milton. Accordingly, the presence of a canon in some form is a necessity.

Criteria for Admission to the Canon

While some debate whether the canon should even be in existence, most disagreements concern what should constitute the great books canon. Adler maintains three criteria for admitting works to the Great Books canon. First, the works must be

> 'essentially timeless and universal, not confined to interests or circumstances that change from time to time and from place to place. Secondly, they are worth reading carefully many times, for pleasure and profit. Third, they deal with problems of thought and action that confront human beings in every age.'

Adler's third criteria could also be restated as "'a work must contain "a certain number of ideas"'".

The question must now be raised as to whether it will ever be possible to have one canon coupon which everyone agrees. According Katha Politt , a university English professor, the apparent answer is no: "Books cannot mold a common national purpose, when in fact, people are honestly divided about what kind of country they want."Terry Eagleton, a literary Marxist literary critic at the University of Oxford skeptically answered the question of whether there could be one canon by saying:

> It depends on where you are standing at the time. People's reputations vary. As long as you realize that this is our criteria but it may not be someone else's...We forget the unconscious guide lines. We judge in the context of what we think is important.

Based on the response after Adler and the Britannica editorial board released their revised list of 517 Great Works, one canon does not appear in the near future. Many individuals were upset at the lack of eastern, African American, and Latino works on the list. For the first time, four females were included, though many felt the number should have been far higher. Nevertheless, Adler insists that the Great Books editorial board, which included both an African American and Mexican American among other minorities, reached over ninety percent agreement in selecting its updated canon.

Discussants and students are still left with the decision as to what canonical list to use. Should Adler's list be adopted and its contents be treated as the supreme authority? Or should one completely discard the biased list which only propagates the racist white male perspective in favor of a feminist or minority canon? Perhaps the best solution has been proposed by Dinesh D'Souza in his "Multicultural Reading List" which appeared in the *Wall Street Journal*. D'Souza advocates maintaining the traditional Western canon, and either incorporating non-Western or minority works or rather studying those works alongside the canon.In conclusion, it is evident that whatever canon an individual or institution decides to adopt, some works will be included which maintain positions which are contrary to held beliefs. However, this apparent contradiction need not deter the student or discussant from canonical study or Great Ideas discussion. In fact, even if one's beliefs stand in stark contrast to the beliefs upheld to the canon itself, one can develop intelligently and creatively through canonical study. Finally, the purpose of the canon is not to provide one with a collection of viewpoints synonymous with one's own, but rather to provide one With what Joseph Schwab calls a polyfocal conspectus, "a view-affording doctrine on reality" which equips students and discussants alike with the ability to make informed decisions in a variety of practical situations.

A Preliminary Compendium of Useful Sources for Further Considering the Questions of the Canon

Serials

Caster,Wendy. "The Classics: Are the literary classics of the Western world still vital to our   education? NO." *San Diego Union-Tribune.* Mar. 20, 1991. Opinion, p. B9.

As a Jew and a lesbian, Caster responds to Adler's exclusion of minority writers from the canon. Caster bases her claim for minority inclusion on the assertion that minority writers such as Toni Mo"is on and Gabriel Garcia Marquez write about the same universals that Shakespeare writes about, while remaining more relevant to the contemporary reader than the Elizabethan dramatist.

Crequer, Ngaio. "Literary canon… a ten-year scheme for improving the mind." *The Independent.*　　　 Dec. 27, 1990. Home News p. 6

A simplistic, concise British response to Adler's revised canon. Crequer is not critical of inclusions or exclusions, but is slightly wary of the Great Books plan as a whole. The article might be useful for providing a brief introduction to students unfamiliar with the canon.

D'Souza, Dinesh. "A Multicultural Reading List". *The Wall Street Journal.* September 24, 1991.

D'Souza believes that non-Western works should indeed be studied, however not at the expense of the established Western canon. He claims that non-Western should appropriately be studied either through integration into the canon. or alongside the canon. According to D'Souza, it would indeed be incorrect to adopt the approach of schools who require only non-Western courses or schools who engage in the depreciation of the Western classics. D'Souza also offers a list of non-Western "great books" which include works such as Confucius' <u>Analects,</u> Achebe's <u>Things Fall Apart</u>, and Paz's <u>The Labyrinth of Solitude.</u>

Grossman, Ron. "Aristotle of Academe: Perhaps its time for American colleges to rethink the great 　　　 thoughts of Chicago's Boy Wonder". *Chicago Tribune.* Nov. 17, 1989. Tempo, p. 1.

Grossman's article is not concerned with canon itself, rather his work accomplishes the greater purpose of effectively communicating the the Jong term effects of a canonical education. He does so by a concise reminiscence of the days when the college of the University of Chicago was under the auspices of then presidentRobertMaynardHutchins. According to

Grossman, Hutchins, along with Adler, created a unique atmosphere where "education was too important to be left to educators."He claims an education steeped in the canon freed students and inspired creativity, rather than being restrictive. Grossman believes that the solution to the current educational "crisis" may indeed lie in returning to the canonical model which Hutchins developed.

Politt, Katha. "Canon to the right of me... " *The Nation.* Sep. 23, 1991. Vol. 253, No. 9, pg. 328.

Politi offers an intelligent and balanced account of both sides of the canon issue. One of the articles strengths lies in Politt's experience as an educator. Asa literature teacher, she offers a realistic view of the educational process as it relates to the Great Ideas, rather than simply purveying idealistic. Politt finally reaches the conclusion that it is impossible to arrive at one satisfactory canon of Great Books when people are divided on the issue of what type of country they want.

Segal, Eric. "Starting with Homer". *New York Times.* Feb. 27, 1983. Sec. 7, p. 10, col. 1.

Segal's article is an introduction to the 1983 <u>Oxford Readings in Greek Tragedy,</u> which he edited. The most useful features of the article are the brief, clear descriptions of the major 20th century attempts to arrive at an acceptable canon.

Venant, Elizabeth. "A Crumudgeon Stands His Ground; 'Great Books' Editor Mortimer J. Adler   Rejects the Growing Challenges to His List of Western Books". *Los Angeles Times.* Dec. 3, 1990. View, part E, p. 1, col. 2.

Venant presents a thorough examination of the changes made in the 1990 revision of Encyclopedia Britanica's list Great Books. She also is successful in describing the process and criteria used to proclaim a book "great. " One particular strength of the article is its inclusion of Mortimer Adler's person/ responses to questions on why certain respected works, especially by minorities, were left out of the canon. Another strength lies in the presence of Adler's critics suggestions for canonical inclusion. Such critics include Henry Lewis Gates, E. D. Hirsch, and Jane

Tompkins, and suggested inclusions, respectively, are Du Bois'
The Soul of Black Folk, The Bible, and Lucas' Star Wars.

Before and After: Two Longer Works for Consideration Before and After Embarking an Organized Collegiate Great Ideas Program

Tartt, Donna. The Secret History. (New York: Penguin, 1992).

> *If nothing else, Tartt's novel is a thoroughly enjoyable read.*
> *Fortunately, it's also much more. The Sunday Times is*
> *appropriate in saying that her erudition sprinkles the text like*
> *sequins, but she's such an adept writer that she's able to make*
> *the occasional swerve into Greek legends and Semantics seem*
> *absolutely crucial to the examination of contemporary society*
> *which the book undoubtedly and seriously is , for all the fun it*
> *provides on the way...brilliant. "*

> *The Secret History has the rare power to make scholars and*
> *laymen alike wish they were engaged in the often elite, but*
> *always rewarding, study of the classics. Tartt's novel could serve*
> *as an excellent, though slightly manipulative, tool for motivating*
> *capable students and discussants into entering the dialectical*
> *world of the Great Ideas.*

Gaardner, Jostein. Sophie's World.

> *Sophie's world can most be appreciated after completing a Great*
> *Ideas Colloquium, or at least after a majority of Great Ideas*
> *perspectives have been evaluated The work provides a enjoyable*
> *yet thorough integration of the ideas of a number of canonical*
> *authors, ranging from Aristotle to Thucydides.*

University Great Books Lists To Consider

*St. John's College
Columbia University
Pepperdine University
* Thomas Aquinas College
Stanford University's Cultures, Ideas, and Values Program
* Shimer College

Other Sources

Any of Adler's numerous books on the Great Ideas (e.g. *Six Great Ideas, Syntopticon)*
Alan Bloom's *The Closing of the American Mind*
E.D. Hirsch's *Cultural Literacy: What Every American Needs to Know*

"For heroism tempered with common sense is a far cry from madness;
reasonableness is to be preferred to recklessness."
-Song of Roland

XXXI
MELVIN SANCHEZ

Jacob wrestled with the angels and like so... we wrestled with the text....

"Then the man said, 'Let me go, for it is daybreak.' But Jacob replied, 'I will not let you go unless you bless me.'" Genesis 32:25

Wrestling is always a struggle in much the same way that reading is a struggle for many beginning readers. The beginning readers of the classics will encounter a very similar struggle with the texts. The Great Books Colloquium will necessarily give the freshman student the opportunity to struggle, be frustrated and be intellectually blessed with the texts. We learn from Plato's *Meno* that frustration is a necessary step in the process of learning. Plato's theory of learning is later laid out (with greater detail) in the *Republic*. The struggle with the text is, in a sense, a struggle with God. A struggle with something beyond and more powerful than one's self. The classical *corpus* is certainly a greater entity than an individual. Something that one can always go back to and learn from. Something that will always be there and that one can reference and quote. Perhaps the text is sacred like the "Thou" in Buber's existential thought.

On a starry night in the fall of 1994, around four or five freshman climbed to the top of the roof of a Pepperdine dorm house. Their goal was to better understand some sections of Plato's *Republic*. They were all freshman being introduced to new ideas. They came from different states and from different backgrounds. They knew that they could be there all night and have material to discuss and perhaps never come to conclusive answers much in the same way that Plato's interlocutors could continue a discussion for several hours. They understood that wrestling with the text was something that could happen all night. Something that could happen until daybreak. In some sense, they were mirroring Jacob's contentious night with the angel. Just as Jacob demanded a blessing, there must have been, at least at a sub-conscious level, a sense in which these youths demanded a blessing from the text.

"After he had sent them across the stream, he sent over all his possessions." Genesis 32: 23

The ignoring of material possessions happens automatically when one becomes immersed in the text. The bodily needs are often forgotten. Plato thought this is why the study of philosophy was meant for the soul (i.e., the mind) and not the body. Perhaps Jacob saw that a clear mind was necessary before one can wrestle with God. Besides the religious connotations that the ignoring of material possessions may have, engaging in the classic texts makes us look at a bigger picture. A picture that reflects meaning beyond what jobs we will have, how much money we will make and how many children we will have. Seeing this bigger picture by engaging the authors and their struggles will make education meaningful.

"Then the man said, 'Your name will no longer be Jacob, but Israel,[a] because you have struggled with God and with humans and have overcome.'" Genesis 32:28

What does it mean to overcome? How do students of the Great Books overcome their struggles with the texts? I think overcoming struggles with the texts means finding meaningful interpretations which will get us through the night. Since interpretations are endless and since there are no definitive interpretations (there are no definitive *translations* either!), meaning can be found in interpretations that speak to specific time periods and which can speak to us at certain points in our lives. Kierkegaard's Knight of Faith may speak to us when we are faced with choices that may appear to be irrational but for which rationality does not seem to have a better alternative (when, for example, we enter long term commitments without drawing up rational calculations of how much these commitments will cost and how long they will last). Kant's categorical imperative may speak to us at a time when a rational and universalist decision seems to be a better alternative than indulging our one sided egoism or selfishness. Kant's categorical imperative may also speak to us in a time of political divisiveness and hostility to specific groups…where an emphasis on universalism and globalism seems more rational.

"The sun rose above him as he passed Peniel,[c] and he was limping because of his hip." Genesis 32:31

If there are any wounds from wrestling with the texts, they are proud battle wounds. Wounds from which one has learned. They are up-building. They make us better in the long run. When one reaches the end of the course, one realizes that the struggles with the texts have been worth it. A curriculum based on the classics certainly gives us a broader picture of how education can be fulfilling and historically informed. Just like Aeneas' journey, it shows us that the struggles have been worth it for the foundation of something greater.

"In accordance with this determination, he passes over with great pain and agony, being wounded in the hands, knees, and feet. But even this suffering is sweet to him: for Love, who conducts and leads him on, assuages and relieves the pain."
-Chretinen de Troyes, *Lancelot*

XXXII
CLAY STOCKTON

On Cooking
A Memoir of a Great Books Education

I spent my formative years steeping myself in books—the Great ones, many just okay ones, and sometimes even a great one. I'm proud to say that nevertheless, in adulthood, I've managed after some struggle to become a moderately useful person who can make things with my hands.

For instance, when I became a father, I learned to cook. Now, when you cook a lot, one of the first things you learn is the importance of caring for your knife. We've all seen chefs sweeping their blades along a honing steel, one side then the other, again and again, raising a big fricative din with an emotion somewhere between joy and obsession.

They do that because they appreciate what happens to knives over time. A knife is a simple machine, a wedge with a handle: they're sharp because their blades taper to the most acute of angles, just a few molecules wide—and as long as that edge keeps its Euclidean perfection, no onion is safe. But, as chefs know, steel proves flexible with use and pressure, and the edge ends up bent to one side or the other like a collapsing wave.

That's where the honing steel comes in. By drawing the blade along that grooved rod, a chef pushes the fallen molecules to the other side—which is why the back-and-forth matters. There's no quicker way to dull a blade than honing it on just one side. The trick is to over-correct one way, then over-correct to the other, over then over, *but a little less each time*, until the edge trues.

As it turns out, the mind is a blade, sharpened on one side by books. In my case, I spent my formative years reading Dante without any meaningful knowledge of Italy, Milton without England, Nietzsche without Germany. I read Euclid as if no mathematics came before, just as I read Hegel without ever, somehow, getting to Marx. I read exactly one volume from the Global South—in an elective. I read, in short, a body of writing that a few obscure Midwesterners of European extraction, men who harbored very specific fascinations and suffered from the concomitant blind spots, touted as not only great books, but *the* great books. And those books honed me on one side.

It would be a long time before I learned to ask what had honed the other.

*   *   *

When I was an undergraduate at Seaver in the 1990s, the campus had very little in the way of ornamentation. I wish I could say it partook of a Shaker simplicity, but honestly the place felt more like a nice mall, designed to project the impression that you were getting value for your dollar. If a magnificent, invisible hand were suddenly to lift Pepperdine University from its seaward basin by the Pacific and set it gently down anywhere other than Malibu, it would have been *dull, dull, dull.* (Don't believe me? Try to remember what the satellite campus in Culver City looks like.)

The Malibu grounds had the uniform architecture and anonymous landscaping of an office park: a few perfunctory fountains, some shiny fields kept behind cordons, but no truly prominent or striking feature except for the hundred-foot tall monolith at the entryway, out of which someone, in what always struck me as a theologically significant use of negative space, had removed a large, cross-shaped section. The blank where the broken body could have been seemed to say: welcome to a place where we will not be talking overmuch about the suffering that led to all this bounty.

I only remember the campus having one icon depicting a flesh-and-blood human being, and that was the statue of Christopher Columbus pointing out to sea, presumably at the Indies that he, much to the relief of India, never found. It was odd, having only one statue of one person on campus, and then to have it be that person. Quite obviously it was a donation, perhaps even a *condition* for a donation. I understand that in recent years the statue has become an object of controversy, but in the mid-1990s, at the height of the then-novel concept of political correctness, Columbus stood undisturbed and mostly unnoticed. He always seemed clean, though I never saw anyone cleaning him; whoever had the job of removing the gull droppings must have also had the job of staying out of sight.

I tried to write about the Columbus statue once for the *Graphic,* the year they let me have a column. I had acquired a good readership with my first two contributions, the first a fizzy satire of campus dating life and the second a harder-hitting piece (I wishfully thought) that talked about the job offer that Pepperdine had recently given to Kenneth Starr. Starr, as the reader will recall, was at that very time serving as special counsel in the Whitewater investigation, which is to say, as the public face of a network of Republican politicians, operatives, and donors whose ultimate objects were the personal humiliation and political downfall of Bill Clinton, who'd had the temerity to become President without ever having been a member of the aristocrat caste. My column pointed out that it was one such Republican donor, a Pittsburgh newspaper magnate (remember those?), who just happened to have put up the money for the endowed chair into which Starr's well-larded haunches would descend. Nobody wrote about that sort of thing at Pepperdine, at least not then, so the column made a bit of a splash.

Then came my third column, my ill-fated attempt to describe what bothered me about the art on campus, or lack of it. If ever Wilde's theorem that "a little sincerity is a dangerous thing" needed proving, my poor, belabored column would have done the trick. All the extant copies are thankfully destroyed, and I don't recall many particulars, only a diffuse sense of outrage, and then the ending. Oh boy, the ending. The ending was an overlong description of the Columbus statue, written in the manner of an Imagist poem attempted by a twenty-year old moron who really liked Pearl Jam. If anyone I knew did manage to read the whole thing, they had good enough manners not to tell me.

What I didn't know how to say back then about the Columbus statue was that it was mortifying, the way it might be mortifying if one were to see a man emerge from a public restroom stall with a small glob of semen on his shoe. Some details tell an entire story—even if the story is one we all would rather stay hidden behind a partition. For me, the Columbus statue was a detail like that. It threw open the door on an unwelcome observation, namely, that Pepperdine as an institution found nothing particularly controversial in the primacy of Europe, not to say of Europeans. The catalyst of a genocide stood proudly on campus grounds in bronze, for no evident reason other than that wealthy persons of Italian extraction wished to see him standing there, and their money was good. No particular affinity drew the school to him—*it's not even Catholic*— but neither did any particular commitment exclude him. Many could have: a commitment to looking seriously at the suffering that led to bounty, for example. Even a consistent ahistoricity would have done the trick, for a statue of a person is a statue about history.

The only history on display on the campus where I read the Great Books was an uncannily clean statue of Columbus. He was there because his descendants were people with influence who felt proud of what he'd done, and those he'd done it to were dead.

*   *   *

Aside from tending one's knives, anyone who cooks must learn to shop. As I read once in a great book, "the quickest way you can become a better cook is to buy better ingredients." (Thomas Keller, *Ad Hoc at Home: Family-Style Recipes*, Artisan Press 2009, p. 7.) In a world of finitude, shopping is the economic expression of spiritual values. Show me how you spend your treasure and I will show you what you treasure; your receipts are the map of your heart.

Those who cook, especially for their families, feel this fact intimately as they traverse the market, basket in hand. Stopping at the fishmonger, we ask: Is it fresh? Check for clear eyes, not cloudy; examine the fins and tail for signs of incipient sliminess; hoist the whole body up to your nose and breathe in a big snoutful—it should remind you of the high seas, not low tide.

But freshness is only a first-order question. You can feed your child a fresh fish, but if you want your grandchildren and great-grandchildren to eat fresh fish too, you have to ask: Is it sustainable? First, rule out bad species—no snapper, no sea bass. Then, find out how it got to market: wild-caught or farmed? if wild, caught where, with what, in what season? if farmed: what was it fed, how was it penned, how far has it been trucked?

These questions are essential for anyone who wants to leave fish in the oceans for the future, which is to say, anyone who wants there to be a future. The market will seek to supply what we demand, so we owe it to ourselves and to each other to think hard about what we desire and be careful what we ask to consume.

I hardly ever ate seafood growing up. My mother and stepfather, both transplanted Midwesterners who somehow found themselves living coastside in California, found fish malodorous, regarded shrimp as kin to cockroaches, and, as for crab, lobster, squid, octopus, mussels, clams, oysters—all these were unmentionably exotic and, for practical reasons, inedible. Who did we think we were, *Rockefellers*? Once or twice a year, my mother baked a sheet of processed, battered fish sticks and made my brother and me choke down three or four, "for variety." We hated them and when we were little we cried as we chewed. It would be a couple decades before I realized that it was worse for Mom. My mother has many allegiances, but variety for variety's sake is not among them; why would she put up with all the tooth-gnashing unless she felt she had to? For her, those must have been nights of creeping humiliation, when she had to reach to the back of the freezer because she felt she had nothing better to feed us. I rush to say clearly that my mother and stepfather were never truly poor and my brother and I never suffered real food insecurity the way that, say, my father had. But we pinched pennies and we didn't have nice things.

I never knew that, oddly enough, until I came to Malibu on scholarship and discovered just how nice *things* could be. I don't remember a single sentence of Aquinas, but I still remember my first good olive. Briny, firm, the color of garnet, and glazed with oil, I ate it at Tra di Noi in the Colony in the spring of 1995 in the company of a well-dressed, slender Jewish girl whose wide-set eyes and ski-slope nose enthralled me (though, dear reader, I would later learn the latter was her sweet sixteen present). She had grown up a few doors down from Gerald Ford, during whose administration I was born, and somehow she was first-name friends with Clint Eastwood. Rachel, I'll call her, picked up the check. She had told me that she would pick it up when she invited me out to Tra di Noi, perhaps because I had suggested we have lunch in the cafeteria, where I had a meal plan. Rachel was the first, but not last, friend I made at Pepperdine who came from that sizable tranche of the student body that was truly wealthy. These were the kids who came to Pepperdine not because they were devoted Protestants like my Oklahoman roommates were, nor because they had received nearly free tuition in exchange for boosting the average SAT score like I had, but rather because they wanted a fun launchpad to an MBA or suitable marriage, and Malibu was, like, way nicer than USC.

Rachel was not fully of that world, nor any other as far as I could tell, but she opened it up for me, not least of all when she helped me get a job bussing tables at a high-end seaside glamour restaurant called Geoffrey's. There, I saw someone famous nearly every shift, in the days before reality television began mass-minting celebrities as if they were coupons for the Sunday circular. I cleared the plate of that decade's James Bond and I refilled the ice water of the man behind the Tonight Show desk; I brought lemon wedges for the heroes of Spielberg movies; my tongs placed hot rolls on the side plates of rock stars and comics, producers and models, and, one time, Dr. Dre, who smiled nonstop and loved to talk about Amsterdam. And more edifying than any celebrity sighting was the food. It was at after-hour staff tastings that I sampled my first sole, my first oysters, my first caviar. Soon I was sucking the heads of prawns, had acquired a taste for sparkling wine, and was rapidly growing accustomed to practically everyone around me being beautiful like the people in magazines.

Though I was not beautiful myself, I was breathless and adaptable, and I found ways to make myself agreeable, so my circle broadened, even touching the outermost reaches of The Industry. I found myself partying at Demi Moore's house (while Demi was out of town). I found myself hitting on Minnie Driver (at a gas station, and before Good Will Hunting). I found myself skipping Great Books one afternoon to drink retsina at a nearby Greek tavern while, next to me, Tony Danza of all people—my mother's television crush!—smoked an illegal cigar.

And one night I found myself skinny-dipping with the proverbial Girl Who'd Filmed a Pilot, along with Rachel and a few artsy friends, in a heated pool that jutted out from a modernist mansion perched above the Coast Highway. The house belonged to a rarely glimpsed sixth-year senior who would later receive a Scottish castle as a graduation present and, before he turned thirty, overdose and die in it.

The superabundance of Malibu, where money, beauty, and youth seemed plentiful as the sunshine, did not, I found, lend itself to a careful reckoning of one's risks. The Malibu I had entered was like an inverted Stanford Prison Experiment, where instead of guards and detainees, one was assigned either the role of the louche scion of a savvy stripmall investor or that of their eager, entertaining hanger-on. The Great Ideas in the Great Books could help you become something—but whatever you were reading, the environment you lived in was going to make you *be* something.

Somehow, improbably, my own environment had become the Malibu of wealth, concupiscence, and consumption, where, if you played your cards right, you could drink at Duke's for weeks and never see the bill. It was in that Malibu where I found myself getting my first-ever F grade on a quiz, then my second, and then . . . well, then they stopped making an impression. I found myself on academic probation, then off it, then on it, then off it, then on it; I never quite accepted that no matter how good my papers were, the squares really were going to hold my attendance against me.

I wish that bad grades and occasional hangovers were all of it. They weren't. The night I turned 21, despite having by then built myself a very solid intellectual foundation upon the pinnacles of Western literature, I found myself getting bounced from a pierside bar, having achieved my goal of drinking 21 drinks, compassionate Rachel leading me out by the arm before the bartender had me thrown out or punched out. I found myself living in a dry mansion in drunken London with a bunch of other Great Books kids, pounding subsidized whiskies all day in another university's nearby windowless pub, and capping off my summer abroad by spending all night rolling across a Hyde Park lawn with a girl (a Great Books girl, as it happened) who was not my girl. I found myself coming home to Malibu and getting my girl pregnant. Later, I paid the bill that had to be paid. In some ways, I still pay it.

So let me say it one more time: we owe it to ourselves and to each other to think hard about what we desire and be careful what we ask to consume.

*　　*　　*

At the time I asked for admission to the Great Books program, I was 18, still living under my parents' roof, and I had all the foresight, wisdom, and judgment for which recent high school graduates are justly known. If memory serves, I signed up for Great Books because it was optional. It seemed like it was supposed to be hard, but I figured I would be smarter than everyone else. You can see how well that worked out.

I distinctly remember liking that it was a bit show-offy. I expected that I would talk to other freshmen and it would come up that I was in Great Books, and they wouldn't actually *say* "whoa!" but, somewhere in their bodies, some kind of whoa-response would pass through them like static electricity and I would be confirmed in my invulnerable superiority to all those who might intimidate me.

Later, as I became a much more serious and level-headed sophomore (this was before the drinking really started), I appreciated that by studying the Great Books I was chiseling my name on an exclusive roster—chiseling, because of course the roster was made of marble and set upon a slab beneath a portico of Doric columns—anyway, this roster, it was the list of those of us who were *serious* about things that were *real*. It was we who could aspire to objectivity, who could hope to shine Woolf's "white light of truth" upon the problems of the modern moment (whatever those would turn out to be; probably something to do with the information superhighway), and it was we who held fast to an important tradition of ideas whose place in the intellectual fundament was confirmed by their longevity there, and which could lead us toward the good, true, and just, *sub specie aeternitatis*.

Perhaps it's no surprise that, to maintain a tribal identity that specific, we needed a pretty specific idea of what a great book was. It resulted in some notable omissions. For instance, although we read political philosophy (Machiavelli, Hobbes, Locke, Burke, Rousseau) and some economics (Adam Smith), and even a smattering of Hegel, we read not a page of Marx. I don't remember us even having a conversation about *why* we wouldn't read Marx—though in fairness, I could very well have been down at the tavern that day, moistening my false consciousness. But I suspect there was no such conversation, because neither did we read Freud nor Darwin, who, with Marx, form the three-legged stool upon which this secular world sits. More Wilde, in paraphrase: to skip one parent of contemporary thought may be regarded as a mistake, but to skip all three looks like careful omission. Especially when we instead used the time on . . . let me see here . . . Ralph Waldo Emerson, an absolute *giant* in the literature of Massachusetts, and no less than the third most influential Transcendentalist, depending whether one includes Walt Whitman. Whom we also did not read.

The oddest thing, in retrospect, is that these omissions didn't seem all that odd at the time. The canon was the canon was the canon, and it had stood the test of years, and that said something, didn't it? If I'm being honest, I also had a vague sense that other Great Books programs probably covered many of these missing texts, so any perceived gaps, I told myself, reflected nothing but the quirks of my (to this day) quite beloved professor. And indeed, the Great Books themselves—that multi-volume, leather-bound commodity sold door-to-door to respectable households in the 1950s, from which the pedagogical project would borrow its branding—do indeed include those missing writers.

It was only when I wandered well outside the perpetual sunshine and seaspray of Malibu that I started to see anything resembling a design behind what got called Great. Visiting a high school friend at a U.C. campus one weekend, I was shocked to find him reading a multicultural history of the United States—not because he had a particular interest in multiculturalism (he had none) but because it was assigned to every single freshman at his college, all three thousand of them—more than the entire undergraduate population at Pepperdine. No matter: I'd already sussed that though we were few, we were proud, and ample for holding Thermopylae. I told him that I was in a Great Books program—*highly* selective, I lied—and that we were reading nothing but Greeks that semester. To my dismay, it was all too evident that he did not feel a single iota of *whoa*. All he did was grimace and tell me that that was weird. (Later, when I went to law school in Berkeley, my friends in the Women of Color Collective would have little trouble locating a different adjective: that, they said, was *racist*.)

But of all the omissions in Pepperdine's peculiar instantiation of the Great Books ideal, the strangest, to this day, is Shakespeare. He would seem to fit the Great Books bill to a tee. One might object, I suppose, that he didn't write "books," but that's a mere quibble: Homer didn't even write. And of course we read plenty of drama (the improving, Athenian kind). No, the objection to Shakespeare wasn't fundamentally one of genre, but of pedagogy. It turns out there was very little we could *do* with Shakespeare; we certainly couldn't do what we were used to, which was to plow through our texts highlighting any passages germane

119

to the twelve or so ideas we'd become accustomed to treating as the ones that mattered (they came on a mimeographed list, if I recall correctly). The Great Books, I came to understand, were delivery mechanisms for Great Ideas, and Shakespeare had none—just great characters.

That's not precisely phrased, I suppose. It isn't that Shakespeare had no ideas, nor that he had only small ones. It's actually that Shakespeare is *too* full of ideas. One character spouts an idea, even a Great Idea, and another character opposes it in "words as hard as cannonballs," to quote a Massachusetts eminence. Nor is Shakespeare very improving. An image of a good or great man may wander through one of the plays, but as often as not he is undercut, and generally speaking, the villains and clowns are just as vivid. The didactic element in Shakespeare is almost entirely missing: rigor, nobility, and a prominent concern with justice may be ideals in the Republic, but in Shakespeare they're the virtues of Shylock. No, in Shakespeare the didactic element is superseded by the poetic element, which finds its expression only by working itself against the strictures of genre, a firefly of imagination that lights up when trapped in the glass bottle of a comedy, history, or murder play.

I would have had a hard time saying it at twenty, but now in middle age it seems plain to me that the Great Books project is not one that places much value on imagination. The mental operation we performed in those classes was something I would learn a dozen years later in law school to call "issue spotting." In law school, one doesn't read a fact pattern so much as one threshes it, beating it with an abstract flail until the wholesome wheat of material fact falls free of the chaff. Great Books was great training for that; it just so happened that in the chaff, unnamed then but obvious now, was feeling, motive, history (which means politics), class (which means politics), culture (you get it), and that gross embarrassment, the live, irrational body, that "heavy bear that goes with me." Great Books trained me that so much in the vastness of human experience was, in the final analysis, irrelevant. For isn't that the opposite of Great? Not "low," not "bad"—irrelevant. Shakespeare, too. He turned out to be irrelevant—or not, at least, as relevant as Emerson, or even Aquinas, of whom I can recall no single word.

The Great Books project, then, turns out to be a project of erasure. Not only or primarily of non-Europeans, though it is that too, maybe even by accident. But its defining feature is its erasure of that which its professors have deemed irrelevant—for classroom convenience. It's a pedagogical contraption, concerned with isolating a canon, so that associate deans can isolate a curriculum, so that assistant professors can isolate a syllabus, so that students can take courses and complete exams, so that tuition can be collected and degrees conferred, followed by jobs being obtained, student loans paid off, property gained, propriety displayed. Details may vary in the individual case, but that, it seems to me, is roughly the gist. I like to imagine sometimes that the Great Books canon would have been more inclusive if only respectable homes in the 1950s had had wider bookshelves.

*　　*　　*

Cooking offers no opportunities for perfection, but nearly infinite opportunities for correction. In cooking, one learns that, while there's no substitute for good tools and excellent ingredients, many deficiencies in those areas can be overcome with seasoning.

The first thing that told me I was starting to become a passable cook was that I began seasoning well—with salt at first (and always foremost), but with herbs and aromatics, too, and acid and heat. Imagine my delight when nearly everything I cooked got better with a few drops of vinegar; that bitterness, so intolerably sharp on its own, like an embarrassing or shameful memory, turns out to lend an essential vividness and subtly support the present savor.

The same with my trusty African pepper powder. It came into my life after I saw that Mark Bittman (in his 90s recipes, anyway) seemed to put a dash of cayenne in anything fatty or unctuous. I tried it at home, and about fell sideways from my chair when I made my first good quiche: that buttery crust, filled with 14 eggs, a half-dozen rashers of browned bacon, ample shavings of Emmental, and a full pint of cream, succeeded only because a dash of violently hot chili cut through the somnolent fat, the way anger can sometimes cut through complacent bullshit.

Seasoning is one of the reasons I love cooking; it is the opposite of Platonism. It's not just the rank materialism, though I do love that. (The forms, in all their empty beauty, are most certainly calorie-free, and just try to feed your hungry baby one. Truth? Virtue? No thank you; we'll have the chicken wing platter.) My body loves the palpability of food, but what my mind loves is cooking's generalized disdain for purity. Not to be confused with wholesomeness, mind you—cooking is very concerned with the health of the body; some say preparing food is akin to practicing medicine. When I say cooking disdains purity, what I'm talking about is the way that it prizes hybridization, bastardization, even adulteration. For the cook, purity has all the appeal of a bowl of undressed lettuce. And in cooking, the word we have for de-purifying is *seasoning*: the artful introduction of foreign elements to make something merely wholesome into something beautiful.

Seasoning is also valuable in itself, as an inculcator of character. It is an act that always rewards and often demands the most exquisite attention, judgment, and patience. Here's what it looks like: taste, then correct, then wait; then taste, correct, and wait. Not until it's right; until it's done. The cook exercises constant, feverish care, for the unexamined dish almost certainly will not be worth eating, and executes innumerable interventions and corrections, because a dish never comes out right just because you read the recipe correctly. Cooking unfolds in time, which is to say, in history, and as such it's subject to all the contingencies and vagaries of anything else that happens outside the covers of a book. On Sunday, I go to the butcher and buy cutlets; I salt them and dredge them in eggs and breadcrumbs, heat my oil, and brown them to perfection. My baby claps. Next Sunday, same cutlets, same crumbs, same oil, same pan. The cutlets come out soggy; my baby cries.

That's what it means to be part of history, living in the body. Our essential condition is to be acted upon by the forces of entropy and chance, and none of this, none of us, really lasts; a great book is, in the long view, as fleeting as a great meal, and all those who have thought the great thoughts and read the great words end up as the same kind of food, the kind the earth swallows. But in the interstices between oblivions there can be pleasure and meaning—provided we know how to whip them up. And doing that, I've found, is a learned skill: practicum, not colloquium.

Thank you for reading my essay, which, as I've said, is about cooking.

"I hold that Divine Providence is related and closely connected with the intellect, because Providence can only proceed from an intelligent being, from a being that is itself the most perfect Intellect."
-Maimonides

XXXIII
MARNIE SUGDEN

Being a part of the Great Books tradition at Pepperdine was more than impactful, it was life altering. It sparked a deep interest in understanding the Lord, His creation, and great ideas. A resulting quest for lifelong learning has been a blessing in my and my children's lives.

When I began Great Books at eighteen, my academic strengths were outside of the humanities. If a question could not be methodically calculated, I was unsure of my ability to contribute. At the outset, simply understanding the vocabulary within the source texts was difficult. Because I was insecure about contributing to these class discussions, I listened a lot.

The welcoming, albeit unnerving, circular seating arrangement was new as well. Each class member was able to see and be seen. We were not lectured or talked to about a particular text, but rather we were in a group discussion, led by a master.

Dr. Gose would pose questions. Ideally, silence followed for individual thought. As the discussion began, I was impressed by so many articulate classmates. Although, often in opposition to one another, these young adults honed their skills of clear and respectful communication, with an open mind to hear opposing views. They were not intimidated to speak up or ask a fellow student to clarify his or her perspective. In time, I was inspired to join the conversation; I stepped in with questions at first, and eventually offered some opinions.

Dr. Gose's encouragement to "be good" has found a home in my heart these last twenty years. His keen ability to listen, learn alongside, and guide us young people through the classics was a true gift.

My husband and I are currently raising three daughters to seek truth, beauty, and goodness on our own homeschool journey. I cherish the foundations that were established in my time participating in the Great Books Colloquium at Pepperdine.

"That which we hold by faith as divinely revealed, therefore, cannot be contrary to our natural knowledge."
-Aquinas

XXXIV
JOHN SWANSON

Great Books – In Medicine?

Before I started my undergraduate studies, I knew I wanted to work with kids and likely wanted to be a pediatrician. Why then, would I choose to take four semesters of Great Books when nearly all of my Biology major colleagues took the single "English 101" course? Part of it was the desire to read great works. I loved nearly all of the great American writers that we studied during high school so now was my chance to study greats from other nations, genres and time periods. Mostly, though, it was a requirement for the Honors Program – who didn't want to graduate in 3 years when you were paying for a private school education on your own dime? (Of course, in the end, I still took 4 years!) Although my intent for taking part in the Great Books Colloquium may have been selfish, in the end, it gave and has given back much more to me than I to it.

During the last half of my intern year, I figured out what I wanted to be when I grew up – a neonatologist (pediatrician caring for sick and premature newborn infants). I was taking care of a boy named Nathan who developed an infection of the intestines just prior to being sent home. His development of necrotizing enterocolitis required many surgeries and he ultimately passed away. He died peacefully in the arms of one of his primary nurses as his family lived hours away and did not have the ability to make it back to the hospital. This event, this process of dying, gave a fire to my passion and demonstrated to me the Art of Medicine.

Both Plato and Aristotle, two authors I never stole a thought of prior to Great Books, spoke of what a physician was. Actually, they wrote of what a Physician was. In *Politics*, Aristotle wrote that there are three kinds of physicians – an ordinary physician, one of the higher class, and lastly the intelligent man who has studied the art. Hippocrates, one who we think of as the Father of Medicine, wrote that the Art of Medicine consisted of the patient, the disease and the physician. Only by treating all three of these components can we understand the difference between the Art and Science of Medicine. The interaction between patient, physician and disease is the key to understanding Medicine.

My time in the Great Books program laid the foundation of my understanding of Medicine and more importantly, my practice of Medicine. As I think back over the last 15+ years of my medical career, I can see how Great Books shaped me as a physician as well as how it has directed my career. I continually find myself telling residents and fellows in training that the entire patient, including the family, is our true calling. Although we combat a multitude of disease processes and must learn intricate physiology, in order to truly understand Medicine, we must treat the entire patient. In my line of work, this includes the parents, siblings, and extended family. Only by incorporating ourselves as physicians into our patient's lives do we truly understand how best to "treat" the disease. Whether this is getting on the floor to play with the toddler siblings of the baby in front of me, or holding them as they pass to the next world when there is nobody else around, do we practice Medicine instead of medicine. Without Great Books, it is doubtful that I would have this greater appreciation.

"For we ought not to lend or do any good deed through hope in man, but only through hope in God."
-Aquinas

XXXV
ED WHEELER

My knee-jerk response, selfishly, is to characterize my greatest appreciation for my Great Books experience as that it was the first time that I felt that I was allowed to speak and be heard in a classroom. So as not to appear that I am indicting the sum of my undergraduate experience I should clarify that I have communicated verbally in other classes. That being said, when I think back on GB I recall the sheer joy of discourse. Unlike the requisite espousing of opinion, exhibiting that I had read a book, or regurgitating what the professor delivered, I had the opportunity to share my understanding of text, feelings about that understanding, and apply this understanding to my life and environment. I can't think of any prior experience in any other academic setting including my post graduate studies.

To go beyond the nostalgic but meaningful recollection above I would say the element of Great Books that has provided the greatest impact is how it altered my personal and professional life in regard to the notion of introspection or self-appraisal. The canon stands proudly on my office shelf and has for decades. I will still pull one out to find an underlined section that might shed light on a given situation. This is not necessarily to provide a solution or answer a question but more often to assist me in understanding my own decisions or actions. I find I can often reconcile my feelings or emotions around something as momentous as life's meaning to something as mundane as why a book or movie makes me sad or happy.

Cheers,
Ed Wheeler

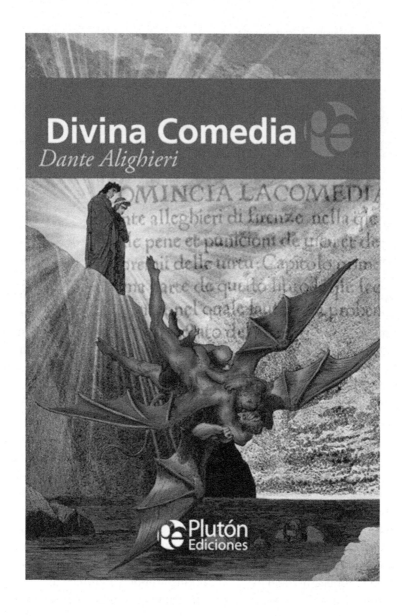

"…the light of God so penetrates the universe according to
the worth."
-Dante, *Divine Comedy*

1995

XXXVI
PAUL BEGIN

Interview of Paul Begin by Michael Gose

Gose: I have found that the best predictor whether a student will like Great Books is whether they appreciate Monty Python. Can you find humor in either or both?

Begin: Both. Irreverence is one my most valued life skills. In fact, it may be my only skill.

Gose: So far you are the only Pepperdine GB student to have returned to the faculty to teach Great Books.

Begin: I have taught many courses in the Hispanic Studies sequence, First Year Seminars, and Great Books. First thing to note is that the Great Books students are predominantly the best students that I have – the most engaged, hardest-working, earnest. I must raise my level of teaching to be ahead of their questions and do Socratic dialogue well. So, selfishly, Great Books has forced me to be a better teacher, both in preparing for graduate work and also in being an intellectual leader. I also find that many (not all) GB students have often developed a more subtle sense of humor. I try to emphasize the importance of beauty and humor. After all, the data that I have seen shows that, above all, a healthy sense of humor is essential for future success.*

*Here we define success as having as much fun as possible and laughing often.

Gose: For our readers, would you relate your story about reading the classics, ivy league competition, and your university program at the University of Virginia?

Begin: I arrived to the University of Virginia in 2000 to do a degree in Spanish literature, there were 11 other students hoping to receive a masters followed by a PhD. I cannot recall all of the pedigrees of every student, but for sure there were students who came from Princeton, Yale, Georgetown, and Emory. They had read Derrida and knew about Michel Foucault. My fellow graduate students also had specific courses by renowned faculty on narrow topics such as, "Left-hand Cuban writers living in exile with their terrorist cats." I had taken general classes on Spanish literature and culture and thus read the classics there, too. Mostly, I had spent my undergraduate time choosing between different types of surf wax and neoprene suits. (Use Sticky Bumps for cool water and get whatever suit is on sale during the November sales.) BUT I had also taken Great Books! I could read for hours on end. I could cite texts. I could engage in dialogue *and* witty banter. I could traffic in Aristotle, Plato, Rousseau, Mill, Marx, More, and (reluctantly) St. Augustine, among others. These thinkers had major influence in the Spanish intellectual history that I was studying. It was obvious to me that the more "fundamental" education of Great Books was more useful than the spotty system of specialized classes taken by my colleagues of other schools. I think GB also helped me to express myself clearly and to disagree when appropriate.

Gose: Did GB contribute to your decision to become a professor? Or was there any particular great book that influenced you?

Begin: I can answer both at once: It was Faulkner. Something about reading Faulkner for the first time in college (we were not introduced in high school) opened my mind to the mystery of literature. He was the most mysterious and captivating of the readings in GB IV. I had to work to come to an understanding. I read over passages multiple times. I gained a lot from discussing him with others. I found my professor's tactics of storming out of the classroom because no one had read properly to be simultaneously disturbing and motivating. In the end, I enjoyed the work and found the payoff worthwhile. So Faulkner plays a large role in my inspiration for graduate study. Coincidentally, Faulkner had been a frequent guest professor and visitor to the University of

Virginia, where I did my graduate work. He was dead when I arrived, of course, but the connection always felt personal, even if it was imagined.

Gose: Any advice to any future, current, and past GB students.

Begin: I have rarely been unsure of myself but Great Books was intimidating. I took it because I wanted to read all the great authors while in college. My high school had not provided much in this regard, unless you consider Vonnegut and Keller all time classics. (Maybe?). I even did a book report on a book title *My Name is Dave and I Am an Alcoholic*. I wanted the challenge and the intellectual cache. So, I jumped in.

Professor Victoria Myers gave me a C on my first paper. Her comments were direct and humiliating. She made me sit down with her to review my paper. It was painful but necessary. I was spouting off without anything to back up my ideas. She gave me an intellectual slap in the face, put some smelling solutions under my nose and forced me back into the ring. I also thought the stakes were high during discussion, so I sometimes refused to participate unless I was really sure about things. Why all the seriousness? Especially when I had spent my whole life trying to scare people, especially my grandmother (my paternal grandmother, not my maternal one – she made the food I liked)?

Here would be my advice, and not only for Great Books: It is better to read carefully as much as you can than to read more but not feel grounded in the information. With solid reading, you can enter the conversation with more solid footing. Highlight the jokes and make note of them. When conversation dies down, you can always say, "So what did you think of X passage?" Catch them off guard. It shows you read and that you know what is most important.

"You can find the right path by listening to your own spirit, which tells you: 'This is the way home.' I pray God that he may accompany you and bring your wandering steps to safety."
-Petrarch

XXXVII
JOHN CARIGNAN

My experience in Great Books affected my life in ways I would never have realized at the time. I entered Pepperdine as a Sports Medicine major thinking I was going to make my mark in the world as an athletic trainer. I loved biology and sports and figured this was my way to turn two loves into a career. Of course I also love literature, so entering Pepperdine I wanted to challenge myself and take Great Books instead of the typical Freshman seminar and entry level English.

One of the genius elements of Great Books at Pepperdine is the students ability to choose the professor they wish to take for each semester of the series. Great Books could be whatever experience you want it to be. My first semester professor left me wanting. He let the class discussions go in directions that didn't feel in line with the works and he gave very little guidance with writing assignments, so I made sure I tried a different professor for semester two.

Second semester was better, it was more of what I expected a college English class to be, lots of reading, intense class discussions, and more writing then I could have imagined, but it still wasn't totally what I was looking for. I went looking for a third professor in three semesters. It was during this semester where the program became real and memorable. I will never forget the second day of class, it was a moment that I will carry with me the rest of my life. We were given a reading assignment and we all came into class read to talk and answer whatever questions the professor posed. None of us had taken a class of his before, so we really didn't know him yet as a teacher or a person. He asked what the author had to say about happiness, a girl very confidently raised her hand. She was a smart girl, a girl who had probably always been at the top of her class, a girl who always came up with something profound and pungent to say, and she answered the professor like she must have a

132

thousand times before in other classes, I think what the author is saying… That's all she got out before the professor cut her off in a loud annoyed voice, almost a yell, "I don't care what you think!" As I think back on the moment, there was an audible gasp let out by the class, but I'm sure that was just in my head. I had never heard a teacher tell a student he didn't care what a student thought, and I'm pretty sure no one else in that room had either. Didn't he just ask? Why would he do that if he didn't care? "Don't tell me what you think," he finished after a pause just long enough to make most question whether they were in the right class or not, "tell me what the author says. Use his words."

I changed my major junior year, college science and me did not get along. I finished my fourth year a few credits short of a degree in Telecommunications and decided I needed to take some time off of school. I bummed around Los Angeles for a while, working in record stores and enjoying life, but that started to become tired and I realized that I needed to be doing something with more purpose. So, I looked back at my college experience, thinking about the classes I enjoyed the most and felt the most alive during, and I glanced over my transcript to see what classes I had taken and passed, and very quickly something became abundantly clear. I had Cs and Ds in science and history and video production, but in Great Books I had As. When I told stories of my college classes and my college professors it was of my Great Books classes. So, I went back to school and became a high school English teacher.

I love my job. It's not always fun, in fact it can be pretty frustrating and depressing at times, but I love what I do and I know that it's where I should be. I tell my students every year about that professor who told the girl he didn't care what she thought, use the text. I'm sure she never signed up for that professor again, she most likely thought that class in the same way I think of my first semester, but for me that class helped me find my way. If it wasn't for Great Books I don't know what I would be doing right now, maybe I would have found my way to teaching anyway, but I know for sure having the choice to take those four courses added to my college experience in a way that allowed me to figure things out.

"Nothing brings so much honor to a man who rises to power as the new laws and methods devised by him." "From this rises a question: is it better to be loved than feared, or the reverse? The answer is that the prince should be both feared and loved if possible… it is much safer to be feared than loved, if one of the two has to be given up. For it can be said of men in general that they are ungrateful, talkative, tricky, and deceitful, eager to avoid dangers, anxious for gain."
-Machiavelli, *The Prince*

XXXVIII
SARAH ROCKEY

As I mulled over what I was going to write about Great Books, the only words that came to mind (repeatedly) belong to James Wright: "I have wasted my life."

Obviously, my subconscious is not a fan of this task.

And I don't blame it. What can I say about something that is so much a part of me that the attempt to analyze just that part led to an analysis of my entire life? And an existential crisis the likes of which I've never experienced? When I try to analyze or quantify the impact of Great Books, everything somehow sounds so elitist. And exclusive. And irritating. And in many ways it is.

But.

I read the texts. I sat in the circle. I participated in the discussion.

So I know it's so much more than Canon worship.

I mean, it is 100% Canon worship, but that's not all it is.

Socratic dialogue was less discussion and more

> dissection.

>> Of the text.

>>> The idea.

> My brain.

>> My beliefs.

>>> My heart.

And that's why it has stuck with me. I probably couldn't name even 30% of what I read. But I can tell you that, as a teacher, I have often been cut by the memory of liberty and license. A context for understanding the abuse of power, even at its most subtle, was carved into my psyche as I sat in that circle.

And when I'm touched by the beauty of creation, I remember "being understood from what has been made." The first Bible verse that was really my own because of the analysis I had to give of it in Great Books. Considering I've been sitting in a church building 3 times a week my entire life, that's saying something.

And when I'm having a particularly arrogant day, my subconscious likes to push to the forefront our class' discussion of *Candide* when every single person, save one who would not back down no matter what was thrown at her, argued the exact opposite of the point. Because we were too literal. We saw the tree and missed the forest. A really, really big forest. For a fairly small tree. It was a humbling experience, but a valuable lesson.

Which brings me to my overall point. Or observation. Or whatever.

Great Books taught me to look at the whole picture. It taught me to listen, not just hear. It taught me to take a good, hard look at myself. It taught me thinking critically has nothing to do with being critical. But most importantly, it taught me that if you read the wisdom of thousands of years and don't walk away with a better understanding of yourself and your fellow man--and a little compassion for both--you missed the point. Maybe "I think, therefore I am." But so does everyone else.

And now I kind of hate Great Books

But I'd still take it again.

Every time.

"Presumption is our natural and original malady. The most calamitous and fragile of all creatures is man, and at the same time the proudest."
-Montaigne

135

1996

XXXIX
CREEDANCE KRESCH

My recollections of The Great Books Colloquium are unique in that I was an only child, my father started the Great Books program at Pepperdine, and eventually I decided to take his class for Great Books IV. Certainly I cannot be expected to sort out all of the daughter memories from the student memories. But clearly Great Books had its influence. I was an Art major as an undergraduate. A couple of years later I returned to school for an M.B.A. Despite my lack of an undergraduate degree in Business or Economics, I was somewhat surprised by my competitive advantages in the MBA program. I was used to reading long (and dare I say tedious) materials; I was frankly a much better writer than most other students; I was used to working in a group with the objective of understanding and getting it right.

Further, in college Great Books allowed me to take four discussion based classes, instead of the likely alternative of lecture classes. I am still in contact with some of my classmates from Great Books. Two of my very favorite teachers, Gary Hart and Victoria Myers, were Great Books professors. My two children both love to read. My daughter, now ten, says that she plans to go to Pepperdine and take a class from "Papa". As my father celebrates the legacy of 100 years of Great Books, I know that his emphasis is on the legacy handed down person to person. This year he has two students whose parents were in his earlier Great Books classes. I know nothing would make him happier than if his granddaughter or grandson continued the legacy.

"Lovers and madmen have such seething brains,
Such shaping fantasies, that apprehend
More than cool reason ever comprehends."
-Shakespeare, *Midsummer Night's Dream*

XL
MONIRA PARKINSON-COLE

Per Eric Thomas, "There is a limit you will not be able to go past if you don't understand the importance of reading." I could not have said it any better myself. There is a certain understanding a well-travelled person comes to due to exposure. They have seen something different beyond their city limits and have a better understanding if not appreciation for what they have learned and how that knowledge contributes to their personal growth.

When I think of the Great Books Colloquium series at Pepperdine, I reminisce about how far my mind travelled in those four semesters. I went to many places and I am a better person for it. It was through the pages of *I and Thou, Who's Afraid of Virginia Wolf, The Divine Comedy, Gulliver's Travels, The Canterbury Tales, I Know Why the Caged Bird Sings, Being and Nothing* and many other works that I grew into the person I'm today. The debates and challenging questions we poured over in class taught me to think differently, to stand up for my beliefs and to read in between the lines.

I still have those books and they stand proudly on my shelf as a reminder of my journey. I will reference them from time to time to remind myself of an important point or to teach my children about the power of words and thought. As the world becomes more technologically advanced, I pray that Great works literature do not get lost and that we find a way to create more beautiful words that will be forever intertwined in the human legacy. The wisdom and history of those works are the very catalyst of human advancement. I preach less screen time and more reading in my house and will continue to do so because I want my children to travel through the pages of Great Books and find their own destinies.

I am eternally grateful to be a GBC alum and for the community of professors and students who will always be a part of me.

"A pair of star-cross'd lovers take their life;
Whose misadventured piteous overthrows
Do with their death bury their parents' strife."
-Shakespeare, *Romeo and Juliet*

1997

.

XLI
WILL JOHNSON

With age I do not reflect on the great ideas anymore as things to be pondered, discussed, questioned, and ultimately understood. At this stage of my life the pursuit of philosophy for philosophy's sake is a luxury that time rarely affords. However, I feel that the Great Books program has influenced my life path in many immeasurable, and wholly positive, ways.

What made Great Books great for me was not the books (though I thoroughly enjoyed many of them) but that the friendships that I made while arguing (as the hours passed in the night the discussions became increasingly heated and often ended up in arguments) the great ideas became some of the greatest friendships of my life. You truly get to know someone when they are passionately defending their definition of good and evil and how either, neither, or both of those things has anything to do with truth, justice, virtue, or happiness.

I definitely do not talk with these friends as much as I would like but they are those true friends that you can not see in five years but feel like you are caught up with in five minutes. It is not the minutiae of life that we want to share when we see each other but the broad strokes of the greater things we are working towards. The day to day fades away and we spend a few hours discussing the same ideas we always have but framed through current events and the decades of experience we have shared.

The biggest compliment that I can give the Great Books program is that I hope that when my children are of age that are able to take part and pursue the understanding of those ideas with their friends with the same enthusiasm that I did with mine.

I am determined to prove a villain,
And hate the idle pleasures of these days.
-Shakespeare, *Richard III*

XLII
YUNA KIM

I remember the day Dr. Gose asked if anyone was thinking of pursuing a Ph.D. degree during one of our class discussions. I made sure to keep my hands firmly planted beside my side as I had absolutely no intention of doing so. Yet, here I am, finishing up my 6th year as a marketing professor. Many things have changed since I was in college. In terms of how business is taught, in this age of technology, the focus is on how to scrape "big data" from the online world and use it to understand the human (consumer) mind. In terms of the students, I am constantly cautioned to convey information in short, concise formats and not to expect Generation Z, a generation that has an attention span of about 8 seconds, to read more than few lines of text at a time. As I break down my course material into smaller chunks of information, I can't help but wonder, how is Great Books doing with the new generation?

I sincerely hope that students will continue to recognize how special the Great Books Program is and take advantage of the (what could possibly be the last or only!) opportunity to become philosophers. I really do believe that I was more of a philosopher, or lover of wisdom and knowledge, when I met with my Great Books cohort every week to read and discuss the great books in college than when I was a Ph.D. candidate. What I realized after entering graduate school and spending endless days and nights learning statistical programs or living in fear of publishing or perishing is that Ph.D. candidates, who are supposedly in pursuit of discovering knowledge, simply do not have the time or peace of mind to read a great book, ponder on it, sit with others who have also read and pondered on it, and spend a few hours discussing, not criticizing, but purely discussing, the ideas that emerge.

When I received Dr. Gose's invitation to write a short reflection on Great Books, I realized how much I miss the time and place that allowed me to read and write about great ideas. A time and place that allowed me to read and write without worrying about getting published or promoted. I also realized that I still have most of the books from my Great Books days neatly placed on my bookshelf. Apparently, even though I don't have the time or peace of mind to read the books again, I still want to hold onto the experience. It seems that, having experienced Great Books, as Plato would say, my soul will always yearn to fly home on the wings of love to the world of ideas. But, for now, back to grading!

"'Tis pride that pulls the country down."
-Shakespeare, *Othello*

XLIII
CHRISTINA LITTLEFIELD

I have many fond memories of my semesters in Great Books. I remember breakfasts in the Caf after my first semester 8 a.m. class where my classmates and I would continue arguing over the Greek philosophers over omelets and waffles. I remember taking such issue with Dante's picture of purgatory that I wrote my essay in the form of an imaginary dialectic between Dante and Martin Luther. I remember becoming so obsessed with Jane Austen's *Emma* that I wrote a 30-page analysis of her satire while overseas in London. And I remember my delight in the *Brothers Karamazov* turning to distaste as the pages went on, seemingly without end, and it became clear I was the only one in my class beyond the professor slogging through.

But what I remember most, and continue to cite to my own students, is a particular point Dr. Michael Gose made that first semester as we were discussing Plato's *Republic.* Gose pointed out that when Plato was making fun of the sophists for being full of hot air, he was making only a slightly veiled fart joke. And that if Plato could make fart jokes, we could critique Plato. And if we could critique Plato, we could critique anyone.

This ability to critique one of the world's greatest philosophers, while still articulating his continued wisdom for humanity today, was freeing. It meant that I didn't have to agree completely with Plato just because he was Plato. It also meant that I could fall in love with his realm of forms while psychoanalyzing his negative view of human nature and ripping apart his advocacy of censorship. This broadened my critical thinking skills so that I could look at any subject from multiple angles and make a critical assessment of the good, the bad and the ugly. This in turn aided my own personal growth, my journalism, my church history scholarship, and my own teaching as I aim to develop critical thinkers.

I cite Gose and his point about Plato's fart joke often in my Christianity and Culture classes, as students often get hung up on Thomas Jefferson. In my sections we study civil religion, or how the sacred and secular mix in forming the beliefs of the nation. Reading Richard Hughes' *Myths America Live By,* students learn, usually for the first time, how the man who gave America the glorious words of the Declaration of Independence, "that **all men are created equal**, that they are endowed by their Creator with certain unalienable Rights, that among these are Life, Liberty and the Pursuit of Happiness" also promoted the idea that blacks were biologically inferior and that Native Americans should be wiped from the earth because their civilizations were unnatural.

Students immediately want to abandon Jefferson entirely, but it's Jefferson's rhetoric that future Americans use to fight for greater equality in terms of race, gender and even class. The Plato-fart-analogy helps them see that Jefferson is just a man, a man shaped by the prejudices of his time, and we can and must critique him. But we can also critique the bad and the ugly while holding on to the good Jefferson gave us. That way we see him and others less as two-dimensional heroes and more as three-dimensional humans; critical thinking tears down false idols and allows for truth to reign.

Great Books lets students explore the wisdom of the ages, but more importantly, it develops critical thinking skills that lets them sort the wisdom ... from the fart jokes.

"For, since we are all priests alike, no man may put himself forward or take upon himself, without our consent and election, to do that which we have all alike power to do."
"Christ's body is not double or twofold, one temporal, the other spiritual. He is one Head, and he has one body."
-Martin Luther

XLIV
JILL WINQUIST LOVE

Participating in the Great Books Colloquium was one of the best decisions I made while attending Pepperdine – right up there with traveling internationally, choosing lifelong friends, and meeting my now husband of 16+ years. Though I was a science major at the time, I learned the most in my Great Books classes because I invested the most time and energy into them. Though many of the book titles and concepts have faded from my memory over the last 18 years, my life was forever changed by the Great Books experience. Below are just a few highlights for me.

The polyfocal conspectus. Great Books (and Dr. Gose in particular) taught me about the polyfocal conspectus, the process of viewing a problem or idea through multiple perspectives. It's a simple concept, yet I have found this to be valuable in any environment. It helped me to learn how to analyze an issue from multiple perspectives, something that has served me well in solving problems for graduate school, work, and relationships. (Do the ends justify the means? Is it for the greater good? Is it right for all, or just some?) The process has also enhanced my understanding and respect for other people. I have a deeper appreciation for how generational, gender, cultural, religious, and socioeconomic differences affect people's experiences in the world and shape their worldviews and priorities. As our world has become inundated by social media and echo chambers in recent years, it has become more important than ever for me to remember that people view the same issue in different ways. The polyfocal conspectus has allowed me to hold onto an opinion loosely as I seek to view political, religious, or business ideas through another perspective. While I may not change my position, I am able to understand and appreciate the reasons why someone else may draw a different conclusion. I have become a more patient, tolerant, and respectful citizen thanks to the polyfocal conspectus.

Engaging in the peripatetic. One semester, Dr. Gose shared that he walked around the track in the mornings, and he invited anyone in our class to "engage in the peripatetic" with him some time. The Aristotelian idea was new to me. Other than scheduled class outings or the occasional greeting while crossing campus, I'd never really interacted with a professor outside of class. Yet one foggy morning, I laced up my running shoes and met Dr. Gose and another fellow student to walk around the track. I don't remember exactly what we talked about, but our conversation probably alternated between concepts from our current reading and what was happening in our lives. I realize now that breaking down the physical barrier between "learning" and "living" is how intellectual ideas can most easily be absorbed into real life. I only went walking with Dr. Gose once, but it expanded my idea of engaging with a teacher or mentor in new ways and taught me to be open to learning. I appreciated the invitation to learn from my professor in a more casual setting, and it reminded me of Jesus and his disciples. Jesus used examples from real life to teach powerful concepts, and now that I'm a parent, I'm mindful of engaging in the peripatetic every day to cultivate a love of learning in my children.

The Socratic method. Thanks to the small class sizes in Great Books, there was pressure on us students to actually read the required material (something I admittedly didn't always do for other classes). When reading for Great Books, I focused on absorbing and understanding as much as I could. I underlined and highlighted sections, dog-eared certain pages, and even wrote notes or questions in the margins. I did those things because I knew that I would need to support my positions in class. Dr. Gose would ask students, "So what?" multiple times to get to the heart of an idea or position; though it intimidated me very much at first, I came to appreciate that the possibility of being in the hot seat forced me to be prepared and to actively engage in the learning process at all times. I also learned not to be afraid of changing my opinion if I found that there was no longer enough evidence to support my original position.

These lessons have prepared me well for graduate school and real life. In matters of faith, politics, business strategies, parenting tactics, and more, I always try do my homework and truly understand why I believe and do what I do.

Curiosity. This is closely linked to my appreciation for the Socratic method. Great Books cultivated curiosity – and the more I learned, the more I wanted to learn. In the nearly 20 years since my last Great Books class, I value curiosity more than ever. I seek to surround myself with curious people in both my personal and professional life. I have found that curious people aren't afraid to ask questions to challenge the status quo, push boundaries, gain understanding, and even encourage others to deepen their own understanding of their positions. Curious people aren't afraid to make mistakes because there are lessons to be learned from them. They keep learning about their craft, other people, and the world. They also appreciate the curiosity in others. Now that my son is four years old, I am able to tolerate the incessant "Why?" questions because I know that he is simply curious and trying to make sense of the world. I'm constantly amazed by the insights and revelations that he shares, and I love that he connects the dots differently than I do. It's wonderful to see him begin his journey of lifelong learning with such enthusiasm, and I want to do my part to make sure he is never afraid to ask questions.

The wisdom of the head and the heart. There were so many exceptional books that taught me important ideas, but the great book that impacted my life the most is Hard Times by Charles Dickens. In it, I read about the wisdom of the head and wisdom of the heart. It clarified for me that intellectual knowledge and matters of the heart (e.g., compassion, empathy, and more) do not necessarily need to be at odds; rather, one can and should take both the head and the heart into consideration. In business school, I learned about IQ and EQ and how great leaders were high in both, and I was reminded of the wisdom of the head and the wisdom of the heart that I'd learned from Sissy Jupe's character in Hard Times. Around that same time, while still in business school, I was laid off from a financial services start-up that I'd been a part of for two years. I was devastated because I loved working on such a challenging and stimulating endeavor. Upon further reflection, though, I knew that my heart wasn't truly in the work. I enjoyed the work but did not feel that I was really contributing to the greater good, nor was I utilizing my unique set of skills and passions to my potential. During my unemployment, I took a course at the business school career center and set my sights on a career that would utilize the wisdom of the head and the wisdom of the heart. This led me to the senior care industry. I started my new career by working in sales and marketing for a continuing care retirement community for a few years as I finished my MBA. I also earned my certification to become an administrator of retirement communities and soon after obtained my master's degree in gerontology. Six years ago, my coworker and I started our own business to consult with families who need help navigating the confusing world of senior care. I am able to use my knowledge and experience to help families make good decisions regarding care options, insurance coverage, legal preparation, and other age-related issues. Part of my work is to come alongside a family to remind them that they are not alone, answer questions, and simply listen. Every day, I utilize both the wisdom of the head and the heart to bring peace of mind to families during a stressful and often sad time of life. I enjoy the challenge of balancing the logistical parameters along with the emotional and relational factors as I guide families to make decisions that are right for them. Though end-of-life matters are not always pleasant, I find great satisfaction and joy in minimizing stress and enhancing the quality of life of aging adults. I am certain that I would not have chosen this vocation if the wisdom of the heart was not equally important to me as the wisdom of the head.

Conclusion. When I was an incoming freshman, I chose Great Books because of the intellectual challenge. I didn't realize that it would lead to a lifelong pursuit of wisdom – wisdom of the head *and* of the heart. I also gained tools to grow in wisdom by being curious, doing my homework, searching for understanding, seeking multiple perspectives, and remaining respectful during debate. I hope that these tools have helped me to be a better wife, mother, friend, consultant, and follower of God. I am so grateful for the Great Books curriculum and those who teach the classes, for my life is better because of the experience.

"There are and can be only two ways of searching into and discovering truth. The one flies from the senses and particulars to the most general axioms, and from these principles, the truth of which it takes for settled and immovable, proceeds to judgment and to the discovery of middle axioms. And this way is now in fashion. The other derives axioms from the senses and particulars, rising by a gradual and unbroken ascent, so that it arrives at the most general axioms last of all. This is the true way, but as yet untried."
-Francis Bacon, *New Method*

1998

XLV
MICHELLE LIU CARRIGER

'Trying, Testing, Leaping, Failing'

The year after I graduated from Pepperdine, I was living in Japan, teaching English in a mountain village. Emma was one of the first, closest friends I made, the only foreigner in her town as I was in mine. Emma was a graduate of Cambridge University in English and so was her boyfriend, Edward, who came to visit Japan in the dead of winter. Sitting around Emma's low table, we were basically children so freshly launched on the world, we thought we were adults. It was a sort of cosmopolitanism—Irish-by-way-of-northern-England, American-by-way-of-Kansas, now in the middle-of-nowhere Japan. We had made it to fancy schools, we were pretty accomplished for very young people, learning how to be adults away from college. I remember vividly the sound of Edward and Emma's incredulous laughter when I told them about the Great Books Colloquium. I gathered that what was uncool about having read a ton of Aristotle, Augustine, Aquinas, and other folks whose names didn't start with 'A' was that *Great Books* were now recognized as a terribly old-fashioned and really even retrograde concept. The literature readers of Cambridge University, despite being the inventors of canons, certainly were not reading stuff like that any more and suddenly I felt very old-fashioned, very outsider, and very small compared to Emma and Edward's laughing self-assurance about their own path and the rightness of Cambridge's vision when it came to books. And the truth is, I don't use my Kierkegaard too much. Like ever.

But time passed, I went on to graduate school in the Humanities and I started reading some of the things that Emma and Edward must have read: Judith Butler, Badiou, Baudrillard, Bourdieu, Benjamin, and other theorists whose names don't start with 'B.' Over time, I realized that maybe what I learned from toiling through 'great' books wasn't a list of cool quotes, or a useful familiarity with Empiricist philosophy, but methods of reading, methods of puzzling, thinking, learning to be in the fog of uncertainty and be okay with that. That last one actually I think is a good lesson for life, not just academia.

Now I'm a professor at UCLA with an Ivy League PhD and I don't teach Great Books per se, but do find myself trying to inculcate the same lessons I learned from all those texts. How to read slowly, on paper, for depth as well as breadth. What you miss when you deem everything "tl;dr." How do you read a text expansively for what may come along, rather than something strategic you want from it? How do you sit with the discomfort of weird texts, opaque texts, hard texts, annoying texts? How do you hold on to what's important and let go the rest? How do you put texts in conversation with each other? How do you read them for philosophical and knowledge insights, but how might you read them instead as documents of a society or a culture? I think I also learned some stuff that not all my professors necessarily enjoyed: challenging people in discussion (including professors), trying something out in discussion and maybe being wrong, learning how to be brave enough to attempt a leap, trusting that I will learn something during the flight, not that I needed to have everything hammered out in advance.

These are the things that I value in my job as an academic, teacher, and researcher and these are tendencies I also value in myself to the extent I am able to practice them. I suspect there are other ways to learn these things, but the way I learned them was by agreeing to jump into a great big sea of ideas and words and authors without a raft of Cliff's Notes or secondary textbooks.

Even Emma came around eventually. We've stayed friends for all these years; she's a novelist and teaches writing for NYU in London and I even stayed with her while researching my PhD dissertation in London several years ago. I brought up that moment when she and Edward had laughed at the very phrase "Great Books" (Edward, by the way, had gone by the wayside long before). This time, the rigidity of young knowledge had worn off, and Emma thought she herself could have used more reading from the moldy old canon.

Years of thinking through the task of educating students—for Emma, in the craft and art of writing, for me in theatre history and performance studies (and writing, since virtually all academic thinking is still expressed through writing)—had both of us thinking differently about Books and their Greatness. The point about the political valences of selection and inclusion in something as sweeping as a canon of Great Books is well-taken, but we might also look at the Canon as descriptive not prescriptive: something like a vast primary archive of what has mattered. I have all kinds of texts that I would add to that vast library of *what has mattered*; a major question, maybe THE most important question, might be to examine what has mattered and all the reasons why it was this and not that which has been added to our shared store of knowledge and insight. Why whole groups of people are so wildly underrepresented in our lists of what has mattered. Those are all questions that belong with the canon, not outside it.

The invitation of the Great Books thus remains: an invitation to join the most pressing, most difficult, most important conversations ever had by humans on this planet. (Indeed, it encompasses the questions of what are humans, and what is this planet. Why take them as givens?) It takes a gesture of real faith in a student as young as we were when we embarked on the Great Books Colloquium to imagine that we would be able to rise to the loftiness of that opportunity. Indeed, I think much of the value of it wasn't that some of us did rise, but that we also learned the value of trying, of leaping, of failing. That's pretty much what life on this planet seems like to me:
you could read the manuals, but you'll notice that life doesn't conform to the manuals' instructions. What you really learned from that reading wasn't the rules but a method of trying, testing, leaping, failing and being okay.

Art done by Michelle Liu Carriger circa 2000

"The notion of God is prior to that of myself. For how would it be possible for me to know that I doubt that I desire—that is, that I lack something and am not all perfect—if I did not have in myself any idea of a being more perfect than my own, by comparison with which I might recognize the defects of my own nature?"
-Rene Descartes, *Meditations on First Philosophy*

XLVI
KRISTINE

There's nothing quite like an empty lot in Colombo. The unchecked greed of greenery and the sapphire blue shade under the unmolested palm trees suggests the need for some lolling about in honor of poorly executed land deeds. Wholly alluring, as if an acre of Milton's paradise has made it into the 21st century. Milton. With a decent editor that book could have been 17 pages long. Too many superfluous descriptions. Not that I would ever do that...

But no lolling today. I am just a face in a train window, winding its cobra slithering way out of the capital, but with the noise level of a particularly agitated murder of crows. Six hours to go. Yet how much more glowingly alive this is than all the blank mental pages that I accrue with my airline frequent flier miles. A train in Sri Lanka is always a train in Sri Lanka. Never a moment of geographical incertitude in this teardrop country. Virgil would never write about a 777 plane dumping him off at a terminal filled with internationally repetitious "lifestyle" brand stores. Virgil. He could work with this. This train is a weak vessel, subject to all the bored invasive gods you would need for a founding myth, some even now hounding the train as it ascends from pounding white sun into the soft witchery of white clouds relaxing on top of neon green rolling waves of tea.

Tea pickers in orange and pink and green and yellow and blue are smiling back at the kids hanging out the train windows and doors, their waving hands full of tea leaves. When our black freckled exhaust passes by they will go back to plucking, filling the post-train quiet with a hymn of leaves. The lush shushing like a thousand librarians half-heartedly taking bookish children to task. Though the women whose jewel-glorious saris lavishly ornament the hills of green with such élan, are likely to have only a primary education or less. Sharing tin shacks that are hardly their own and years away from attempting to enter an elitist university library like Woolf writes of. Woolf. It's as likely as not that if she sipped tea at The Orchard with the Grantchester Group, it was Ceylon tea from Nuwara Eliya, plucked by the great great grandmothers of the women I see.

I remember drinking my first cup of Ceylon tea one winter, the ruby colored brew with mellow tones seducing me like a well-tuned viola suddenly heard in between the usual Assam and Kenyan violins. This, I averred, was the best tea I had ever had. So, it was serendipity to find myself here in "Serendib". On a black passport no less, which meant an embarrassing skyrocketing of my comparative wealth translating into a six-bedroom house and a housekeeper named Kusum, who sits next to me on this rattling train. Who, and this hurts my soul, has grown up drinking corrupted tea sold on the local market. Obviously, I buy her all the tea she needs, and presently we are cutting out all possible villainous middlemen by heading to the source. Over the last two years, Kusum has unexpectedly and thoroughly tentacled into my heart. Perhaps I need Aristotle to tell me what to file this friendship under. Aristotle. He would probably be able to tell me why this diplomat's best friend and constant travel mate is her 53 year old housekeeper. Not that I actually require answers.

Much of what I love about Sri Lanka is the inexplicable. I do not know this yet, standing (tort law free) at the open train door to better inhale my tea heaven as it whizzes by, but when we finally arrive at our hotel tonight, I will find myself eating dinner while compelled to listen to a live band whose lead singer has decided he would rather whistle all night. And thus, I will go to sleep with a mix of the train's jarring dance along the rails still echoing in my bones and the longest available version of "Lady in Red" swirling through my brain in a regrettably unforgettable warble of a human whistle. I can't think of anywhere I would rather be though, inhabiting this tea factory turned hotel at a crisp limpid 6,300 feet above sea level. If I had to find my garden to inhabit, Voltaire would find me somewhere in the hotel's 25 acres of tea, enjoying nature's peace stippled with a constant supply of Sri Lankan ironies. Voltaire. I share his Weltschmerz. I mull too often over the inventory of my internal cicatrices, accrued by an invisible sjambok in places as strange as Kandahar and as familiar as Minneapolis.

But I believe the world will be set to rights at the end of this train ride. That my journey will eventually deposit me in a hidden tea garden full of droopy clouds that like to sleep in late. I will sit in pricelessly comfortable silence next to Kusum, and we will share a pot of Ceylon tea brewed at tea pickers' strength, so that even a moderately obese mouse will be able to tap dance across its surface. And I will get rid of the bored invasive gods who managed to follow my train all the way from Colombo to Nuwara Eliya.... Yes, somehow, I will find a way to shed all these dead authors and simply enjoy my cup of tea.

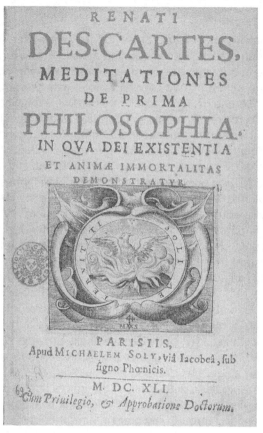

"I am nevertheless subject to innumerable errors...Thus I clearly recognize that error as such is not something real which depends upon God, but only a deficiency...mistakes on my part occur because the power that God has given me to discriminate between the true and the false is not infinite...consequently, when I come to examine myself closely and to consider what are my errors, which alone testify that there is imperfection in me, I find that they depend upon two joint causes, namely, the faculty of knowing which I possess and the faculty of choice, or rather of free will...whence, then, do my errors arise? Only from the fact that the will is much more ample and far-reaching than the understanding...thus it happens that I make mistakes and that I sin."
-Descartes, *Meditations on First Philosophy*

XLVII
KIMBERLEY KIRKSEY

I have always enjoyed spending time with the greats. Whether it be through the sounds of Rachmaninoff, Puccini, and Mozart or the words of Dante, Plato, or Karl Marx; it all made me feel quite worldly. As both art forms and I ruminated on love, the universe, as well as life and death. In hindsight, I ponder the actual worldliness of the narratives extolled.

Art done by Kimberley Kirksey, circa 2000

That all this good of evil shall produce,
And evil turn to good; more wonderful
Than that which by creation first brought forth
Light out of darkness! Full of doubt I stand,
Whether I should repent me now of sin
By me done and occasioned, or rejoice
Much more, that much more good thereof shall spring,
To God more glory, more good will to men
From God, and over wrath grace shall abound.
-John Milton, *Paradise Lost*

XLVIII
PAULO RODRIGUEZ

My first memory the Great Books course was the excitement of finding out I was able to add it to my schedule just 2 days before school was to start, followed by the dread of finding out I had to read half (all?!) of the Iliad and write a 5 page paper on it by the first day of class. I was always an avid reader and always a self-proclaimed "bad writer," so I had to jump right in and immerse myself in the grind that would be Great Books in order to reap the benefits. The benefits, of course, being the exposure I would get so many great works of literature and philosophies throughout history and the analysis that would follow. The ancient Greek and Roman works stand out, as do Kant, Nietzsche, Kierkegaard, Kafka, Thoreau, and de Beauvoir. I remember that much of the 3rd semester I would read something one week and be totally convinced of that philosophy, but turn around the next week and be convinced of a nearly opposite worldview. It seemed fickle of me, but I suppose this is what college should be about: learning that there are a number of valid ways of understanding the world and human nature. At the end of the four semesters, Dr. Gose asked us to create a final project with very few limitations on what this creation could look/sound/smell like. I chose to write and perform a song. It was not particularly "deep", but I remember the experience of recording it with much fondness. I spent hours in a friend's dorm room trying to produce something that I wouldn't be too embarrassed to share with the class. It was set to Jewel's song, "Jupiter," and I consider it a success.

I continue to be an avid reader of fiction, non-fiction, biographies, and classics. In the last year, I have discovered a podcast called Philosophize This! which takes listeners on a mostly chronological journey through the world of philosophy from the Pre-Socratics to The Frankfurt School of thought (as of this writing) and beyond. I listen to an episode, and then re-listen and take notes. I feel like I'm creating my own Great Books course—the podcast edition. It feels good to feel like I am still learning, still expanding my mind, and still allowing myself to see the world through a different lens.

"Freely they stood who stood, and fell who fell...
When will and reason (reason also is choice)
Useless and vain, of freedom both despoiled,
Made passive both, had served necessity..."
-John Milton, *Paradise Lost*

XLIX
LEIGHTON COWART

Great Books III Expressive Outcomes
December 2, 1999

When asked to write about Great Books, my first inclination is to highly praise the program, this semester's class, the university for offering it, and every professor that has so much mentioned the program in passing; I am restrained from doing this, however, by two considerations. The first is from personal experience: early on, I recognized that praise for one's efforts may be good for emotional well-being but tends to be didactically useless unless accompanied by some instruction on how to continue doing well in whatever is being considered. The second consideration derives from the program itself: given its emphasis on rationality and discussion, I suspect that if one can't find something intelligent to say about Great Books then one probably didn't pay attention enough to be able to praise it anyway.

I will start by describing how I have been able to use Great Books perspectives outside the classroom over the past three semesters; not because I think that its practical usefulness is its only function, but rather because such a discussion will provide a convenient springboard to being able to describe the way I have been able to use it to better understand myself.

Great Books has improved my socialization, in a sense; being able to quote classical texts at random (though appropriate) points in a conversation has earned me the following social benefits: Dr. Coodey threw chalk at me once; Dr. Maddox has told me to shut up three (possibly four) times; and I even received the coveted 'Uh-huh' of Indifference from Dr. Brock.

Aside from these, the dialectical techniques taught in GB have proved immensely useful in discussions outside of class. I note a marked contrast between these discussions, in which no particular viewpoint is advocated, and debates, where there is disagreement between the participants; the dialectical method is immensely more useful, I think, in terms of both of enjoyment and productive discussion; I've noticed that people tend not to feel obligated to preach when all viewpoints are being analyzed, although there are exceptions, such as when they mistake analysis for the advocation of a viewpoint they happen to take exception to.

In "discussions" of this sort, I realized this semester that very few people actually disagree with me; they disagree, rather, with some annoying person in their dorm, or their parents, or their older brother with a degree in philosophy who is occasionally a mental bully, or the liberal scholars in some field or other who expound the silliest theories; and because I say something that resembles whatever their phantom demon has repeatedly insisted upon (or so they think), I am suddenly put in a position of defending not my viewpoint, but myself and, often, something I never said. Mill, of course, predicts this simultaneously fascinating and nauseating facet of human nature: "In proportion to a man's lack of confidence in his own solitary judgment does he usually rest, with implicit trust, on the infallibility of 'the world' in general . . . he places on his own world the responsibility of being in the right against the dissenting worlds of other people" (p. 326). People seem to feel obliged to convince others to think as they do, for whatever reason; for this reason, I believe the issue at stake is not knowledge or opinion, though that clearly may be the topic argued: I think one may, looking at a higher level of abstraction, ask why a conflict is taking place, and recognize human nature at work. What precisely this says about human nature, I'm not so sure.

The dialectic approach has also enabled me to approach issues without any undue influence by emotional commitment; I tend now not to have any adverse emotional reaction in conversation, which has greatly improved my understanding of other opinions (Mill and possibly Milton would be pleased); this is in no small part due to my summer reading of Adler's <u>How to Speak, How to Listen</u>, when I realized to what extent useless anger impairs understanding.

Some things still infuriate me, however, and more so than they did before I took Great Books: I am especially irritated by uneducated opinions, for example; I was criticized once during a class at church for quoting Kant within context of the discussion ("Kant isn't biblical", they said). "You," I wanted to say, but didn't (according to Emerson, I probably should have, but maybe he would have been satisfied with my few choice words in Latin), "describe movies and books and classes as 'good' based solely upon whether they happen to entertain you--the Kierkegaardian concept of aesthetics, an existentialist idea, no less--and you criticize me for referring to Kant?" A foolish consistency may be "the hobgoblin of little minds, adored by little statesmen, philosophers, and divines," but a foolish inconsistency is no better and is adored only by its possessor.

Still in the spirit of Mill, this semester of Great Books has been for me an exploration not so much of works of literature as of my own system of interpreting reality. Some people can, or at least claim they can, just know whether a given action is right or wrong; I do not have, and have never had, such a luxury, at least beyond the obvious (for example, I would through instinct readily agree, as J.P. Moreland suggests, that torturing babies is wrong; but this is not especially useful to me, since I tend not to wake up wondering, "Shall I find and torture a baby today?"). So far as I can remember, in every moral decision that I consciously made there were criteria which I used, consciously or unconsciously, to choose a course of action. The Great Books sequence has made the implicit standards explicit, and elucidated the similarities and differences between them; and I have not since experienced the crippling opposition of conflicting priorities as I did before---not a conflict between mind and appetites or emotion, as Plato describes, but mind against mind---since I am better able to sort out the issues. This isn't to say my life is simpler. I actually encounter more dilemmas than I could have imagined before I came to college, but I no longer feel that pressing imperative that one action is strictly right, the other entirely wrong, and I will be cosmically penalized if I make the wrong decision.

I have also begun to notice how truly interconnected everything is; a vague statement, to be sure, but I intend to clarify it. Coming into college my freshman year, I imagined the various majors to be very discrete with very little overlap; I recall writing about this in my last expressive outcomes paper, so I won't go into detail about that semester; I'll summarize instead, saying simply that I found more overlap among all subjects, more than I could have imagined before. Early in this semester, I seriously considered changing my second major (math) to philosophy because I didn't like the idea (which I later identified as Smith's) of specializing in an esoteric field whose only opportunity for discussion was with other specialists; I had a vague mental image of myself, years later, standing in front of a blackboard and sharing with an uncomprehending class all the obscure math jokes, like the one about the isomorphic cow and the horse on the tin roof (or maybe it was a spherical cow and a cat on the tin roof... whatever). But I quickly realized how much my classes were interconnected.

Discrete Structures, the class where math majors learn to write proofs, has influenced my writing style more than anything else; I have always had what I consider to be a healthy distaste for the pathos of rhetoric, but now, instead of using it to support points I suspect are weaker than others as I used to, I rely almost exclusively upon logos. I'm sure Dickens would object to this, and I realize it may not be appropriate for every situation; but in the context of academic writing (especially in Great Books), I have found it immensely useful. It almost seems like the material taught in Discrete is secondary the hidden objective of teaching its students how to think logically.

An even more surprising contribution to my thought about the ideas comes from Formal Methods, the computer science logic class, which I often criticize because it often emphasizes the form of a logical argument almost to the exclusion of its function; my pet story, play "the world's smallest violin" if you like, comes from the time when I lost half credit on a problem for using an asterisk for multiplication instead of a dot. Hence my shock when I realized that I was achially implementing principles I learned in class, specifically Dijkstra and Knuth's emphasis on efficiency. For example, people ask me why I took Great Books: of course, I don't answer that question (though if you're curious, I signed up because Julia told me I'd enjoy it), but rather the implicit question, "Why have I continued to take Great Books?" Here is where I use Dijkstra: Socrates, I suspect, would take the opportunity to educate the person or group about the ideas, the basis of the dialectic, and the principles of deeper thought. Socrates was not a double-major taking eighteen units. I recognize that, given the odds against my usual audience understanding my reasons within a reasonable amount of time, my efforts may be used better ("more efficiently") elsewhere; so, instead of enlightening them, I give them a brief statement instead.

I eventually decided to keep my math major, not only because I found it useful, but because of its inherent fascination: somehow, it is intrinsically linked to the real world (not for nothing did Plato place mathematics immediately below the forms, I suppose). There is an old joke among natural scientists: "The engineer thinks his equations are an approximation of reality; the physicist thinks reality is an approximation of his equations; the mathematician doesn't care; and the computer scientist is too busy debugging his $#@! program to worry about such abstract issues." Up until the past couple centuries, nearly every major mathematician was a philosopher of sorts, and many philosophers were amateur mathematicians; it's fascinating material, and as Dickens suggests, I would readily prefer Euclid to DeFoe.

This is not to say, however, that the approach I take to reason is entirely, or at least consistently, direct: though I have never been especially partial to Robinson Crusoe, I grew up reading Tolkien and Asimov; my heroes weren't "normal" archetypes like soldiers or men stranded on islands or pirates; they were cloaked wizards with long beards studying runes inscribed on unspeakably ancient doors, explorers in zero-gee suits exploring the blackest reaches of distant space, dragons, trolls, ogres, unicorns, sentient humanoid 'bots, aliens, and the hapless federal agent who was constantly attacked by vampires. Given this discrepancy in my thought processes between reason and fancy, how do I, in fact, think? This is the question I am confronted with. I tell myself that I am majoring in computer science because it interests me, and most days I think I am correct. (The other days, I suspect Smith is influencing me to find a profitable niche in society.) But when I ask myself why it interests me, visions of immense starships enter my head, sailing silently through the void toward the ends of the universe; in a way, I think, computer science offers me a way to participate in science fiction. Who knows, maybe I'll visit Mars someday.

As far as enjoyment, this observation about myself is quite useful; but it does not help me at all when I try to figure out how I think. Can I simply approach reason directly and find truth there, as Plato and DesCartes suggest? Or is there more to it, as Dickens insists? For the sake of simplicity, I would love to be able to say (without lying) that I value knowledge, all knowledge, for its own sake, and that I dedicate my life to the acquisition of truth; but then I notice that a story about a talking mouse holds my attention far longer than an article on plankton, and I recognize the symptoms of wishful thinking; but not a day later, an entire book on the Evans-Ventris debate on the linguistic origin of Linear B grabs and keeps me for still longer.

Am I rational or not? I am certainly *capable* of rationality, but I don't exercise it every single moment. I suspect it wouldn't be such a dilemma if I didn't think differently at different times: I think differently depending on whether I'm doing a proof, or reading a story, or drawing a comic, or listening to music (except in Great Books, where, like Pavlov's canine friend, I have been trained to pull out books the moment my feet pass through the doorway). Why? What is it that makes me human? At least I am able to recognize that this is a question that Great Books asks, and dismiss the immediate worry that I'm crazy (at least for that particular reason). Perhaps my problem is that I am looking for a Boolean answer to a complex question: it may not be the case that anyone is able to say, Yes, I am rational, or No, I am not (Boolean= True or False only, nothing between).

Another part of my problem is that I intuitively sense that a solution is just out of reach. In my life, I have usually been able to know, when I don't understand something, whether the problem is: that I didn't pay close enough attention and will be able to understand after a small amount of study; that I am psychologically capable of understanding, but don't yet have the prerequisite instruction; or that I don't see how a conclusion or solution is possible, and if I will ever be able to understand, that point will come only after a long period of time. So far as I can remember, this feeling has never been entirely wrong, although it has been close once or twice. And my intuition tells me that a solution (whatever that may be) to the question of my identity is possible, but that I am not quite ready to arrive at it yet. How do I know this? I don't know! I'm not comfortable simply calling this intuition a feeling, since in my experience it has been entirely independent of my moods; but at the same time I balk at categorizing it under reason, since I don't know how it works.

So after nearly three semesters of observation and analysis of the classical views of human nature and what it means to be human, I feel no closer to complete understanding; I don't know whether the proper approach (assuming one exists) would be to look at humanity and narrow down to the individual, or to examine the individual and broaden the scope to society at large. This ignorance after study is much like Socrates, I suppose. I am reminded of the plaque Dr. Coodey placed on his door:

"Contrary to what you might expect, we do not have all the answers. After years of study and research, we are, if anything, more confused than we were before we started. We believe, however, that our confusion inhabits a higher plane than yours, and that it concerns more important matters."

Reading over this essay, I am quite fond of parts, not so pleased with others, and there are parts where I am appalled that I am capable of writing such unintelligible gibberish; yet this is a useful (I wouldn't dare say "good" without defining the term) experience for me, in that it exposes my ignorance in my definition of self. Actually, according to Adler, "self-definition" is almost a contradiction, since only ideas can be defined; people must be described. So I'll call it my concept of identity instead. I realize that at this point in my life, I really have little idea of who I am (or what, for that matter); but in my process of discovery, at least Great Books has given me a conceptual foundation to build from.

2018 update from Leighton: "Dr. Colson was right, I used way too many semicolons at that time in my life"

Life is hard and Great Books is useful. Twenty years after my first semester and that's the best I can do. Even as Great Books trains you to be kind of an asshole, it teaches you humility toward things that genuinely deserve respect, if not always deference: honest and rigorous wrestling with hard issues. Great Books also trains you to define your goddamn terms so you don't waste people's time. My oblique approach to definitions comes more from the asshole part of the training than the dialectic part of the training.
Studying the canonical Great Works™ has the advantage that the

authors are dead. They don't care if you buy their books or how their names are trending in social media. Almost all the time, these works actually care about the subjects they claim to care about, and not some dubious hidden curriculum that's at best orthogonal to the interest of their readers. Arguing in good faith like this is what I mean by honesty: when Kant titles his work *A Critique of Pure Reason*, you can bet your 401k that he's going to be talking about pure reason because he thinks pure reason is really [forking] important. And obviously they also don't knowingly make false statements, which could be bucketed under honesty, but is about as meritorious as a driver not deliberately swerving onto the sidewalk to hit pedestrians. We should expect that.

As a failed logician, I know a bit about rigor, but you have to zoom out from the abstract nonsense to see that what mathematicians and philosophers (both professional academics and streetfighting thinkers) have in common is looking as hard as they can for where their ideas fail – not (always) to discard them, but to map out the scope of where they're useful. We read *Republic* not because we want Plato's ideal form of government to travel within five hundred yards of our representative democracy, but because the framework of ideas he built to support it is transferable to many other things. It's freakishly unlikely that any of my ideas will survive me more than ten or twenty years, but maybe the way I got there will help someone with issues I haven't even imagined. That thought makes me want to drink slightly less when I think of all the time I've spent writing over the years.

The thing about wrestling is that it takes time and training. Dante found himself lost midway on life's journey, maybe at 35 or 40. There are no Spark notes for what you do when your wife develops a debilitating neurological condition and needs both hips replaced. The only consolation you're likely to find is knowledge that people have gone through massive amounts of pain for millennia, and individual lives go on, and society carries on. Whether I side with Augustine or Nietzsche on the nature of suffering is less material than that they tried to respond to it.

Finally, hard issues are the ones immune to platitudes. When Google changes the gmail interface and it's impossible to navigate, you repeat the mantra that "If you're not paying, you're not the customer, you're the product," and you realize that it is altogether right and just that you suffer for your choice of email provider, because that is not a hard issue. A hard issue is reconfiguring how you respond to sensory input because of persistent audial and visual hallucinations. No words help that, but knowing that Descartes followed a similar line of inquiry when pursuing Truth (or Trust, as I understand it) at least gives you the vocabulary and grammar to partition off pieces of yourself that are still trustworthy.

Humility toward the Great Works™ leads me to be fine with only writing Pretty Okay Bumper Stickers. I affirm that life is shit, and that it's important to do good work, and that those two statements are not in tension.

Advice is like scripture in that it's trivial to apply harmfully. But I will say: Make your choices now, wrestle with the hard problems of existence now, so that when the day comes when you have to, they won't be new and you won't be under as much time pressure. We all die, so far, and we have a chance to make it matter. Great Books doesn't give you everything you need. It does give you a fighting chance.

Best of luck to you.

"He confined the knowledge of governing within very narrow bounds; to common sense and reason, to justice and lenity, to the speedy determination of civil and criminal causes…"
-Swift, *Gulliver's Travels*

1999

L

SHANNON CORDER

Kant's Scategorical Imperative

I had a moral dilemma.

A dilemma about poop.

Granted, this wasn't an ethical question that would require me to call Ruth Bader Ginsburg. In fact, should I have had the means by which to contact RBG, there are probably much better questions I could ask. I wasn't determining states rights, gun laws, or if life began at conception or birth. But I still took the subject quite seriously.

The question was, when I walked my silky terrier, Lando, and I picked up his dog poop, did I have a right to dispose of that dog poop in a neighbor's trashcan?

I had a list of ethical guidelines for other dog poop related scenarios. Whenever possible, use a biodegradable bag so that Sir Furpant's digested kibble would not last the many millennia that a plastic bag would. Always actually pick up all dog excrement, unless it was not larger than a quarter or if the consistency was closer to a liquid than a solid. Do not actually walk onto another person's property to use a trash receptacle without prior permission. (Leaning over a fence was a gray area.) And never EVER use a recycling bin for fecal disposal. (The only acceptable place to recycle crap is network television.)

But, what if it's trash day, and a trash bin - technically owned by the city - is sitting on the curbside, on public property? As that bin is in the custody of a particular household, does that mean that household's members are the only ones allowed to discard into it? Did it matter if the can were full or recently emptied? Was the purity of one's trash can more or less important than the ability of a human being to walk the streets unencumbered by intestinal waste? If one makes the life choice to be an animal guardian, didn't that make that person responsible for proper waste disposal? But did making sure the poop ended up going to a landfill cover responsible waste disposal? Was it also my responsibility to house the odiferous poop when in my own trashcan or dumpster? Was homeownership a privilege that allowed one to have their can poop free, should they choose? But was such ownership equally available to all persons from all backgrounds or was a certain amount of luck or privilege involved?

Was it possible I was over thinking this?

Perhaps I wouldn't have pondered this so much if a) I didn't spend so much time walking my dog and b) if my neighborhood's homeowners didn't have such strong opinions about whether or not their beloved trashcans were being violated.

The neighborhood yards were speckled with polite signs asking that dog owners clean up after their pooches. Then, other yards sported signs showing a dog in a posture of defecation with a red "buster" sign over it. I wanted to ask their owners for more explanation; were they asking that dogs not poop anywhere, ever? Were they asking that dogs not poop in the immediate vicinity of the sign? Just on their lawn? Were they ok with dogs pooping on other people's lawns, but there was something special about theirs that necessitated it remain excrement free? Or, was it their way of asking folks to clean up the poop, but with a simple and elegant visual rather than text? Did they realize how much dogs love to pee on these signs?

Some owners put signs on trashcans directly with varying levels of indignance suggesting dog owners think twice about depositing stinking sacks into them. The pièce de résistance, however, was a professionally manufactured sign attached to a fence over a homeowner's bins that read: "CAMERAS ON PROPERTY NO TRESSPASSING TAKE YOUR S*** HOME WITH YOU!!!" At least, that's the gist of it. I wanted to take a picture of it, but I'm a little frightened of those homeowners.

But I digress. There are just so many delightful ideas surrounding the ethical implications of pet waste disposal and we haven't time to explore them all.

Back to the question of the morality of disposing of a baggie of dog poop in a neighbor's garbage. If only I had another soul with which to dialog over my quandary. I'd already decided Ruth Bader Ginsburg was out. Maybe someone with more time on their hands? Perhaps unlimited, eternal time? Ah, yes! Of course. I could invoke the Ghost of Immanuel Kant.

After laying out his favorite foods -- room temperature water and a butterless loaf of German *Vollkornbrot* -- I said his name three times while looking into a wooden-framed hand mirror and he appeared.

ME: *Vielen dank*, The Ghost of Immanuel Kant. I appreciate your materializing on such short notice.
THE GHOST OF IMMANUEL KANT: *Bitte schön*; it is my pleasure. I vas in the middle of a very boring game of cards with some other philosophers. I cannot prove it, but I think Hobbes vas cheating.
ME: But, that's unethical!
KANT: It depends - vat do you mean by ethical?
ME: Well, that might be a conversation for another time. I have a question for you.
KANT: How can I help?

I explained the moral quandary to Herr Kant. He listened politely, nodding from time to time, making a face once upon the mention of my rule regarding the bagging of liquid dog feces. He seemed to take me seriously.

ME: So, that's my question. Well, a question that seems to lead to several more questions.
KANT: If you have more questions than answers, you are doing something right.
ME: Is this a question you've encountered before in your studies?
KANT: I do not believe so, though Hegel's cat used to poop in my yard, and it brought us to strong vords more than vonce. (*Thinking.*) How vould you say that the categorical imperative applies in this case?
ME: Ah, yes! An excellent question. (*Googles categorical imperative. Holds phone out of sight.*) Well, I think as long as I was... "Acting in accordance with the maxim through which --"
KANT: -- Are you reading that from Vikipedia?
ME: I... yes. But to be fair, ven, I mean, when I studied you last, it was literally a different millennium.
KANT: (*sighing*) Okay. Let me ask this. What if everyone put their doggie doo-doo in other people's trashcans?
ME: Well, it wouldn't literally be every person; it would just be dog owners or caretakers. And since they would only have access once a week - assuming they're not trespassing in order to deposit the trash - the impact would not be that large. I mean, it has to go somewhere. Still 6 out of 7 days would either see the waste housed in their own trashcans, if they made it all the way home before throwing it out, or in the can of a different neighbor who had their trash day on a different day. It seems the volume would be minimal and would not

prohibit the person assigned that trashcan from using it fully themselves.

KANT: However, it might create a strong odor.

ME: I mean, it's a trashcan.

KANT: *Ja.* That is correct. But vill the neighbor go through this thought process? Vill they have the assistance of a several hundred-year-old ghost or vill they most likely have taken a Great Books course?

ME: ...Probably not.

KANT: So, vat can we conclude from that?

ME: Only put the poop in the trash --

KANT & ME: -- when they're not looking!

KANT: *Toll!* A *wunderbar* assessment.

ME: Thank you, and thanks for your help.

KANT: *Kein* problem. Now, are you going to eat that *Vollkornbrot*?

ME: No, sir, that's all you.

And so, another great moral problem was solved, though, as the Ghost of Immanuel Kant had suggested, not all people's ethics would be my ethics. (Sure, the categorical imperative is SUPPOSED to be universal, but not everyone has read Kant.) Were I to get into an ethical discussion with a neighbor, I probably wouldn't have the time to even define our terms before getting chased down the street. Perhaps politeness was a better consideration in this case. I mean, unless no one was looking.

"This is the origin of that great "leviathan"...for by this authority, given him by every particular man in the commonwealth, he has the use of so much power and strength conferred on him that, by terror thereof, he is enabled to form the wills of them all...by natural force, as when a man makes his children submit themselves and their children to his rule, as being able to destroy them if they refuse..."

-Hobbes, *Leviathan*

LI
JUSTIN SCHNEIDER

Great Books Thoughts

When I think of my time studying the Great Books, the images flash forward, and I am once again in the cave. The images dance in front of us, and we try to name them. I also remember clearly the sense of fear and trembling when I stuck my neck out to answer questions or present them in class. I always had a sense that I was Isaac and my professor was Abraham with the clenched fist, hoping it would "work out." Exam days also revealed the anguish, forlornness, and despair of my life. Most of all I remember "good" was not so good.

No other courses in my undergraduate career or law school career have impacted me as deeply as my time spent with the Great Ideas in Great Books. The colloquium at Pepperdine was the heart of my liberal arts education, and I made sure it bookended my time. I started as a freshman and then waited until I was a senior to complete the colloquium. The grades I received my senior year (less so my first year) are the marks I am most proud of from college. I am a man of significant privilege. I openly acknowledge that I have not had to work to receive a lot of the "blessings" I have. But I worked my tail off as I wrestled with the texts, argued with classmates, and was often humbled in the process. I credit this process of refinement as a key factor in allowing me to recognize and acknowledge my privilege while fueling my journey towards empowering others.

Which brings me to where I am now. I often wish I could be back in the cave. In the cave there was connection and comradery. Out here in the light, I am less convinced that the world is spiraling in a positive direction. The words I thought I had for the world around me were sufficient then, and now I find myself more often speechless. I see in myself a new Adam every day: able to stand, yet free to fall. Yet the more I live, the more I see my own self-reliance as too narrow and wanting. I realize that the great ideas I have in my head still rolling around need community. As the leaders around us resemble Yahoos more and more, I know I need to find those of our form who choose kindness and compassion.

I am grateful for my classmates and professors who challenged me and molded me wittingly and unwittingly into a person who thinks about Great Ideas and who is willing to let them affect the ways I live my life and serve others.

"If we submit everything to reason, our religion will have no mysterious and supernatural element. If we offend the principles of reason, our religion will be absurd and ridiculous."
-Pascal

LII
AMANDA TIPTON

September 11th happened near the beginning of my third Great Books semester. I was a theater student, a technician, and we were building rubble in the scene shop that day for a show about Beirut. That's the sticky little detail that always comes back to me about that day the absurdity of a bunch of college students artfully rendering foam cinder blocks and rebar in Malibu, California while war arrived on our doorstep. We didn't know yet about IEDs, Wounded Warriors, or that we'd still be functionally at war 17 years later.

9/11 quickly changed our Great Books book list for that semester. My class felt strongly that the spectacles we needed to put on in those moments were not those of Locke, Voltaire, or Hume. We wanted to understand the religious worldviews around us from the original texts themselves. We wanted something closer to the source than what we were being told about Islam as filtered through news reports and political speeches. And not just Islam- we were hungry for all of it. We wanted to grapple with Hindu perspectives, Taoist perspectives, and Confucian perspectives. We wanted a much wider religious understanding as quickly as
possible.

It's easy to question if our impulses were virtuous, or just a reflection of where we were at the time- still innocent, still young, still playing at war in the Pepperdine scene shop. Great Books can seem impractical and passive. After all, sitting around discussing Platonic forms is a fairly affluent, privileged and inactive, well, activity. Do we really need to understand the Quran to work to protect our Muslim neighbors from abuse? Do we need to know the tenets of Sikhism to stop the guy yelling at another for being a "terrorist" because he's wearing a turban? When do we put down the books and *do* something?

Nearly two decades later, however, I am certain of the practicality of the Great Books Colloquium. The books themselves are more than incidental, but the part of Great Books I use every day isn't what I learned about any particular author; it's how I learned to work through understanding each perspective. It's the wrangling, defining and clarifying. It's learning to look for how each perspective considers big ideas.

Today, American perspectives have become crystallized and fragmented. It seems sometimes that we'd all rather go around with our goggles welded to our faces than engage with a polyfocal conspectus. Great Books for me today is less about being able to talk about Rousseau's view of Human Nature and more about being able to see the Christian Evangelical view of Human Nature, or the Progressive Liberal view of Society vs. the Individual. Practically, we need to wrestle, to look for truth -- or even Truth, to define our terms, to provide evidence, and to use specific language. We need to be able to have the same debate, to talk *with* instead of *at* one another, to melt our ridged perspectives. Great Books for me today is still questioning myself when I use phrases like, "we need to." Oh, we do? Why? It's knowing that I am still standing somewhere even when I try on the glasses of another.

Great Books isn't just about understanding the perspectives of another - it's about understanding yourself. That is imminently practical. I remember beginning the program and being concerned with the validity of each perspective. I remember using phrases like, "I don't buy that" a lot. As the semesters progressed, I learned more to see the humanity of each perspective - whether or not I "bought" it, the author did, and why was that? That was a far more interesting question. At some point though, as we move from black and white to a sea of gray, it still needs to resolve into some kind of picture. I still need that place to stand while I wrestle. I still want to tell Hobbes that I don't think life is, "nasty, brutish, and short," even if I understand that he did. I'd much rather hang out with Locke and his Truth and Beauty.

Great Books gave me the mental tools to not only question my perspective, but to stand and defend it. I believe it's important to make the fake rubble- to tell the stories that help us consider and have conversations that lead us away from war and violence. I also believe sometimes we've got to put the books and the plays down and do something about actual war and violence. And I finally believe that my perspective is no less valid because it just happens to be mine.

"Man being born with a title to perfect freedom and an unrestricted enjoyment of all the rights and privileges of the law of nature equally with any other man or number of men in the world, has by nature a power not only to preserve his property — that is life, liberty, and estate…"

-Locke

LIII
CORRIE ZACHARIA

I wish I remembered more from Great Books class. I wish I had at my disposal a few eloquent phrases that I could quote for you now. I wish I remembered more of the great authors' names even, so I could make intellectual sounding references. But I don't. (sigh). Here is what I do remember about Great Books class: I couldn't please the teacher like I could in all my other classes. I tried and failed. I got my first B in Great Books and I was mad. What was this strange code that I could not crack? I was an A student... or was I?

Did I deserve to be an A student if I could not sit in the tension of opposing great ideas and ponder the truth present in each? Did I deserve to be an A student if I skimmed through the text without stopping to weigh the perspective of the author? If I did not have the patience to try it on as a lens through which to view contemporary issues and even my own life? No. I deserved that B, and one day I decided to stop crying about it and go for the A. I was willing to dig deep. I was willing to do the work.

I needed to stop rushing, stop performing, stop being prescriptive with the world and with myself. A-level Great Books work forced me to be *descriptive*. No more "should's" in my writing. Suddenly, finally, almost as quickly as an inhale, I began to feel the freedom of it! I was allowed to play with ideas, to compare and contrast. My black and white prescriptive world swirled into a more complicated gray, and truth appeared in winding strands shining silver through the murky waters. Did not all of the great authors grasp that truth and spy it from different boats? I liked sitting in certain boats more than others, but I learned from taking a turn sitting in all of them. I learned to stop and to play with ideas. To stop grasping for the "right" answer. To stop, identify a pattern, make a case for it, then watch in wonder as the shiny strand emerged, even if just for a momentary glimpse.

I remember a dreaded final in-class essay shifting to a joyful experience as I let go of my fear and started with the title "I ate DOTS in Great Books Class." Yes, DOTS the candy. I connected it to my topic, and guess what? I got that A.

"But though this be a state of liberty, yet it is not a state of license..."
-Locke

2000

LIV
JONATHAN BAKEWICZ

**Knowing the Good: Or, how to tend your garden and
why Great Books is the best of all possible academic endeavours**

I'll be brief. I know you and I haven't much time. You see, we're both
going to die. Shadows and dust, wisps of smoke curling skyward. All we
can hope for is that we become a pleasing offering. Yes, I realize it's
uncomfortable; so is Great Books. I'll explain, and I'll use small words so
that you'll be sure to understand, you warthog-faced yahoo. (You see?
Very uncomfortable.) So is most of life by the way—hard and
uncomfortable. You might not know it yet, but it's good to see, for all
seeing is perspectival seeing, and even far better to see and know (by
presence and absence) the Good.
Don't live hand to mouth. Escape from your malaise of existential
humanism. Think. Think! Ah, but you don't know where to start.
Good, good, Good! That's where it begins—and ends. Where you can
stop pretending you have it all figured out. Start by understanding what
somebody (hopefully an author of a Great Book) is saying on her/his—
yes I know it's a binary—own terms. Start listening *well*. Why, why
bother? I'm glad you asked. You thought I might say because it's a
good in itself, and it is, but thanks to Aristotle, it's so much more.
Do you really believe that accounting or biology or journalism degree
will help you discover truth, know freedom and liberty (or license)?
Understand the relationship between emotion and reason? Probe the
depths of good and evil? Sort through how an individual should relate
to society? Figure out why a hero is a hero at all? I'm not picking on
accountants, scientists or journalists here; God created us ants, spiders
and bees alike; what I am contending is that you will be a better

accountant, better scientist, better journalist, better human person by taking Great Books. Why? You learn to ask intelligent questions, and, ahem, maybe have something to say (hopefully unoriginal) because you understood an idea that someone much smarter than you came up with a long time ago. You learn how to analyze, how to ascertain the *why* behind the *what*. You gain a competitive edge because you will be able see where anyone's ideas come *from* a mile away.

Great Books has made me a better attorney. Understanding and listening, making connections, seeing issues as they are, could be, might be, through a lens called the polyfocal conspectus. Ding, ding, ding! Read a Great Book, read a client. Hear a client. Serve a client. Be good. Repeat. Ibid, your honor.

And it's not just my career, but so much more! I watch movies better. I enjoy food and drink better. I'm a better father because of Great Books (ask my eight year old; after all, she is smarter than you, asks better questions than you, and just watched her first Monty Python movie). But you don't even know what 'good' means yet….Maybe I'm a better husband because of Great Books? My wife says so; I'm still not convinced. Point of information: Great Books—if you let it—should utterly change how you approach everything in your life.

"Ha, ha, ha! You will be finding enjoyment in toothache next," you cry, with a laugh. "Well, even in toothache there is enjoyment," I answer. And, indeed, I will ask on my own account here, an idle question: which is better—cheap happiness or exalted sufferings? Well, which is better? Perhaps I have become virtuous? Perhaps you will? Likely not; becoming, maybe. I'd wager me more so than you, because I have taken Great Books.

"But though man in that state has an unrestricted liberty to dispose of his person or possessions, yet he has not liberty to destroy himself, or any creature under his control."
-Locke

LV
RACHEL HOFMAN

Bob's test scores for this term were 80, 78, 80, and 82. Ann got 100, 98, 100, 60. Who is a better student? If you were their teacher, what grade would you give each?

Carl and Della go shopping for shoes. They see a sign in the window that says, "Buy one, get half-off the second pair." The pair Carl likes costs $40, the pair Della likes costs only $20. When they get to the register, the clerk tells them that the total is $50. How much should each pay?

13-year-old Emma loves geometry; 14-year-old Frank, not so much. For Emma, math is more beautiful and pure than anything she's ever actually encountered in "real life." Frank just wants to know "when we're ever going to use this in real life."

***

When I took Great Books more than a decade ago, the notion that much of my professional life would be spent grappling with questions like these would have been laughable. But "life is what happens when you're busy making other plans," or something like that, and here I am, enjoying my 11th year of teaching junior high--mostly math.

And while we didn't calculate percents or bisect angles, I believe Great Books, more than any other course I took in college, prepared me to do this job well. For how could I make wise decisions about

Bob and Ann, without first grappling with what it means to be "good," or what it means to learn? How could I appreciate the variety of student responses--mathematical and otherwise--to the "problem" faced by Carl and Della, without first having learned to appreciate that "justice belongs to the highest class of good things?" And how much less prepared would I be to engage and inspire both Emma and Frank, had I not inquired, with Plato, with the existentialists, and with so many in between, into the nature and meaning of "real life?"

Anyone can assign math problems to students. Good teachers help their students learn to solve them successfully. But great teachers embed the problems--and all they represent--in a much larger story. I believe Kierkegaard said it well: "to be able to land in just that way, and in the same second to look as though one was up and walking, to transform the leap in life to a gait, to express the sublime in the pedestrian absolutely—that is something only the knight of faith can do—and it is the one and only marvel." I am thankful that, however short I fall in my quest to act as a knight of faith, my Great Books education at least allows me to aspire to greatness.

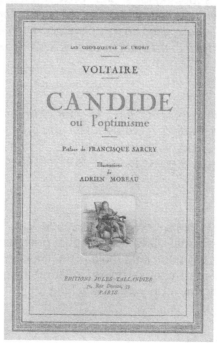

"I also know that we should cultivate our gardens. Let us work without theorizing, 'tis the only way to make life endurable."
-Voltaire, *Candide*

LVI
MATT JEWETT

In the nearly 20 years since I took the Great Books courses, there is rarely (if ever) a day that goes by that I am not reminded of the various lessons, ideas, and lines of thinking that I was exposed to for the first time at Pepperdine. In fact, as time goes by, I think I am far more aware of them now than I was while taking the courses and reading these Great Books. Specific details, immediate recollection of the specific author and context have faded a great deal. However, I regularly experience the joy of recognition when certain ideas, concepts, or writers of the Great Books come up.

The joy of recognition comes up frequently in social settings, whether it is related to Great Books or not. I see the look in people's faces as they light up when I bring up a topic that is familiar to them. In those moments, I take joy in theirs, and am grateful to Great Books for making me self-aware of what that joy means and recognizing it in myself and others.

My education and career have led me into the world of Real Estate and Property development. There is not a day that goes by where I am not dealing with private property rights and interests. Most people I work with assume that the rights to their land are the result of natural law. Many do not think of it in those terms or recognize the impact that John Locke has had on their "right" to build their dream home on "their" property (even if they did not personally mix their own direct labor with that particular piece of land).

However, inasmuch as I work with property owners and advocate for their "rights", I also must remind my clients that we are a part of a Social Contract and that they have their own stake in the common good. Yes, an individual may want to build that here, but how does that impact those people over there? And if those people over there wanted to build whatever they want on their land, what would that do to the value of your land? How would their actions impact you? This little reminder (courtesy of Rousseau) is often helpful to provide clarity, context, and understanding, when developers have been undergoing a sometimes frustrating and seemingly endless environmental review process or are compelled to reach out to the local homeowners to get their feedback and critiques.

Generally, I do not ascribe to Machiavellian principles when it comes to interpersonal relationships, employer/employee relationships, or the relationship between a ruler/political leader and the governed. However, I professionally represent property owners and advocate for their interests to the government. I also sit on my neighborhood council and represent my community and their interests to the government. In recent years, as my involvement with my neighborhood community has grown, I have gained a deeper appreciation and respect for Machiavellian principles in a democratic society. I believe it can be and often is more effective for the leaders who are supposed to represent the will of the people to fear the wrath of their constituents. Many polite, articulate, and intellectual conversations backed by pages of facts and figures can be had about the impacts that the new condo project will have on local traffic, density, safety, and community well-being. However, I have learned that this approach frequently falls on deaf ears, lip-service is paid, and nothing substantive changes.

Facts and intelligent arguments...backed by the force of people who are angry, threatening lawsuits, recall votes, public shaming, and the threat of having a tarnished legacy and not being re-elected are very effective tools to create change that the constituency asks for. It may very well be true, that in order for representative democracy to function effectively, it is in fact better for our representatives to fear us rather than love us. In a representative democracy, the people are The Prince.

In my personal development, the most pervasive lesson that I associate with Great Books is recognizing the importance of defining one's terms in any type of conversation or debate. Many unproductive arguments have been avoided through the importance I now place on understanding what people mean when they say something. I also try to check myself to ensure that I use words that accurately convey what I mean. To be fair, there have been more than a few arguments that have been created by my relentless insistence that others define their terms for me…to their endless frustration with my nitpicking on this point. My wife will vouch for this.

I have boiled this down to the phrase, "words have meaning". It is easy for us to take that for granted and forget that we don't always precisely mean what we say. "Meaning" can get to be a lot to unpack for most of us in our daily lives and much conflict is created when people use or understand words differently from one another. We forget that words can carry different meaning for different people, based upon our own world views, experiences, presuppositions, etc. If words are devoid of meaning that both parties understand, there can be no "real" communication or shared understanding in any social, professional, political, or religious discussion. Without that, we cannot accomplish anything meaningful together.

Because words have meaning, I view the words "sorry" and "Good" (and a whole lot of other words) in a completely different manner than I did before being introduced to the works of Kant and Plato. I still use the word sorry in a colloquial context because it's often easier ("I'm sorry to bug you again about this deadline that you missed"). I am aware of it when I use it in this manner and it bothers me sometimes, but I'm not sorry about it. On the other end of the spectrum, I am also more thoughtful when I intentionally and accurately use the word sorry to express deep regret and my desire to have made different choices. Because of that awareness and my understanding of the weight of that word more fully, I hope that I am able contextualize and elaborate on my feelings of regret more fully. My goal in this manner is to help others understand my feelings of sincerity.

I use the word good like most people do. However, even in text message exchanges, when something strikes me as deeply praiseworthy and profoundly "True" (another word I won't elaborate on here), I will often use the word "Good". Yes, that is a capital "G" and I owe it to Plato. A Platonic understanding of "Good" also provides some color, diversity, and deeper meaning to rote Biblical references like "God is Good". It is not because God behaves in ways that we agree are noble, it's because it's axiomatic. God is Good. The Good (rightly understood) is the end. It is not a means to anything else. It is the supreme virtue that all other virtues point to. As I write this, I am looking at a framed picture on my wall that states:

GO INTO THE WORLD
AND DO WELL, BUT
MORE IMPORTANTLY
GO INTO THE WORLD
AND DO GOOD.

It's a constant reminder of what I want to strive for in every aspect of life every day, and I have a deeper appreciation for it because of my understanding of what "The Good" is. Yes, it would be more accurate if it ended with "AND BE GOOD", but then the poetry and word juxtaposition that creates interest would all be lost. And sometimes, poetic artistry, at the expense of precise terms, can be a more effective tool of communicating great ideas. I think I learned that from Milton.

"...the three great evils, boredom, vice, poverty...but we must cultivate our garden..."
-Voltaire, *Candide*

LVII
KELLY PIPPIN

To prepare for writing this reflection, I pulled out a black, dusty portfolio from the back of my closet where I keep all my meaningful academic work, much of it from Great Books. In Great Books III and IV, while sitting in our socratic circles, Dr. Gose would often talk about entering into the "Great Conversation." He emphasized that writers and thinkers speak to each other over time and across geography; the texts resonate, and wrestle, and we—through our thinking and discussing together—join in. For me, I have found that the conversations which stay with me from Great Books, the ones with the most profound impact, didn't necessarily happen in class, but occured on the pages of my word processor during an all-night writing session or in a Blue Book bought fresh from the student store. On those blank spaces of promise, I pieced together some of my most important, and even personal, dialogues.

I was never the best talker in Great Books. Philosophy did not come as naturally to me as literary study, and I would often sit quietly in class as bolder students debated some ontological point. But I found my place in the conversation when I wrote. Great Books changed my writing forever: it taught me the thrilling architecture of argument; I learned to identify an essential problem and then pursue an answer; I learned that it didn't *really matter* if Charles Dickens had Rousseau in mind when he created the hopeful child Sissy in *Hard Times*. What mattered is that both men had questions about the nature of childhood innocence and the process of education, about the way our ability to reason can be thwarted by our emotions and imagination—especially when we're confronted with hard realities. These human concerns are universal and timeless, and how thrilling to be able to say I think Dickens was right: to be happy, one must be hopeful, even if irrationally so.

One story in particular sticks with me, fifteen years now after it occurred. It's my most cherished academic memory. And the story is this: I took a final. It was the Great Books IV final, the last one of the whole colloquium. In a room on the second floor of the Cultural Arts Center, Dr. Gose gave us a slip of paper with two words on it: "Discuss Momma." That was all it said. I had my books from the semester with me and an empty Blue Book. Nothing else—no computer or phone or even a snack. Dr. Gose told us we could take as long as we wanted; that he would go home after two hours, but we were free to stay and slip the final under his office door when we were finished. "With a little luck," he said, "this will be a fun experience."

The prompt asked us to think about the character Momma, Maya Angelou's grandmother from *I Know Why the Caged Bird Sings*. Throughout the novel, she operates within the traditional and oppressive bounds of her status as a woman and an African-American. The novel makes it clear, however, that Angelou sees her grandmother as a hero, a figure of power and strength. There was my problem: how, when Momma is bordered and penned and *so accepting* of her circumstance, can she be a symbol of power? My scratch paper for the final (which I still have in my portfolio) shows me planning my way down many dead ends: I tried out a Locke and property argument...I tried to fit Virginia Woolfe into it, which clearly didn't work. . . Momma's power is real, not hypothetical, and it doesn't hinge on a circumstance like an imagined room of one's own . . . And then I found it: Momma is a Kierkegaardian knight of faith. She finds freedom in duty, transcendence in devotion. She is a paradox: strong yet silent in the face of persecution, driven by a leap of faith in eternal justice.

Finding this argument was as exciting to me as any other moment in college, as thrilling as a leap in the Heidelberg river or my first Songfest or my first college date. I stayed in the room for a full six hours. Everyone left, the sky grew dark, but I carefully wrote and rewrote, with nowhere else I wanted to be. As I slipped the Blue Book under Dr. Gose's door, the janitors were locking up, and I headed home, hungry and euphoric.

I think about that night often, especially now that I'm an English teacher, and I see students race through in-class essays, confident they've aced a deceptively simple prompt. Or they ask me questions like, "How do you know William Golding was *actually* thinking about Hobbes when he wrote this?" Or, of course, the most common one: "When are we ever going to use this in real life?"

I worry this is the trend in current thoughts about education: that the humanities are archaic and useless; that the classroom should be a laboratory where students use "real-world application" to learn skills for future profitable work. But when I think about my Great Books final, there is nothing in that memory that finds exact "real world application." When will I ever again have six hours to do nothing but think? To interact with a text, to create, and then to emerge, after a long time, with new awareness. Great Books was, for me, a vital incubation period: a space in which a fledgling human worked on becoming more fully human—a space to discover the great conversation and work out my place in it, with fear and trembling and exhilaration.

"God makes all things good; man meddles with them and they become evil."
-Rousseau, *On Education*

2001

LVIII
MATT DUFFY

The words of the Blogger, the son of Twitter, king of the Internets.

Vanity of vanities, saith the Blogger, vanity of vanities; all is vanity.

What profit hath a man, or a woman, or even one who prefereth non-binary gender identification, of all the Great Books he hath read?

Though he may have a rough idea of what a "polyfocal conspectus" is, still he shall have absolutely no clue about what a "colloquium" is.

Both the great king in his lofty tower and the lowly retail worker at Best Buy, whose job shall presently be stripped of him by an autonomous Amazon warehouse robot, avail themselves to stream "Game of Thrones" on HBO Go rather than read the books -- verily, even George R. R. Martin himself doth tune in every week with eager interest to find out what happeneth next in his beloved fantasy series.

And what book, in all its Greatness, though it wax on and eloquently in its description of delicious foods, can match the rich visuals of HD Netflix spectaculars like "Chef's Table", or the light drama and charm of "Great British Bake-Off"? But this, too, is vanity.

Yea, even the freshman in his first semester of Great Books can plainly see that "The Iliad" is the Greatest Book ever written, and it was all downhill from there. Actually, now that I doth think on it, "The Courage To Be" by Paul Tillich is surely the Greatest Book ever written, but unless ye took Great Books, ye shall find it utterly incomprehensible.

And indeed I confess that I totally did not read "King Lear", like, AT ALL. Is that one any good? Or, like the wind that forever circles the globe, like the celestial sun and moon and stars that may or may not circle the globe, do not both the wicked students and the good alike end up getting a "B" for that semester regardless of whether they actually read "King Lear" or not?

For all is vanity; yet, even still, wisdom belongs to the wise and folly to the fool. I should think that would be pretty self-explanatory by now.

There is nothing new under the sun. Virgil ripped off Homer, and Dante ripped off Virgil, and Milton ripped off Dante, and Pixar rippeth off them all in "Coco", and winneth an Oscar for it. Such vanity.

Gael Garcia Bernal was surely Great in it, however. Which remindeth me that I need to watch "Mozart In The Jungle". Canst believe it is already in its fourth season? To everything there is a season, except of course to shows which are untimely cancelled. Truly, a show which was never even greenlit in the first place is better than a show canceled before its time, like "Deadwood", which endeth in a most peremptory and unsatisfactory manner, and whose only hope is a disappointing and pathetic internet message board fanboy-driven revival many years after, like "Arrested Development" or "Veronica Mars". For crying out loud, they bringeth back "Roseanne". "Roseanne"!

For I have seen that the same fate awaits all, both the star Great Books student and he who took a much dumber and obviously useless elective, like Pottery or something. All must endure the Reality TV presidency and the asinine tweets of this moronic, corrupt cretin who lacketh even a sixth grader's understanding of spelling, punctuation, and Captilization. Vanity, amirite?

Then I commended mirth, because a man hath no better thing under the sun, than to eat, and to drink, and to be merry: for that shall abide with him of his labour the days of his life. Or, like Voltaire says at the end of "Candide", "tend your garden."

Also, for those who, like me, find it hard to actually make time to sit down and read a proper book nowadays, I commend listening to

Audiobooks and excellent Podcasts. For example, lately I have been listening to "Moby Dick" (http://www.mobydickbigread.com/) and, man, it's Great!

Vanity of vanities, saith the Blogger; all is vanity. Be admonished: of making many Great Books there is no end; and much study is a weariness of the flesh. Let us hear the conclusion of the whole matter: #qohelethrants #greatbooks #vanity

EMILE,
OU
DE L'ÉDUCATION.
PAR J. J. ROUSSEAU,
Citoyen de Geneve.

TOME IV.

GENEVE.

M. DCC. LXXX.

"The worst education of all is to leave him hesitating between his own will and yours, constantly disputing whether you or he is master; I would rather a hundred times that he were master."
-Rousseau, *On Education*

LIX
ALISON JARBO

My last Great Books class was nearly 15 years ago—a lifetime ago, really. Since then, I have graduated from law school, married, and had three children, among other things. Despite the passage of time and several cross-country moves, a bookshelf in my home office remains filled with all of my annotated Great Books. Though I haven't had the luxury or privilege of reading those books in many years, I have never forgotten the most important thing Great Books taught me—how to be a "Great thinker."

It would not be an exaggeration to say that I implement on a daily basis the analytical processes I learned in Great Books. After graduating from Pepperdine University, I went on to earn a Juris Doctorate (with a focus on Philosophy and the Law) and have been practicing law since. The process of analyzing a primary text (typically a rule/statute or case law) and applying those ideas to a current problem is the essence of practicing law.

But Great Books has impacted me in more personal ways as well. It has shaped my faith, my parenting, and my inter-personal relationships. Living a life of faith means a daily dive into *the* source text—the Bible— and applying God's word to my daily life. Other great thinkers who have wrestled with the Great Ideas have enhanced my Biblical knowledge and faith. (Tim Keller is a personal favorite. I get giddy reading/listening to his apologetics, which frequently reference the worldly philosophers and identify the worldviews underlying common objections to Christianity.) In essence, Great Books taught me how to study the Bible.

Great Books also taught me how to critically examine my worldview and expose inconsistencies in my own thinking. As a parent, I am continually analyzing whether the activities/books/experiences to which we expose our kids reflect our worldview or communicate something else entirely. I am constantly asking, as my Great Books professor did, "What is it/he/she saying?" I don't yet discuss Aristotle or Milton with my kids (ages 5 and under), but we are regularly engaged in a Great Conversation. I want my children to wonder, ask questions, learn from others, and apply what they've learned to their lives in a way that allows them to express their worldview in a logical, respectful, helpful way.

I often wish I could return to my Great Books class, now that I have lived more life and have a fuller grasp on my own worldview. Kierkegaard's Fear and Trembling takes on a whole new dimension after having kids of one's own. Likewise, my views on the Great Ideas—in particular, the relationship between society and the individual, freedom/responsibility, justice, and human nature—have been greatly enriched by life experience. But that's the beauty of Great Books. It equipped me with the tools I need to walk over to the bookshelf in my office, open Plato's Republic or Milton's Paradise Lost, and see what those books have to say

---

"With every piece of premature instruction which you try to force
into their minds you plant a vice in the depths of their hearts.
"...never make him say, 'Forgive me...'"
-Rousseau, *On Education*

2002

LX
JONATHAN CRABTREE

Two years after I graduated from Pepperdine University, and almost three years since the last time I had done so, I once again sat in Room 202 in the Cultural Arts Center on the Seaver College Campus. The blinds along the long back wall were open, it was sunny and clear outside, and the Pacific Ocean sparkled and shone a deep blue. And just like he did those two semesters I spent with him in the Great Books Seminar in 2005-2006, Dr. Michael Gose strolled into class with his wooden toolbox full of classroom supplies–paper, pencils, and blue books–placed it on the table underneath the chalk board along the long front wall, and occupied the front, center seat in the oval of desks.

The "Great Book" under discussion today was one of my favorites that he had introduced me to through his Seminar–*Fear and Trembling* by Søren Kierkegaard. It was only one of the many reasons I had returned that day, however. This was March 2009, near the end of my second year as a participant in the Teach for America program in Los Angeles. If you are unfamiliar, reader, with this program, let me introduce you. It is a nationwide organization that sends mostly young, naïve college graduates, much like I was, into underserved and low-performing school districts across the nation with the goal to "close the achievement gap" by improving student achievement. At that time, the organization defined improving student achievement primarily as improving students' state achievement test scores. Yes, those seemingly endless, mostly multiple choice-style tests that often come nearly two months before the end of the school year, leaving teachers to figure out what to do with the kids for another six to eight more weeks, as if the test was the final arbiter of what students should and do know. I am no longer a part of the organization, but I have friends within and have noticed their recent strides to create a more comprehensive program with a much more robust definition of student achievement.

In any case, throughout those two school years, I was a mathematics and science teacher at a charter middle school located in South Los Angeles. For a boy from the Midwestern suburbs of Indianapolis, the concrete sprawl that sits within the rectangle bordered by the 10 and 105 freeways to the north and south, and the 405 and the 110 freeways to the west and the east, was a different world. On a daily basis, for the first time in my life, I was a minority, a stranger. That was true racially, culturally, and in the context of being a Teach for America member, philosophically. Out of a staff of ten people, there was one other Caucasian besides me. Further, 98% of my students were African-American. And philosophically, in terms of my Teach for America cohort, I was one of a small percentage that had ever heard of Jean Anyon, much less her theory of the "four types of schools," or who could define "epistemology" and discuss the viewpoints of some of the major contributors in history on the concept. These were, of course, common discussion topics in my Great Books course with Dr. Gose.

For a teacher, the Great Idea of epistemology, specifically the idea of how one comes to know what one knows, is one of the most important ideas to grapple with. This is because it influences the very methods the teacher uses with students, how one gathers evidence on how students are progressing in their understanding, and perhaps most importantly, how the teacher views students. As a very basic example, consider how you view your own schooling and learning role. When you were a student, did you consider it your duty to take in facts from an expert, store it in your memory, and give them back to the expert when requested? Or did you consider it your duty to discover facts, ask questions about them, and process the answers to these into your own viewpoint on them? Or did it depend upon the circumstances?

I realized quickly that what Teach for America was trying to do was to lift "working-class schools" in these underserved districts into the camp of "middle-class schools." Because Anyon defined these schools based on the type of social rungs the school was preparing its students to occupy, this intention seemed good. Why not try to help students to become part of the next more upward class? All the same, this did not sit well with me. My students, I thought, should be learning the same skills and habits as those students who attended what Anyon dubbed the "affluent professional" and "executive elite" schools. On top of this, the epistemology espoused by the organization, specifically how students come to know and to create knowledge, and the methods encouraged by these, both seemed to me to be very lean.

Wonderfully, my principal wanted our students to learn the way those in the affluent professional and executive schools did, and encouraged me to build a curriculum that did so and in a way that reflected a richer epistemology. I figured that I could gain inspiration and take examples from another classroom session with Dr. Gose. He was the most credentialed educator I knew, taught me to add perspectives on the Great Ideas from so many authors into my "polyfocal conspectus" to help me in my encounters with those who held different views than I did, and he also had experience at an experimental school in Los Angeles proper, the city in which I then worked.

***

After taking a seat with the class, Dr. Gose introduced me, a stranger to everyone but himself before now, to the students in his class that day. He did not miss the opportunity for his usual banter. I was his one former student, he mentioned, who needed to come back a second time to the class, because I "did not get it the first time through." He glanced at me and flashed a mischievous grin. I smiled back, fully understanding at once he did not mean it.

This momentary unspoken exchange between us was a very "I-Thou" moment. I gathered very clearly a significant truth in that brief flash of time. From my year under his tutelage, I knew well that Dr. Gose did not believe that one could read a text such as *Fear* and understand it completely the first time. Many times over, he expressed to my class his belief that thorough re-readings and discussions, often and with different groups of people, were crucial to sharpening one's understanding of the Great Ideas within such works. In fact, he had been teaching the Great Books Seminar the same amount of time I had been living. I was born in 1985, the same year he began the program at Pepperdine. I could only imagine how often he had read this particular text alone and discussed with a different group. So I took the ribbing as I figured he'd intended—a playful way of expressing his admiration at my desire to engage with Great Ideas even outside of the requirements of his course.

Or, maybe he did truly mean it as he expressed it. After all, he would not have been incorrect. It always seemed to me when reading the Great Books that there was something I had missed by the time I had finished.

You see, for most of my first twenty years, I lived, in the words of Göthe, "hand-to-mouth." Here and there–in class, on the playground, at church, or maybe just on my own–I would encounter one of those Ideas that have been an essential part of the foundation for human thought throughout history. God. Human Nature. Justice. Good and Evil. Perhaps I might pick up on the name of someone who had expressed influential viewpoints on these ideas, a contributor of merit in an ongoing conversation that has spanned the past several thousand years and has shaped the everyday thought of millions of people who have passed through this world–sometimes without them even knowing it. Names like Plato and Aristotle, Voltaire and Locke, or Dostoyevsky and Nietzsche, sounded familiar to me. For the most part, though, I had little to no understanding, and sometimes even outright misunderstandings, of what any of them had actually communicated.

Much like those in Socrates' cave, what I saw dancing on the wall in front of me was nothing but someone else's understanding of the viewpoints of these important individuals, a dim shadow of the actual reality of their thoughts, which I probably could have picked up just by reading their works. To that point in my life, my schooling mostly involved a teacher's carefully structured delivery of someone else's writings. If I were lucky, I might be challenged to learn two opposing viewpoints on one of these Ideas. Overall, because I had not engaged with their viewpoints on their own merits, I was missing so many contexts for why people thought the way they did on a variety of subjects, and thus any way to engage in meaningful discussion on significant topics.

Too bad for me–these different angles on so many of the central concepts that informed my daily thought would have given me a wealth of tools to use to consider and truly understand radically different points of view from my own, whether they came from my friends, my family, my teachers, the national news, or anywhere else. They could have also helped me navigate the complexity of the issues of the day much easier, as popular viewpoints on current events are in some form related to the ongoing conversation about these Ideas. For instance, the idea of the relationship of the individual to society is crucial to everyday living because it influences how a group, or a portion of that group, decides to govern itself, and how members of that group interact with one another. Socrates (via Plato) held on one end that the town is ultimately supreme over the individual, and on the other, Emerson held that the individual is ultimately supreme over the town. And along that spectrum lay the opinions of everyone else. This was the beauty of my Great Books experience–it not only opened up so many different avenues of thinking about ideas that affected me everyday, but it taught me to engage with others' viewpoints and develop my own understanding of what that person is trying to persuade others to think or do based on their own words.

***

That brings me to how the Great Books have helped me grapple with that important idea of an individual's relationship to society today. Since 2010, by which time I had read and viewed enough primary sources to understand a good deal of what had happened during the worldwide financial crisis of 2008-2009, this idea has come to take an active role in my daily thoughts, especially as it regards money. From what I can understand, the simple version of the crisis is that certain large banks relaxed lending requirements for a variety of reasons to such a state that people could incur significant debts well beyond their means of repayment. These banks also made bets on almost all of these mortgages, often taking one side while broadcasting to counterparties that they took the other. They made significant profits for a time off these counterparties, but at a certain point, significant cracks began to appear that threatened them with bankruptcy.

Instead of going through the normal bankruptcy process, where their assets would be sold off to others to pay their debts, they ended up making arguments that their continued existence as is was vital to the society as a whole. Though Congress and the majority of the American people initially rejected this argument, Congress eventually flipped on the issue and voted to give them bailout money–not once, but twice. Some of this bailout money came from taxpayers themselves, who were defrauded during this process by having to pay for the mistakes of the companies themselves, and some came from the United States Federal Reserve. There were some great changes in the financial system that occurred or were solidified in both the United States and worldwide as a result of the crisis. These tended to favor these privileged companies within the financial sector, which exercise a great variety of control over the rest of the population because they control money.

This brings me back to Socrates and Emerson. In *The Republic*, Socrates describes his ideal society, in which individuals fulfill their respective befitting roles and give to the society what they owe it. This is how he defines a perfectly just society. The leaders of the "town," or society, assign individuals to an education track for one of the three main roles within the town. They do so based upon their understanding of the essences, or essential beings, of these individuals. It is important here to note they do so without regard to any of the individual's wishes or desires. In other words, the "town" and its structure (much like an ant colony or a beehive) are ultimately superior to, or greater than, the individual.

Emerson stands on the other extreme. In *Self-Reliance*, he states, "I am ashamed to think how easily we capitulate to badges and names, to large societies and dead institutions. Every decent and well-spoken individual affects and sways me more than is right. I ought to go upright and vital, and speak the rude truth in all ways." Also from that same work, "...a true man belongs to no other time or place, but is the centre of things. [...] He measures you, and all men, and all events." Emerson constantly emphasizes the centrality of the individual above the "town," its stations, and popular opinion.

I have now studied the Bitcoin protocol almost daily for about eight months, starting with the original document that first explained the technology (available at bitcoin.org/bitcoin.pdf). You may have heard about Bitcoin at some point in 2017, potentially for the first time, and potentially through some sort of media publication. It would not surprise me, as it has undergone wild swings in valuation in that time period. But more than valuation, this technology and asset fascinates me because I actually read what the inventor had to say about it, and not just what I can read on the Internet or in a newspaper, or hear second hand from someone else who knows about it. By doing this, I learned that it unifies elements of Socrates's view that individuals within a community ought to fit their respective roles and give back to the larger community what is owed it, with Emerson's view that each individual ought to not capitulate to dead institutions, but should rather "speak the rude truth in all ways" and be the "centre of things" that "measures you, and all men, and all events," or at least those that happen within the Bitcoin community. In so doing, it creates a censorship-resistant, just transactional community for both the individual and community. Using the laws of mathematics, for perhaps the first time in history, Emerson and Socrates meet not as polar opposites, but as partners.

In the original white paper, the author, Satoshi Nakamoto, describes Bitcoin as a "peer-to-peer electronic cash system." It brings Socrates and

Emerson together by creating a monetary system that does not require a trusted third party, like a bank, corporation, or financial clearinghouse, to validate transactions and keep score. Instead, the system is made up of three main roles. Parties that own and transact with some portion of the 21 million coins that will ever be created occupy one role. Miners that assemble blocks of transactions between participating parties—which are time-stamped in chronological order and cryptographically secured via digital signatures so as to ensure participants do not spend the same amount twice—play a second role. And the final role is the community of connected nodes that accepts these validated blocks into a chronologically correct chain, makes it public to all other nodes to show all transactions that have occurred in the system, which is updated about every ten minutes and then added to immediately, making it highly impractical for a dishonest node to go back and change without a significant majority of the processing power of the network.

As a result of this, the network knows about once every ten minutes the status of who owns and has spent what. Miners work on a math problem that requires them to guess a random number. The first to do so is the only winner, since it submits the block to the network and then receives a reward of fees paid by one of the transacting parties and a new amount of coin "minted" as a result of starting the newest block. The community can trust this miner's block because the miner has put money on the line in the form of significant amounts of energy spent to guess the random number. In other words, don't trust people—trust their incentives.

Just like with Socrates's vision of a society in which certain roles are occupied, so the Bitcoin network has different roles to fulfill: the transacting parties, the miners, and the individual nodes. They each play a part in keeping the community going forward, much like a beehive or ant colony, so that each role gives to the community what is owed. Transacting parties owe the miners a portion of their transactions in exchange for keeping the chain of transactions honest. Miners owe the transacting parties the work necessary to make sure that no one double spends their coins. And people or machines that run nodes are giving the community their set of eyes to validate the honest blocks and begin work attaching the latest block to the honest chain.

On the other hand, the primacy of each individual within the community is apparent, in line with Emerson. In essence, each individual is the center that is measuring everyone else within the community. The transacting parties are central to the system, speaking "the rude truth" about the value they want to exchange according to their own wishes, and not those of a trusted third party (a "dead institution," perhaps?) that can decide whether their wishes should be granted. Each individual miner is central because it should "speak the rude truth" about the honest results of each value exchange within a given time period in chronological order so that it can word towards being justly compensated for doing so. And each node is central because it should "speak the rude truth" of which block is most trustworthy, allowing itself, all other nodes, and the transacting parties to validate the miners' work and continue to build upon the most reliable version of the chain. They all act as though they are the center of the community, measuring all else, not capitulating to anyone else because of their "name" or "badge" or "institution," lest the system function otherwise than intended.

For perhaps the first time in history, a community has used technology to synthesize the polar opposite views of Socrates and Emerson on the relationship of the individual to the society. And in so doing, it has shown that both viewpoints are vital to the individual and greater society alike.

***

I am no longer an educator, but I drew upon the Great Ideas when I was teaching to help me understand my role and my students better, and make decisions to be the most effective teacher I could be. I am not in finance nor am I a computer engineer, but I have drawn upon the Great Ideas to help me understand a highly technical financial instrument and the value it could bring humanity in light of the current murky state of worldwide finance. And I will continue to draw upon the Great Ideas throughout my life, because they apply across time, space, and any other barriers one might be able to think of.

"There is a certain disposition in human nature...to barter and exchange one thing for another."
-Smith, *Wealth of Nations*

2003

LXI
JULIE JANG

My husband and I love the television show Westworld. After coming home from our medical residency training and tucking our toddler into bed, we will sneak away with a glass of wine in hand, popcorn in our laps, to watch what happens to a group of sentient androids as they shoot each other and their human creators to pieces. I would be horrified if my son walked in. If you are not familiar with the show, you might think it was the typical sex, violence, and mystery that draw viewers in, but it is so much more. The evolution of one android in particular keeps me up at night, ruminating about ideas of free will, meaning, and consciousness.

Sometimes the ruminations turn into active discussions with my husband. He just started his psychiatry residency, so surely he has opinions about the bicameral mind. I will bring up Descartes, maybe something about metaphysics, maybe the word nihilism. I look into his eyes, and he looks at me with such awe for how smart I sound. Or maybe he looks at me with contempt—I'm not really sure, maybe I'll assign meaning to it later. However, other than the ability to spit out some names and a few associated terms, there is little I know about western philosophy and literature.

Other than the Great Books courses in college, I never had any formal philosophy courses. Now it is more than ten years later, and somewhere between studying about cells, learning about diseases, and having a kid, I can tell you that Brad Pitt played Achilles in the movie, Karl Marx was German, and for some reason I found Nietzsche to be disagreeable. No, I'm being facetious. I remember a little more than that, but I am saddened by how little I remember. And it is not for lack of effort. In college, I bent pages in my books, underlined text, and wrote notes in the margins, so that I could contribute something to say the next day in class. I know I wrote a few essays about something. About a decade later, I even pulled the books off the shelf to refresh my memory, only to think *Nope, not reading* Iliad *again.*

Then there are those pieces of literature I cannot forget. I remember well *Candide* and *Waiting for Godot.* Perhaps it is no coincidence that these were the shortest of our reading assignments, but my love of these comedies would carry on well after any obligation I had to the Great Books courses. For the next decade as a graduate student, my time was devoted to training in medicine and the sciences, yet I still read multiple times *Catch 22* by Heller and *Don Quixote* by Cervantes, with *Catch 22* as a contender for my favorite book. And my mind at this time, sometimes even now, was in such conflict. As a person in pursuit of the sciences, I thought I espoused rationalism and a sense of order. Like a carefully planned set of experiments, I thought I might arrive in my life at some sort of breakthrough--as if *this is it, this is the meaning of everything.*

Yet, if I paid attention more to my choice in literature, I would have acknowledged my inclination towards the absurdity. I hesitate to use the word "absurdity", since the Absurd carries a specific meaning in western philosophy. Remember I did not formally learn about all the semantics, but what I mean by absurdity is just the inherent silliness humanity finds itself. For all our best intentions, our well laid out plans go to waste. It is this absurdity, this lack of understanding of my own life, that I find fascinating. At times, embracing absurdity has me chuckling as I go about my responsibilities, and in other times, it has me paralyzed in anxiety and fear.

This anxiety is best represented when I place myself in the shoes of Vladmir and Estragon. In Waiting for Godot, these two main characters have a choice to make. Do they continue to wait for a person named Godot or do they leave? The intellectual community debates on what Godot represents, but let us just say for now that it does not matter. In their indecision, hilarity ensues, but the reality of the situation is a kind of tragedy. I, humanity, or whatever it is that Vladmir and Estragon represent are stuck. With our free will comes decision and revisions of those decisions, with the net result of nothing—at least that is how it often seems. Perhaps nothing we decide really matters.

These are the thoughts that keep me up at night. Reader, do not mistake them for sad thoughts, because anxiety and fear can also be associated with a state of excitement. These thoughts and my preliminary understanding of the Great Books provide a context as I approach the absurd adventure that is life. As I sit with my husband with our wine and popcorn—how adventurous indeed—my mind will meander through the voices of authors now deceased and my life experiences as I draw parallels between the sentient androids of Westworld and my own being. I do not know what comes next or what conclusion I am meant to draw, but I know I have work the next morning. And, like the eponymous Candide, I must continue to cultivate my garden.

"One of the greatest improvements that has been made upon this machine, since it was first invented, was in this manner the discovery of a boy who wanted to save his own labor."
"...enlightened self interest..."
-Smith, *Wealth of Nations*

2004

LXII
MATT GRAVES

The Individual, The Universal, and The Absolute

In my ten years as a high school English teacher and now an administrator, I have often referenced, to both scholars and colleagues, the myriad lessons learned in my time as a student in my four great books courses at Pepperdine University. Small nuggets of wisdom have often found themselves sprinkled in between expectations on classroom routines, discussions of curriculum, and conferences about student behavior. I recall a particular high school student reaching out to me after her first year in college to confirm that I had indeed been correct when I had told her that she had not truly read anything until she had taken notes on her notes. This particular directive was one that was repeated often by Dr. Michael Gose as the necessary prerequisite for the type of insightful and flexible thinking that was the expectation in his great books seminar day after day. I took up this particular mantle during my six years in a high school English classroom and added to it that simply looking at words on a page was not the same as reading, that reading was a responsive activity that required critical assessment of the ideas at stake in a text. Studying the great books taught me that, above all, great ideas supersede great works of literature. Specific texts impact the world because of the significance of the ideas within them more than the beauty of their prose.

And so it is that when asked to share an anecdote about the impact of my great books experience, my thoughts immediately turned to a single sentence. To the best of my memory, I recall spending the better part of a two-hour class period reading and re-reading a single sentence that sprawled across pages eighty-four and eighty-five of Soren Kierkegaard's Fear and Trembling. I have shared this sentence with many as an example of the type of intellectual work that great works of literature and philosophy demand of their reader. Kierkegaard writes, in translation:

> The single individual as the particular
> is higher than the universal, is justified
> before the latter, not as subordinate
> but superior, though in such a way, be
> it noted, that it is the single individual
> who, having been subordinate to the
> universal as the particular, now by
> means of the universal becomes that
> individual who, as the particular,
> stands in an absolute relation to the
> absolute.

Whether due to the sentence's opaque qualities or my own lack of preparation, I had failed to muster a single pen stroke of analysis prior to class—my apologies to the professor who taught that class and may be reading this now. In my defense there may be few sentences in the canon that contain more depth and complexity, and I have returned to it again and again to make sense of various life experiences since.

As a college student at Pepperdine, this sentence helped me to understand exactly how I was to live as a person of faith in a progressive-minded world that at times challenged and at times encouraged actions associated with Christian belief. The part of me that passionately sought out social justice and desired to disrupt unjust social structures rejoiced in Kierkegaard's affirmation that the "individual... is higher than the universal;" it is not "subordinate" to the established rules but is instead "superior" to them. Of course, my twenty-one year old self declared, this was exactly as it should be. Having fled the homogenous suburban-Minnesota world of my youth for the challenges of life in Los Angeles, I was ready to confront established systems of privilege and injustice wherever they may be found. But Kierkegaard continued on from the individual's superiority; the individual was somehow also "subordinate to the universal." Submitting to the ethical rules of the world, according to Kierkegaard, had some merit; in fact, through this submission, the individual somehow entered into relationship with the absolute, the transcendent. Such is the paradox of faith for Kierkegaard: through relationship with the divine we submit to the laws, and in so doing find ourselves above these very laws. Kierkegaard helped me to find a position of simultaneously affirming ancient traditions while also challenging them when they failed to elevate the individual to his or her rightful place above the traditions themselves. Faith in God appeared to require me to live ethically without being a slave to ethical rules.

There has been no resolving this paradox in the years since I first encountered it in a great books classroom. Life as a high school teacher and administrator in schools serving under-resourced, minority communities has provided me with countless case studies to which Kierkegaard's paradox of faith can be applied. What does it look like to function in an educational system designed to serve students who, many stakeholders know in advance, will not be well-served by that system? As a teacher it looked like submitting myself to the non-negotiable expectations while doing everything in my power to elevate students above systems that had traditionally failed them—an undertaking that required significant reliance on my faith. I did not give zeros for missing work, allowed multiple opportunities for reassessment, and worked to make students the owners of their performance in my classroom. Grades were to be based on ability, performance, and growth rather than on the unspoken rules that often govern classroom success or failure. As an administrator, I have learned that no system is set in stone. An unofficial motto of our school is 'quality education by any means necessary,' a mantra rooted in our belief that students must be necessarily subordinate to our school's systems but that these systems must be changed or thrown out wholesale when necessary to ensure the success of individual students. The individual student is both subordinate and superior to the systems that govern their days because he or she stands in relationship to an absolute beyond both individual and universal.

Ultimately, the great books tradition is about learning to live well. To be fair, it is not the only place in my life where I have been exposed to models of a life well lived, but studying the great ideas has also been far more than an intellectual exercise. Kierkegaard's paradox of faith is just one example of the many ideas I have encountered in the great books canon that has had very tangible implications for the ordering of my life. The great ideas, like the universal ethical rules of Kierkegaard's paradox, are not to be held up as an absolute good to be pursued in and of themselves. They are, nevertheless, worth submitting to through serious study because this work ultimately points to something greater than the individual works themselves, the absolute that Kierkegaard speaks of in Fear and Trembling. In my life, the greatest legacy of critically engaging with the canon of great books is the affirmation of the centrality of this absolute relation to the absolute—above all other systems that have sought to define my life otherwise. For this, I am grateful.

"...those who attempt to level, never equalize. ..the levellers...only change and pervert the natural order of things."
-Burke, Reflections on the Revolution in France

2006

LXIII
KEITH CANTU

What makes a book "great?" There are countless criteria, debated endlessly in academic departments from Comparative Literature to Religious Studies. Also, what causes a book to deserve being placed on a list of greatness for the consumption of undergraduates eager to learn? While these questions are important, I am grateful that in the Great Books Colloquium they were temporarily "bracketed" for the sake of studying textual substance rather than a book or author's social context. Sitting down, engaging a text, reading the ideas and letting them swirl about with the prospect of future discussion was a critically important exercise for me. From fiction to nonfiction, everything from Plato, Virgil, Boethius, Dante, Kant, and Nietzsche to Japanese poetics helped to contribute a knowledge base from which to engage deeper questions about reality and my true nature. If I ask a question like "what does it mean to will?" then all of a sudden I have recourse to a number of authors in the back of my head who have engaged this question.

As a PhD Candidate in Religious Studies, I have had to be a TA for numerous sections on a regular basis. So I will conclude this short schrift with a concrete example on how Great Books has endless value. Last year I taught a course in the Global Studies Department, entitled "Global Culture and Ethics." One of the weeks was naturally on the Kantian contribution to human rights, and the readings were designed to get students to think critically about the notion that rights in the Enlightenment era were not necessarily for all people but often for only landed male gentry of European descent. While focusing on such a ridiculous limitation is important, I was startled that the students in critiquing Kant had no knowledge about the deeper foundation of his ethical system. So I brought in a physical book to my sections, the same "great book" that I had been assigned for Great Books and purchased used at the Pepperdine University bookstore. This book was none other than Kant's *Critique of Pure Reason* (1781), with passages on the "categorical imperative" underlined throughout. I passed the book around and, while discussing certain passages, watched as the students suddenly had an "Aha" moment on the relationship of contemporary affairs to eighteenth-century philosophical presuppositions. This then of course in subsequent weeks led to reflection on the philosophical presuppositions of today that have led to the many complex (and often controversial) constructions of political, cultural, and economic identities. The applications are endless.

My intention has been to demonstrate anecdotally that it is always handy to have a sampling of greatness in one's back pocket (or rather, tucked away in the brain somewhere). It can come to the forefront of any moment, and that depth of engagement will always be valuable, regardless of whether or not the assertions of an author are ultimately found agreeable. I am delighted to have been part of a program that, while always open to question and inquiry as to what constitutes a "canon," nevertheless chose substantive understanding of a text over getting lost in surface-level arguments that have little or nothing to do with its content and message.

"Perform your duty for no motive other than unconditional esteem for duty itself, i.e. love God above all else and love everyone as yourself."
-Kant, *Grounding for the Metaphysics of Morals*

LXIV
CHRISTIANA CHA

I was mystified when I received a letter from my alma mater that was addressed to me by hand and also bore the last name of one of my former professors. I opened it and was tickled to find that it was from a certain "Gose of Christmas Past." I had not forgotten the Gose puns from my Great Books professor, Dr. Michael Gose. Naturally, I do not remember every detail of the books we read, but I remember the puns. So it Gose....

What does one write when there are no instructions? We are not taught to do such things! Even in our Great Books courses, there were always writing prompts (who could forget those timed essay tests? I kind of miss them.). I have struggled to know what to write for this anthology and in that struggle have spent much time remembering how I felt and still feel about those courses. I remember being young and timid about sharing my thoughts, to the point that I was often silent in class. I worried about my grade because participation was part of our overall grade, and I was clearly not participating. I walked down what felt like a long hallway to Dr. Gose's office and expressed this concern. His response was, "I can tell by your eyes that you are following. You're smart; own it."

By the time I was in class with Dr. Gose for a second semester and for my final semester of the Great Books Colloquium, there was no more hiding. This man, who had a reputation for being tough and intimidating, called me out in class and forced me to speak the things he knew I was silently pushing around in my mind. I both dreaded and appreciated it. Each time he called on me, I felt my chest tighten as the words began to tumble from my brain to my clumsy mouth. What if I said something stupid? I was so afraid of this that I can honestly say I never read more fervently for any other course than I did for my two semesters with Dr. Gose.

My first two semesters of Great Books I spent with Dr. Victoria Myers, whom I remember with great fondness. She was petite, warm, spicy, kind, and devastatingly witty if you so much as gave her a syllable of ignorance. To my eighteen-year-old self, she seemed fearless and like she could hold her own in any battle of wits. A Sicilian when death is on the line would stand no chance against her! I wanted to be bold like her. It was partly this desire for boldness that drove me to say "yes" to my friends who begged me to join them in choosing Dr. Gose for our third semester of the colloquium. I had at that point never met Dr. Gose, but I was already terrified of him because of his reputation for "ripping apart" anyone who said anything dumb, ignorant, or unfounded.

I did not grow up with the luxury of safe intellectual environments, for the most part. I learned not to speak unless I was absolutely certain that I was right and knew that I could prove that I was right because I had experienced enough times the sting of being publicly ridiculed. Growing up, other kids teased me and even threw rocks at me because I was different - my parents are immigrants, and though I was born and raised in the United States, one look at me prompts people to ask, "Where are you *from*?" This is what I came from and what my life was like leading up to that year with Dr. Gose. Perhaps you can understand why I was intimidated by his reputation and why I deeply appreciated that his classroom was an intellectually safe space.

I have never regretted my decision to take the class with Dr. Gose, and I have never regretted choosing Great Books over any other colloquia. My Great Books courses were my most challenging and fulfilling courses of my college career. They stretched me and forced me to work harder than I might have had I not been challenged, and I cherish the growing pains I experienced. Dr. Myers and Dr. Gose taught me to think critically, examine thoroughly, and argue fiercely but charitably. These are qualities that I find to be widely lacking in conversations today and that have served me well in every stage of my journey since I left the CAC building for the last time.

The Great Books courses were not simply courses wherein we talked about a bunch of dead people; for me, they were courses where I was nurtured into a trajectory that would lead me to eventually pursue a masters degree in a program where I was one of only a few female students and needed every ounce of that Victoria Myers boldness and spiciness. I learned to "trust [my] compassion." I learned to speak with conviction and confidence, and I learned to not let the ignorance or narrow-mindedness of others intimidate me anymore. I learned to craft sound arguments and stand by them but also to listen well to others and encourage them to "own it."

I think I entered college expecting to come out smarter and more knowledgeable, but I did not anticipate that sitting in a circle and talking about books that might change my life entirely and free me from fear. I am forever grateful for those four semesters and to my professors for believing in me and gently pushing me. The books are great, but the people and experiences have been and continue to be invaluable.

"Act in such a way that you treat humanity, whether in your own person or in the person of another, always at the same time as an end and never simply as a means."
-Kant, *Grounding for the Metaphysics of Morals*

LXV
JOE HOOKER

Great Books did more than any other exercise, class, retreat, or personal reflection of helping me figure out who I really was based on what I really believed. When I first began the Great Books Colloquium, I thought the purpose of the class was to figure out what some of the smartest and most influential people in our history thought . . . And then regurgitate that philosopher's thought into a 3-5 page paper and try to pull off a B+ or better. It took me awhile to figure out the real purpose of the Colloquium was exploring whether the thinkers we were studying were telling the truth or telling the Truth. Were their thoughts true only for the time that they were writing or were their philosophies the Truth for which we are all searching? Or does Truth exist at all?

I still look back with great fondness on the early morning discussions when a small group of people were trying to figure out life, and our only tool was a marked up paperback with words written by a person that had been dead for more than two thousand years. The fierce, contentious debates were only surpassed in enjoyment by the feeling of acceptance upon finding another former stranger who became your ally in pursuing Truth.

My life looks very different than it did when I first began my journey through the Great Books. While at 18 I of course was concerned with finding a purpose in life, eventually find a spouse, etc., I was much more concerned with making it to my 8 am classes on time (which Great Books happened to be one of those) and going to the beach afterwards. Now I feel that I have begun answering some of those larger questions and concerns that were looming on my horizon when I was 18. I know that larger challenges, sweeter joys, and potential suffering lie ahead. But my journey with the Great Books has not and will not stop. Whether it's a new work to add to my quiver or pulling down my battered copy of a well-thumbed Great Books I classic with the notes I made while sitting in a Pepperdine classroom, I know I can use these truly great books to give comfort and guidance.

Grundlegung

zur

Metaphysik

der Sitten

von

Immanuel Kant.

Riga,
bey Johann Friedrich Hartknoch
1785.

"Every rational being must so act as if he were through his maxim always a legislating member in the universal kingdom of ends."
-Kant, *Grounding for the Metaphysics of Morals*

LXVI
REBECCA HOOKER

There is a lot I can say about Great Books - why it was so formative for me. Why I think everyone should take it. I have it narrowed down to a top 10 list in honor of the 10 great ideas we studied in Great Books (which I can't exactly remember, but I am pretty sure there were 10 of them).

1. I met my husband in Great Books*
2. I learned how to ask insightful questions - or at least pretend to know the difference between good and bad ones**
3. I can impress people as an adult with all the smart books I have read***
4. You pick up on lots of cultural references - more than you would even imagine - you continue to realize there are few original thoughts and most everything is recycled from these really smart dead guys (and a woman or two)
5. You get to know people you would otherwise not talk to.+
6. You spend -in my case- many late nights writing papers and trying to craft a sound argument which was not always successful but when I finally got it I felt real pride and I still think about that paper today++
7. You learn how to begin trying to think for yourself+++
8. You get to know some very smart and cool Professors who will become your favorites BY FAR!
9. I am having trouble thinking of a nine but I remember the views from the Great Books classrooms being nice - but really the views everywhere are pretty nice. #Pepperdine
10. It will help you send a fax!!

*really I did. We both chose it as our freshman seminar. I remember as we all introduced ourselves at orientation and most of the 17 students had already read more of the syllabus than I had. I was still an overly confident know it all 18 year old so that did not concern me near as much as the fact that I had to discuss Plato at 8:00 am - DO WHATEVER YOU CAN TO NOT HAVE GREAT BOOKS AT 8:00 AM (or any class really). But future husband and I made eyes at each other and read together late into the night - really that is not a euphemism we were really reading. Then we fell in love and now we have a baby. So if you take Great Books be careful you may end up with a VERY CUTE husband and baby.

**It turns out asking good questions is harder and worth more than having good answers.

***Even though I can not remember most of what I read (I do remember the essence of it) it is fun to casually drop knowledge on people about Achilles shield and what Dante did in Hell and where the term "Yahoo's" comes from (Gullivers Travels)

+This is different than the way you get to know people in Speech class or abroad or in the dorms. You all explore these complex works of fiction together and as they unravel so does each person and at the end you realize everyone is woven together. So even if you never hang out after class or have another class together you will definitely say hi to each other if you should pass by in the caf.

++I was not writing A papers - I was living solidly in B land - which in some cases was fine for me in other classes but I really cared about my Great Books grades and I was trying really hard so it was irritating me I could not get an A. I started writing extra papers on top of my regular ones to practice my writing (which Professor Gose suggested) and after a couple tries I FINALLY nailed one (or he took pity on me). Afterward I made all my roommates read it and rightfully put it on the fridge.

+++ In most every other class you will take you will listen to lots of facts or theories or what have you and then you will memorize them in some way to get them to stick. Then they will float away after a while. Great

Books is different. It is like solving a great big puzzle you don't even know what it looks like or how it fits together and sometimes it doesn't fit at all. But that is ok because lots of things in life don't fit the way you think. (If you already think you do think for yourself - HA - there is nothing new under the sun)

!Ok some are cooler than other - but they were all super smart and really interesting and a WEALTH of knowledge and it is rare to get such unfettered access to them for so long in a such a small group.

!!There is so much crap you have to do for other people and for requirements and ya know to "check the boxes" to get the internships or start some non profit or study for the LSAT etc etc. DO THIS FOR YOURSELF. It is the best thing you will do. And when you are sitting in your cubicle at your first job years from now and spending lots of time trying to use the stupid fax machine (bc yes PEOPLE STILL USE THOSE) and their archaic email system and you look at the clock about 10 times and it has only been 15 minutes you will think back to college and that time you took Great Books and really used your brain and you will smile and say to yourself - I am really glad I did that. Then you will say, "If I figured out &$%^#@^& Kant, and Aristotle, and Homer, and Milton I can figure out any of the #$&#%$ they throw at me!" (including surviving and thriving in corporate America).

"Once again do I behold these steep and lofty cliffs, that on a wild, secluded scene impress thoughts of a more deep seclusion, and connect the landscape and the quiet of the sky."
-Wordsworth

LXVII
KANAKO SUZUKI

As I was selecting courses for my first semester at Seaver College, without much thought, I chose to participate in the Great Books curriculum; the program seemed like a good introduction to traditional classics that one should read at some point, and it served to fulfill several of the general education requirements. I had no specific expectations for the classes at the time due to my shallow understanding of the colloquium – looking back now, I'm grateful that my eighteen-year-old self decided at that moment to be a student of the Great Books program and thus, a student of Dr. Michael Gose. It is not an exaggeration to say that Dr. Gose left a permanent impression on not just my undergraduate studies but also on my current career as an educator. Our encounters from my first days of college until now have helped transform me into who I see myself as today.

Dr. Gose's Great Books classes were some of the most demanding courses of my undergraduate years. Never having had much exposure to the canon of Western classics before Great Books I, I spent many nights on the sofa in the dorm suite, attempting to stay on top of my readings while knowing that I was out of my depth during in-class discussions. My peers seemed to understand the content better (or, at least, they were better at sharing their thoughts). Our classes were centered on a Socratic dialogue model, an inquiry through discussion where students help lead the conversation. Although I loved hearing other's discerning comments regarding the text, I was hesitant to voice my opinion at first due to my natural introversion. However, despite the challenges (or because of them), I came to love Great Books because of how Dr. Gose led his classes. Of course, the text-based knowledge I gained is invaluable; one of the primary and most straightforward goals for taking a class is to study and acquire academic knowledge specific to that content. From Plato to Dostoevsky, the core texts provided innumerable opportunities for us to discuss and analyze the various perspectives of its authors. However, even more than the content, I obtained insight into the many pedagogical practices that Dr. Gose implemented in his Great Books instruction to make his classes successful and stand out from others.

Below, I will list some of the lessons I've learned and the tools I've gained for my own teaching by being a participant in Dr. Gose's Great Books courses.

1. expectations – Dr. Gose had reasonable and appropriate expectations for his classes, and he built a classroom culture where those expectations were upheld. He didn't demand that all students ace his essays and tests; in fact, he promoted a growth mindset that allowed students to fail but keep trying. However, he did insist that students read the text, come to class prepared, and actively participate in class. By having what students would perceive as fair and just expectations, Dr. Gose held his class accountable for their actions, which led to productive discussions and a spirited community.

2. rapport – as any teacher can tell you, building rapport with students can transform how your class as a unit functions. Dr. Gose was very skilled in understanding different personalities and how they function with one another in a classroom setting; he often used this knowledge to build a cohesive classroom culture, like how a coach would masterfully use his players on the field. I remember early on when I was slightly timid about taking part in our animated discussions. Although I did not share this insecurity directly with him, he told me that while I didn't always contribute verbally to each class, he knew that I was thinking thoroughly about the text at hand. Because I felt acknowledged by him, his kind words ultimately made me more confident to take risks and offer my thoughts during dialogue. I am sure that he has done similar for many other students and in return, created learners that were more eager and present. As an educator now, I try to emulate Dr. Gose's ability to establish rapport with my own students and celebrate them for their individuality and strengths.

3. humor and playfulness – although Great Books deals with monumental texts, Dr. Gose kept a playful, lively atmosphere

that invited participation and at times, grand gestures. It made the texts approachable instead of foreign, and students appreciated his comparisons and metaphors as we deconstructed works by Kant and Erasmus. Achieving greatness through rigorous study is of importance, but that doesn't mean it needs to exclude the art of anticipation and surprise.

4. role model – being a teacher in the classroom means the necessity of wearing multiple hats: the instructor, supporter, disciplinarian, mentor and magician to name a few. Maybe one of the most significant of these duties is the one of the role model. The idiom, "do as I say, not as I do" may be appropriate in certain scenarios, but it definitely fails to work in a classroom setting, where students, especially younger ones, continuously look at the teacher to gauge the appropriateness of one's behavior. Having taught middle school, I know I have to be careful that my words match my actions – any deviation may potentially result in confusion or distrust within that learning community. As an instructor of Great Books, Dr. Gose made sure that he shared his own enthusiasm, passion, and curiosity while he aided us in interpreting the content, and all of us were in awe of his knowledge and intellect as we examined ideas within the books. He pushed us to be better students, but he also showed how he took his role as an educator seriously. By setting the tone of the class, Dr. Gose increased learning and productivity by modeling those behaviors.

5. support of student success – while the above traits are all imperative in order to be a good teacher, I believe that a core attribute that all great teachers share is the ability to believe in each and every single one of their students. Research has shown that positive teacher-student relationships support students' academic growth and resiliency. I believe that Dr. Gose wants the best for every student that comes through his classroom; he often tailors his advice to each individual, and he pushes students to aim for ambitious goals. If you are willing to put in the effort, he will recognize that and work to aid in your success however he can. Even though it has been over ten years since I first had him as a professor, I still benefit from his teachings and still remember how his encouragement emboldened me to pursue my own dreams in becoming a teacher.

While I truly enjoyed Great Books for what it was, it would not have been the same without Dr. Gose's pedagogical methods. Taking the colloquium not only introduced me to time-honored texts but also helped me see what an effective teacher looks like in such a class. It is inestimable the effect a great instructor can have on his or her students; I plan to take all that I've learned from Dr. Gose's classes to enrich my own classroom culture and practices. As the books in the canon that we read are considered great, Dr. Gose himself is an epitome of another kind of greatness – the greatness that affects all that come through his classroom doors, the greatness of a teacher.

"Beauty is truth, truth beauty."
-Keats, *Ode to a Grecian Urn*

LXVIII
TRICIA TOMPKINS MCKENZIE

Gadfly

The morning sun peeked through the crevices in the walls and danced across Kurt's face as it did every morning. He lay still for a moment, recalling the last vanishing visions of his dreams and then let out a yawn as he stretched his appendages. Kurt swiveled his head to find his young brother, Luc, still sleeping. Using his back legs, Kurt prodded him in the abdomen and waited until Luc began to stir before ambling toward the light.

He watched the others scurry by. Some herding Younglings, some with longer legs or larger jaws, and some more petite. Kurt had always been one to pay attention and observe closely. In secret, he often marveled at the differences between each colonial. Seemingly minute, and yet he wondered if there was not some meaning behind them. He had once asked his father about this as a Youngling.

"Father," he said, why do we all look different?"

"Kurt, hush!" his mother quickly intervened, "You know better!"

"It's alright, Doris," his father said coolly, "What's this you're going on about, son?"

"W-well," he stammered, "We all do the same things. You and Mister Fitz, you're both Transporters. But you're so different."

"Different?" His father's large eyes narrowed. "He's got six legs, same as you and me. And two feelers, two pincers, and--"

"Yes, but they aren't the same. There must be a reason for it. Your legs are longer than his. And his pincers are larger than yours. Why would--?"

226

"And what reason would that be, son?" Kurt's mother looked on nervously, sensing the tone of aggravation growing in her husband's voice and his abdomen beginning to rise.

"Well maybe he..er..." Kurt's voice trailed off and he slunk lower to the ground. A look of satisfaction spread across his father's face and his abdomen lowered.

"You musn't ask questions when you don't know the answers, Kurt. We don't go looking to disrupt the colony. We have survived for years. Before you or I were born. Before my father's father was born. Don't go making trouble, you hear me, son?"

"Yes, sir."

That was the day he learned not to question a Full-Grown. It was a rule the colony lived by. These rules were not spoken, yet ingrained into their every membrane. He learned this lesson many times over through his mother's hushes and Full-Grown's scoffs. Now, nearly a Full-Grown himself, Kurt resolved to guarding these musings safe inside his mind.

Luc caught up with Kurt at the Morning Gathering and they both filed in behind their parents. Always in single file. First fathers, then mothers, then finally the children in age order down to the smallest Hatchling. The Elders would deliver their daily assignments and boundaries, though they rarely varied, save when Hatchlings were old enough to begin their contributions. *Contribution* was a word that Kurt poured over constantly in the secret recesses of his mind. When he was still a Hatchling he had gathered that contribution was what you would offer to the colony after your day's work. Some were Transporters, like his father, who spent their days collecting food for the Stockpile. Seeds, leaves, fruit, wood-rot, and fungi were meticulously gathered from the flatlands and transported back for safe-keeping. Kurt always enjoyed watching his father and the rest of his Squad work.

The Extractors would use their strong mandibles to cut through plants and rotting wood, and then the Transporters took over. They masterfully worked in tandem with one another without uttering a word. To Kurt it appeared as a choreographed dance. Each in perfect rhythm and sync with the other.

Kurt was assigned as a Seeker. He recalled receiving his assignment when he was phasing from Hatchling stage. Elder Abner had given him his assignment. In that moment Kurt felt proud. Seekers were tasked with discovering new food sources for the Extractors to labor, a noble task. *They have chosen me for this*, Kurt had thought. *My marks must have been high in Instruction, Elder Abner must have seen.* The leaves had turned, fallen, and grown back again before Kurt learned it was happenstance. Assignments were given on rotation. Once one colonial reached Full Maturesence, they would no longer be fit to contribute and would be replaced. Willa's joints had begun to stiffen and buckle, just as Kurt entered Youngling stage. Though she had contributed for many cycles, she was too weary to venture into the flatlands any longer. On the same day that the air left Willa's body and she went back into the earth, Kurt was given his new assignment. It would be his charge until he himself went back to the earth.

Morning Gathering concluded, and the colonials shuffled on to their various assignments. Transporters following behind Extractors, Instructors herding the young Hatchlings, and so on and so on. Seeker was one of the lonelier tasks. They did not work in Squads, but in Pairings so as to scour more efficiently. Kurt was paired with Keane. They had hatched only three days apart. Keane was quicker than Kurt, but Kurt was more careful. Together they covered a large amount of ground and the Elders had commended the pairing for their contributions. Kurt's father took great pride in telling tales of the pairing's conquests to his fellow Transporters during their Stockpile runs.

"My son's pairing found this log, you know" He would say to Fitz as they worked together to roll loads of rotting wood back the Stockpile.

"You don't say, Berni" Fitz would reply, just as he had the day before and the day before that.

"Oh, yes. He spotted it from many stretches" Berni would beam. "This is sure to double the Stockpile, don't you think?"

"Surely," Fitz would say.

In truth it was Keane who had first seen the log, but Kurt never quite mustered the words, or courage, to correct him.

The Seekers were sent in different directions each day and were told to labor until the sun began to disappear. They were given no boundaries, but every Seeker knew to leave many stretches between themselves and the Edge if assigned to its direction, as Kurt and Keane were today.

"When the sun begins to hide, we return to the Colony," his *Instructor had told them in their teaching.*

228

"Where does the Sun go," one of Kurt's fellow pupils had asked. The Instructor paused and straightened her appendages.

"Young ones," she said, addressing the entire group, "The sun will hide beyond the Edge. Just as we return to the earth, so does the sun at the end of each day. It goes beyond the Edge to die. Nothing can live there. Just as new Hatchlings are born into the colony, so a new sun is born into the sky and emerges each new day."

"But--"

"That is all we need know, Hatchlings."

From there the tales of the Edge were born. Wild and fantastical stories exchanged by young Hatchlings, born out of sheer fear and curiosity. By the time Hatchlings became Younglings, the stories had ceased and curiosity had simmered down into resolved truth. The fear, however, remained and grew stronger with each new sun that rose. Every colonial dreaded the Edge, and none would dare to approach it.

"Keep up, would ya?" Keane hollered back at Kurt, jarring him from his memories. Keane was five lengths ahead of Kurt, rather than his usual two.

"Right behind you," Kurt replied, and quickened his scurry. The air was growing colder, and with it, the food grew scarcer. The wind made it difficult to make out from which direction a smell originated. The pairing sought for hours to no avail. They ventured further on, relying on their feelers to scour the scents of the air until they could no longer see the Colony behind them, much further than either of the pair had ventured out before. Kurt, struggling to match his counterpart's stride in the wind, lowered his head and pumped his legs as quickly as his strength could manage. Unknowingly, he barreled straight past Keane, who had stopped in his tracks.

"Hey!" Kurt heard from behind. He halted and whipped his head around.

"Did you find something?" Kurt asked. He looked up Keane, whose eyes were transfixed ahead. His eyes were wide and his expression was one Kurt had not seen before.

"Look," he said, without breaking his gaze. Kurt turned toward the direction of Keane's gaze. Immediately, his eyes widened as well. A chill came over him, coupled by an emotion he had not felt since his Hatchling days. Before the two, the great sun was beginning its descent. What once was full and round, now appeared as a half-circle, slowly diminishing as they watched. The ground extended some ways further, then dropped off and disappeared. There was nothing beyond it, as far as the eye could see.

"Is that the--" Keane began, then paused. He was unsure of the answer, and yet somehow entirely sure all at one.

"The Edge," Kurt said certainly. It had to be. The two stared for many moments as the sun slowly disappeared. It was Keane who broke the silence.

"We'd better get back," he said and turned to leave. Kurt stayed still, unable to move. Mesmerized by the sight before him. This was the sight they had demonized back in the days of Instruction. Certain death, as his mother described it. Where nothing, not even the great sun, can survive. While he had feared the existence of this unknown place for so long, what he felt now was nothing similar to fear. It was beautiful.

Keane had already started back, his voice trailed off as he hurried toward the Colony. A gust of wind blew against Kurt, nearly knocking him onto his back. Wind blew up from the depths, where the sun was falling. It swirled in the air, carrying dust and deterioration with it, then blowing directly toward Kurt. He lowered his body toward the earth and let the dust blow by him, his eyes still fixed on the Edge as he stabilized himself against the wind. It was not only dirt and dust blowing up from below, but what appeared to be larger objects as well.

One landed at his feet and he quickly trapped it in his pincers. It was a leaf, just the same as he had seen his father transport so many times before. It was not brown, nor even orange, but green in color. No charring or signs of destruction.

"KURT!" Keane yelled in the distance. The sun was nearly disappeared now. Kurt turned his body and scampered with the wind back toward the Colony, the leaf still clenched in his jaw. As he hurriedly made his way back, his mind raced.

Where did this leaf come from? Did it truly come from beyond? But, how? How could it be alive? Nothing survives beyond the Edge. Not even the great sun. How could this leaf be green? The air hasn't even left its body. It is not dried or crackled, but nimble and soft. How can this be? Nothing lives beyond.

By the time Kurt returned to the safe haven of the colony, Keane was already surrounded by a simmering crowd of indistinct murmurs. He calculated the distance to the quiet of his own dwelling, but seeing no safe route, relented to joining the crowd. His mother saw him first. She scurried to greet him, Kurt released the leaf from his mouth and buried it under his abdomen. When Doris reached him, she assessed every feeler, joint, and ligament, let out a long sigh and began her chastising.

"What were you thinking, Kurt? Staying out so near to dark? And so close to the Edge?" Her eyes were wide, but not with the disappointment or anger of a mother's retribution. He peered into her deep black eyes and recognized the fear that clouded them. He reached to touch her face.

"We were wrong about the Edge, Mother." He said. The fear shifted to bewilderment, and almost immediately, panic. She stepped back, nervously. By this time the colony had surrounded them. The Elders stepped forward amongst the crowd.

"*Wrong?*" Elder Abner said. He moved in closer and squared his body with Kurt's until Kurt could feel his hot breath on his face.

"Please do elaborate, Youngling" Elder Abner said slowly and quizzically.

"Well, Keane and I saw the Edge. And it isn't a place of death like we were told. We saw the sun as it hid beyond, and it was nothing like we thought. The sky was lit with bright orange and shades of gold. It was incredible. I don't think the sun was dying at all." Kurt looked to Keane and they locked eyes for a moment. Keane lowered his head and stared intently at the ground.

"Oh, no?" Abner said. "Did the sun disappear behind the Edge?"

"Well yes--"

"And is this not what you were taught in Instruction?"

"Yes, but we were also told that nothing lives beyond the Edge. That's not true." The sea of murmurs had hushed into a dead silence.

"Not true?" Elder Abner's tone grew agitated. "Are you telling me you traveled beyond?"

"No, sir." Elder Abner stood taller in a show of triumph.

"Well then, how could you possibly..." Kurt pushed the leaf he had hidden toward the Elder. It was pierced and crumpled from its travels, but deep green with life all the same.

"This has." The Elder crouched low to the ground to examine the leaf, looking it over as though it were an undiscovered species.

"The wind carried it up from the Beyond," Kurt continued. "This leaf was fallen fresh from a tree. It is not dried or crackled. It was alive only moments before it appeared at my feet. There could be life beyond the Edge." Kurt spoke excitedly and he drew short of breath. "Don't you see?"

231

"Could be?" Elder Abner mocked. "You'd risk so much for, *could be*?"

"I just mean if we are wrong about this that we all believed...what else might we be missing?"

"*Enough.*" Elder Abner nearly hissed. He leaned his face in close to Kurt's a second time. "Enough." His eyes were wide and wild. Kurt had watched the wise Elder for his entire life, always calm, powerful, and unwavering. Yet, in this moment, Kurt saw weakness in him for the first time. He appeared to him as frail as the blades of grass cut down and hauled to the Stockpile each day. Kurt stood taller and inhaled deeply. He looked out to the silent colonials around him.

"What if what we know is not the truth?"

Elder Abner stepped back, his gaze unshifting. He stayed quiet for a moment, then turned to search the crowd until he locked eyes with Kurt's father.

"Berni," Abner summoned, "Is your youngest fit to contribute?"

"I--I suppose--he could be, Edler," Berni stammered. "Luc has not yet finished with his Instruction... but--but he's a very quick learner."

"Very well." Abner raised his abdomen in a show of dominance. "From this day forward, Luc will take Kurt's place. He will be assigned as Seeker and paired with Keane."

Berni's head cocked and his mandible dropped. Murmurs from the colonials grew louder.

"But...and my oldest, Elder?" Berni asked timidly. "What of his assignment?"

"He's no longer fit to contribute." He did not break eye contact with Kurt. "There will be no re-assignment."

In all of Elder Abner's cycles, he had never stripped a colonial of their assignment before reaching Full Maturesence. Those who had been replaced would spend their days resolved, waiting for their end days to come. They often remained in their dwellings, only venturing outside for Morning Gatherings or to stretch their weakening joints. This was how Kurt would live out his days. Though his legs were strong, and his pincers sharp, he would live out his days, idly--the ultimate punishment.

The morning sun peeked through the crevices in the walls. He lay still, keeping his eyes closed, hoping for a moment, that this had all been nothing but a bad dream. He would awaken and venture out as he had so many times before. Kurt swiveled his head to find Luc, but Luc had already awoken and shuffled toward the Morning Gathering. Luc had done this every morning since his assignment three suns ago. He would wake silently so as not to disturb his brother. Kurt would lie still and feign sleep until he scurried into the light, then slowly rise and watch the colonials gather from the darkness.

He watched the others quickly pass by. Watching, and observing as he always had. Somehow, they seemed to move more slowly, the Gathering lagged and Kurt no longer felt the urgency in the air. He stayed hidden as the gathering concluded and the colonials dispersed. The Hatchlings hurried past, two by two, their Instructor barking back at them from the head of the long line. The last pair of Hatchlings slowed as they passed the opening to Kurt's dwelling.

They crept slowly, cautiously, toward the entrance. These Hatchlings were nearly Luc's size, they would surely soon matriculate from their Instruction. One stopped a few lengths from Kurt and turned as if to stand watch. The other continued forward in determination, and as she drew nearer to his dwelling, Kurt stepped out and met her in the sunlight. She did not speak but lowered her head and dropped something at her feet, and nudged it forward until it was at Kurt's.

He looked down to the ground. Though it was browning at the edges, Kurt recognized this leaf instantly. Such an ordinary object weighted with such significance. He raised his gaze to meet the young Hatchling's. She nodded slowly, and in that moment, she did not appear to him as a wide-eyed Hatchling, but as a Full-Grown with wisdom beyond her short days on earth. He nodded his head and she turned to meet her pairing. They scurried on to catch up with the line of pupils. Kurt watched them both as they joined their grouping and took their places for the day's instruction.

Kurt picked up the leaf and carried it back inside. Warmth washed over him and his legs tingled. His body twitched as he placed the leaf on Luc's resting place with great precision. He looked around the place and exhaled slowly, steadying himself. He reached the entrance to the dwelling and waited until everyone had cleared from the gathering place, then stole quickly into the flatlands.

He did not pause. Did not look behind. Did not stray from his path until finally, he reached it once again. Just a few lengths from it now, he slowed his pace and inched his way toward the Edge. There was no wind today. The air was still and almost tranquil. He stepped out and craned his body to look over the edge and saw nothing but vast unknown. Doubt crept into his mind, and Kurt began to turn his head back toward the Colony where all familiarity lied, but where his certain death lay also.

Kurt stepped out to the crest of the cliffside. Timidly at first. It was steep and uneven, and Kurt was unsure if his body could manage the climb. Then he thought of how he and Keane would climb up fragile dandelion stems and rotted branches, and he began his descent. With his first few steps he would look down at his feet, careful not to lose his footing. As he pressed on, he thought of the young Hatchlings, and each step grew more steady, more determined, and more resilient.

He walked long past when the sun was at its peak, pausing only to catch his breath and rest his legs. His feverish pace had slowed and settled into a contemplative ambling. He noted the changing of the winds, the shifts in his shadow, and the myriad of colors in the cliffside. At times he voiced his thoughts out loud. With no fear of listening ears or condemnation, he felt free to pose his unanswerable questions aloud, for the first time, out into the open abyss:

Where does the great sun go when it falls?
What assignment would I most want?
Why do we have assignments at all?
What does it all mean?
Why was it I who found the leaf?
Why are the others so afraid of the Edge?
How do I find the truth?

"A fine question, good fellow." A voice said from above. Kurt wondered for a moment if he had answered himself. Had he wandered for so long that he had lost his senses?

"I've been asking myself that very question for some time now." Kurt looked up and saw a small creature hovering above him. He buzzed ahead of Kurt and landed before him.

Kurt looked him over. The being looked similar to his own colonials. Six legs and two feelers, large glossy black eyes, but he had no pincers and delicate wings that vibrated spontaneously as though beckoning him back to the sky, though he had landed firmly on the ground.

"Who..." Kurt began, "What are you?" Kurt asked.

"*What* am I? What *am* I?" The stranger repeated Kurt's question to himself. "I am not sure if I can fully answer your question, but I suppose, to put it simply, I am a gadfly. You've not seen one like me before?"

Kurt shook his head.

"Come with me," The gadfly said.

The gadfly took to the air again and Kurt followed behind, willing his legs to move as quickly as he could.

"It would be much easier if you used those wings of yours!" His new friend called. Kurt stopped in his tracks, perplexed.

"Wings?"

As the word escaped from his lungs and into the air, a layer peeled from his back in a stretching sensation. Virgin wings extended and began to whir and vibrate. Clumsily, Kurt levitated off the ground. He bobbled in the breeze like a falling leaf, but quickly steadied himself flew with even greater force than that of the gadfly. The gadfly looked back at Kurt, and Kurt smiled in disbelief.

"Come, my friend," the gadfly said, "We've much to seek, yet."

"If I was wrong in yielding to persuasion once, remember that it was to persuasion exerted on the side of safety, not of risk. When I yielded, I thought it was to duty; but not duty could be called in aid here. In marrying a man indifferent to me, all risk would have been incurred, and all duty violated."

-Anne in Austen's *Persuasion*

2007

LXIX
NADIA DESPENZA

When I think about Great Books. I think of the very first day of class. I was slated to be in another freshman seminar however, this seminar allowed me to take Calculus my freshman year. I had no idea what Great Books consisted of as I changed my schedule to accommodate my first year as a Biology major but I knew I needed Calculus. I emailed you to let you know I was in your section and asked for pre-work but I received no response. So I went to your class on the first day and I remember that you questioned me with indignation about not being prepared for class. You reiterated that this class required everyone to do the assigned readings because only then could we have an authentic dialogue. I remember, responding with same indignation because I emailed you and intended to be prepared but received no response. After that encounter, I bought my books and read my material. You always required us to sit in a circle and we could only respond to one another with evidence from the text. This was the first time an educator had ever sat alongside me vs. teaching directly at me. I learned to use the text as my "battle weapon" to have a debate about lifelong essential questions that no one truly has the answers to.

Great Books taught me to challenge the world around me. I used history to shape my voice vs. renting my parents' voice. Great Books allowed me to read books that I would have never read as a Black girl from the south side of Chicago. To this day, I tell the teachers I coach to find the "ha" in their readings and in their classroom. I think of how Great Books taught me to critically think and analyze text for the deeper meaning. I learned I didn't have to agree with an author but I could find another author who I did agree with to justify why I didn't agree with the first author. Does that make sense? ha

I can't really put into words all the feeling and appreciation I have for Great Books. However, I know God blessed me with having to change my freshman schedule because I wouldn't be the spunky and critical thinking woman that lies before you without this foundation.

"Death, death, death, death, death."
-Whitman, *Out of the Cradle Endlessly Rocking*

LXX
BRENDAN FEREDAY

Great Books was one of these experiences that I feel like I've cheapened trying to explain, yet continue to in the hopes the appreciation will be shared. I find myself writing or speaking about it in nearly every application or interview I've had. What this program did for me educationally begs an attempt at description. Great Books felt like a perfect storm in how well things seem to align for my educational formation, though I now believe it was more a factor of the program than chance. This class was my educational awakening as I learned to really think for the first time. I figure that the effect Great Books had on me was due to three major facets of the program: by teaching me to recognize patterns, by forcing me to experience different perspectives, and by teaching me to understand the relationships between ideas. I want to briefly explain each.

Patterns: While getting a master's degree in Human Development and Psychology at Harvard, I thought it would be fun to take a class in analytical legal theory (not as fun as it sounds). At the very end of the class, our professor referenced Great Books. His class, he said, wasn't aimed at teaching us the exact wording of arguments or to precisely remember the ideas presented, but, like Great Books, was meant to *expose* us to these ideas early on in our career so that they will be recognized later on. In effect, he was arguing that memorization of information wasn't as important as exposure to the patterns that once seen, can't be unseen.

That wasn't where my head was at upon completing Great Books. When the two years of Great Books concluded, I remember the intense feeling of regret when I couldn't remember exactly what Kant's categorical imperative was and when I found myself frozen after realizing that I didn't have a clue what Rousseau said even after dropping his name in a conversation like I did. I remember wondering what the point of the program was if I didn't actually remember what I had spent all that time learning. I felt like an imposter that couldn't prove those years were well spent.

The content itself was certainly important—many of these authors helped to define Western thought, so a recollection what they said can definitely be helpful. But in the long term, exposure has proved more important than memorization. An introduction to the ideas that are repeated and built on throughout literature helped me recognize the lineage of thought that passed through writers and disciplines—to see the patterns of ideas. I found Buber's "I" and the "Thou" in human development theory. "The Other" from Simone DeBeauvoir's Second Sex, gave me a term for describing current social tension. And once I realized a Great Books author was hiding behind a contemporary argument or saw them cited in a research article, I was sent back to the texts—to my underlines, stars, and margin notes—to see exactly what they were saying and how what they said was relevant to the issue at hand. Once I became aware of the different ways an idea or philosophy shows up in the world and learned to recognize it across contexts and disciplines, the ideas became meaningful in their usefulness.

Patterns are useful because they increase the amount of ways you can understand something. They increase the amount of access points—the number of ways in. You aren't limited to an understanding that just depends on one way of seeing something. If it has been expressed in other ways and in other contexts (is part of a set), I have more data points to pull from, resulting in a more informed and faceted understanding of that idea. Recognizing Shelly's commentary on the dangers of unchecked pursuit of knowledge in an article debating the ethicality of gene editing provided a multi-dimensional understanding of the issue. When reading a psychologist's reflections on group behavior studies, Plato's allegory of the cave helped me understand why individuals tend to remain in specific group roles and reenact negative patterns of behavior.

The time spent in Great Books was merely the start of the journey. The classroom was where I was introduced to the ideas, but I found the greater substance in the return to them. In the repeated revisiting of a text over time, for different reasons and in different contexts, a work begins to solidify in the mind. A good memory of the actual points of each author right after finishing Great Books wouldn't have been as valuable to my understanding as the ability to recognize patterns was. Recognizing patterns allowed me to apply the ideas to real situations, leading to more informed action and, dare I say, better living.

Perspective: While discussing liberal arts and human flourishing at Yale back in 2013, the theologian Miroslav Volf and New York Times Opinion columnist David Brooks claimed that the Great Books program is most instrumental in the way it develops a student's perspective. They held it up as a way for students to "try on" different worldviews like clothes by experiencing the kind of life and view of the world that an author's take on things affords them. It was an opportunity for students to figure out what pieces of the author's perspective fit, and which don't. Through this process, students shape their personal worldview.

Everyone unconsciously undergoes this process through proximity to parents, teachers, and friends. Others share their view of the world with us and we then, consciously or unconsciously, judge their perspectives. If those perspectives feel accurate and helpful, its incorporated into our perspective and built upon. If not, its dismissed or rebelled against. Great Books accelerates this process and refines the muscle that we use to discern by demanding increasingly greater nuance when drawing distinctions between worldviews and judging accuracy. It does this by requiring students to defy that reflex to dismiss or rebel, to not ignore an idea just because it contradicts one's current view of things. We had to sit with each perspective for a bit, to search hard for it's virtues *and* vices. I couldn't digest news (or any claim, for that matter) the same after Great Books. The new reflex was to respond, for example, to an article discussing the negative effects of a political policy with the question, "Well, what could be the positive effects?" Someone's claim that "this is definitely right" is now immediately met with the internal voice searching for how it could be wrong.

This pisses people off, as Dr. Gose promised it would. In school staff meetings, I am the one that questions (internally and externally) the thing everyone takes for granted, that posed the counterpoint to what everyone is sure about. In one sense, I enjoyed being the Socratic gadfly but had to learn (and am still learning) the value of not letting the perfect get in the way of the good. I've had to learn when unsure agreement is better than fully interrogating and exploring an issue, when to ask questions and when to just nod in approval even when I don't fully agree. The internal critique that Great Books instilled remains though. I still internally explore an idea from all sides even if that exploration isn't carried publicly.

This internal conversation and testing of ideas leads to more flexible thinking. I became more willing to take the good even when it was in the presence of bad. To say it a different way, I wouldn't dismiss a whole theory because it contained pieces I disagreed with. This happened unconsciously by virtue of our march through the Great Books authors, stopping at each to see how they fit and felt. I started to see the world a little more deeply as they pointed at different parts of it with differing intensity. Erasmus and Machievelli both illustrated human frailty and folly, but did it in different ways by tending to different manifestations of it in different contexts. Much like how art helps to break the lens of habit that keeps us from seeing any deeper into the world than our present needs afford, the thoughts I was exposed to in Great Books pulled back the veil to reveal a richer, more colorful view of the world.

Much like how my musically inclined friend directs my attention to a previously unnoticed bass riff in a John Mayer song, which deepens my appreciation of the song, these authors pointed out parts of reality and humanity that warranted closer study. As I saw the world the way they did, some parts of their perspectives that felt useful or truthful remained and others fell away. It wasn't a conscious choice, but again, just a matter of not being able to un-see what you have once seen. I was left with a personal world view that is (and in a continual process of becoming) dynamic rather than static. Learning to not hold any perspective or vantage point too dearly by having to continuously change them out for a different one cultivated a flexibility that's marked by a value for ideas based on their ability to accurately portray reality rather than how comfortable or familiar they feel. I became less dogmatic as I was forced to simultaneously hold conflicting perspectives and acknowledge the virtue in each.

Relationships: I didn't just have to cognitively hold what these authors were saying but had to place them in relation to the bigger conversation—to synthesize. The "synthesizing mind" that philosopher and psychologist Howard Gardner identifies as a virtue of a liberal arts education is the mind that can tell how well an idea fits (or doesn't fit) with others. A synthesizer can compare ideas and then integrate them into a bigger working system, weaving them together to form a more truthful understanding of the world that affords more authentic action and living. This cognitive capacity doesn't develop merely by learning new information; synthesizing happens when information is put into relationship with what we already know. This was the demand of Great Books—to connect ideas to other ideas, yourself, and the world.

The class ritual of being handed a story, or even better—told a story by Dr. Gose himself—and asked, "what are the issues?", forced a collision between the world as I saw it and the authors we were reading. News, school policies, interactions our professor had in the supermarket, and even our personal histories were all fair game when it furthered learning how to synthesize, to connect the thoughts philosophers wrote several hundred years ago with the ideas that marked our present reality. In writing this, I remembered how often Dr. Gose would put someone and their personal life in the hot seat. He would ask the kinds of questions that you would ask in a one-on-one conversation, not in front of the class. What I'm pretty sure he was doing was 1) making us feel known by him and the class community, and 2) engaging our personhood in an attempt to trigger personal relationships with the material. This was his way of moving us away from impartially engaging with ideas like we would in any other class, but instead to move us towards building personal relationships with them. This process, though similar to recognizing patterns, is different in the sense that relationships include the comparing *and* contrasting of information, connecting information by virtue of harmony *and* dissonance. It can be described as putting ideas into conversation with each other to help a student better understand each.

The exact moment when I felt the tingle, when I felt 'enlightened' and like my understanding of reality was expanding— when college felt 'worth it'—was when I couldn't initially see the point of a problem that was brought up, but then gradually had the mental mist part to reveal a deep connection to the reading. These "ah ha" moments sprung from the cognitive formation of relationships between information. Realizing that Locke connected to prison reform and to economic policy or that Kierkegaard connected to something said weeks ago to Dostoevsky didn't just endorse these ideas as relevant, but introduced me to the bigger conversation. Over the course of our professor bringing up something that happened at a baseball game, an obscure Polish movie, or the final credits of the black and white film "Pork Chop Hill," I learned to relate the Great Books authors to each other and current ideas, in cooperation and disagreement, to analyze the very dilemmas, problems, and life questions that mark the present moment.

I would argue that we can't really be said to know, let alone understand something, unless we reach this point of placing newly acquired information into relation with the old. Psychology affirms this need for new information to be anchored to something, to fit into some schema, for the knowledge to be retained and used to inform future action. When Dr. Gose would ask, "What would ___ say about this?", we were being guided (prodded) to establish relationships between information by being asked to actually *do* something with what we were learning. Peer pressure forced me to do the mental work, but it was mostly just good teaching.

I became a teacher due to my experience in Great Books. I wanted to be in a position to create what I experienced in this program for others. While this still holds true, I've now realized was more a desire to be like my professor. My experience was a direct product of how he taught. He weirdly made me take Great Books from another professor for a semester, which did allow me to see the consistencies across the program in terms of pedagogy and content, but also helped me realize that I wanted to teach like *him*. What I couldn't initially see was that his ability as a teacher was magnified and given the breadth to work in the context of Great Books. He was able to ask the questions, build the relationships, push for growth, and make the moves that mark the best teachers because Great Books required it. The process commands good teaching. It's a double-edged sword though. The environment that creates the potential for the good teacher to teach well can be oppressive for the teacher that doesn't have the skill or desire to handle the immense freedom and variability of the model. If a teacher isn't committed to reading students, teaching without curriculum, or asking the right questions, Great Books would be a hard slog.

This class made a convincing case for a liberal arts education in the way it taught me to think. It can easily be argued that all learning (and every moment of our existence) involves thinking to some degree, but this learning was different than memorizing information or learning scientific truth. This learning concerned pragmatic judgment. In the judgment, I defined myself by doing work *on* the information. If ownership of learning requires a student to make judgments about what they believe is true, liberal arts (Great Books specifically) uniquely presents students with charged material to make judgments about. The liberal arts concern humans, the way they think and the way they make sense of the world. To make a judgment about a philosophy is more definitive for an individual's internal structure and worldview than say, a judgment about whether a specific molecule is or is not present in DNA. One judgment holds greater implications for their personhood (and soul) than the other. While one may find truth when studying DNA, there isn't as great a need to make a judgment that impacts who you are.

Perhaps most profoundly, this whole experience forced me to own my learning. Early on in the program when I knew there was something profound happening but didn't know enough to articulate what it was, I asked Dr. Gose to tell me 'the meaning' of Great Books. Asking this question revealed my belief that it was the teacher's job to determine meaning, give answers, and pass judgment on learning. Though I wasn't aware of it, I was trying to get him to do the work of determining the value of my learning without realizing that any answer to this question is only meaningful and relevant if it's been the product of my own mental work. My educational career up until Great Books was marked by a need for others to do that work for me—to decide whether my learning was 'good', to tell me what I should care about, to set the standard for good work, and to endorse whether learning was actually taking place. I was overly dependent on my teachers and others to evaluate my learning. In Great Books, I was forced to decide for myself what good learning looked like and then exercise my own agency to move towards it. The process, without hyperbole, was a pedagogy of freedom. I was taught to think.

Great Books is all things education should be. It epitomizes the soul of the university as a place to raise up people that can fully engage with reality by virtue of their ability to see it and themselves. And does this kind of education ever stop? Does it terminate with the end of the class? It hasn't ended yet for me, which is why it's a paradigm.

"...to be a genius is to be misunderstood."
-Emerson, *Self-Reliance*

LXXI
ALEX HAKSO

My undergraduate choice was driven by a line in the university's affirmation statement: "truth, having nothing to fear from investigation, should be pursued relentlessly in every discipline." Great Books ensures hundreds of hours engaging with thousands of years of this pursuit.

The process is not what I thought it would be. Less linear progress, more paradox and tension. Fittingly, I find it simultaneously reassuring and unsettling that the questions I set out to answer have been asked and answered in prose, logical proof and narrative, with divergent conclusions hinging on small differences in intuitions. Expecting to establish a clear view of the world around me, I found a firm foundation for humility. Expecting answers, questions took on new weight. "Take your son, your only son, whom you love—Isaac—and go to the region of Moriah. Sacrifice him there as a burnt offering on a mountain I will show you." Kierkegaard's fear and trembling is well founded.

It has been a decade since I enrolled in Great Books to find answers. I would not have embraced then what I know now: some questions without clear answers are worth thousands of years of thought and art. For the joy of it, I took philosophy classes during my geophysics doctorate, and reread Sartre to my wife on vacation. Studying humanity's great conversation has enriched day to day conversations with colleagues and friends. I suspect that when Dr. Gose reached out to "former" Great Books students for a reflection on the curriculum, the letter landed in the mailboxes of many people who never seemed to successfully complete the course.

WALDEN;

OR,

LIFE IN THE WOODS.

By HENRY D. THOREAU,

AUTHOR OF "A WEEK ON THE CONCORD AND MERRIMACK RIVERS."

I do not propose to write an ode to dejection, but to brag as lustily as chanticleer in the morning, standing on his roost, if only to wake my neighbors up. — Page 92.

BOSTON:

TICKNOR AND FIELDS.

M DCCC LIV.

"There can be no very black melancholy to him who lives in the midst of nature and has his senses still."
-Thoreau, *Walden*

LXXII
TRAVIS PADGETT

"Kant['s categorical moral imperative] will solve 99% of your ethical dilemmas" – Dr. Michael Gose

The Great Books Colloquium was the single most important part of my formal education. Although my undergraduate degree was in Economics, my master's degree is in Finance and Accounting, and my day job is in the Banking industry, the knowledge and tools that were developed during those four semesters continues to enrich and benefit me on a daily basis.

Like many of my classmates, I signed up for Great Books because I wanted to better understand the minds that helped shape western society, and hopefully better understand my own place in the world. Great Books didn't create in me a consciousness of the moral and ethical ramifications of my daily life, but instead gave awareness, focus, and voice to that innate part of myself which we all share. Through (what felt like) countless hours of reading, reflection, and discussion, the tools to engage in a thoughtful existence became absorbed. While I can't tell you every idea that was examined, or every work within the colloquium, I can say without a doubt it was time incredibly well spent.

On the purely practical side, there isn't a modern career where a student will not benefit from being able to communicate effectively, analyze and deconstruct complex concepts, and rationally (sometimes dispassionately) defend a position. Some of the lessons learned were driven by the professor(s) and not the material; when writing, don't say in eleven words what can be said in five. It is important to be able to separate the ideas from the person proposing them, even when they are colored by individual experiences or a moment in history. However, the practical skills (and catalog of ideas) developed through Great Books are that much the richer, having been informed by the deep pool of material used within the program. If nothing else, a young mind will be forced to learn patience at an age where the virtue does not come naturally, a process I found particularly difficult at times.

At the present, in late 2018, there is a sense of terrible division in the United States that permeates both our political/societal dialogue as well as day to day life. Many days, I find myself reflecting on ideas I learned in GB: that man was happiest when living closest to nature, and that the construction of a 'society' has only made things worse (Rousseau); that, first and foremost, we are called to tend to our own gardens (Voltaire); and that we should trust in our own selves above all (Emerson). I also find myself frequently reflecting on Kieslowski's Dekalog which helps me remember just how much is happening within the people around me. I wholeheartedly believe that instruction in the foundational concepts of our society is one of the best tools we have to facilitate civil discourse in generations to come, and one of the best investments we can make in our own future.

Finally, my wife and I became first time parents at the end of 2017, which naturally leads a person to some self-examination. It's a humbling moment, realizing that you'll serve as both the conscious and unconscious example of morality and acceptable behavior for a life. I'm still not sure I'll be worthy of the task, but know I am undoubtedly better prepared for having participated in Great Books than I would be otherwise. I can only hope the program grows in the coming decades, and that my own children get the same opportunity for personal and practical development that I was given.

"Unjust laws exist: shall we be content to obey them, or shall we endeavor to amend them, and obey them until we have succeeded, or shall we transgress them at once?"
-Thoreau

LXXIII
MEGAN REEL

It is tremendously difficult for me to put into words what the Great Books Colloquium meant to me—so much so that I put off writing this for months. One thing Great Books did not solve for me was my overthinking. In fact, the courses encouraged me to think harder and longer about the story I wanted to tell with my words as well as in my life. Dr. Gose was the first professor I met at Pepperdine in 2007, and I immediately knew his courses would transform how I looked at learning, my relationships, and the world.

Both through my relationships in the Great Books courses and studying the great ideas, I was transformed over the years from a naïve eighteen-year-old from Small Town, Tennessee who hardly knew myself to someone who had a strong sense of values and regularly evaluated why I felt the way I did.

My faith in God was challenged and eventually confirmed throughout many readings including the writings of Kierkegaard and Descartes. I had been raised to hold honesty as one of my strongest values, and the words of Kant confirmed why. Plato (and Dr. Gose) transformed the way I viewed the word Good and will forever make me evaluate how I use it. Because of Great Books, the words "be good" are extremely meaningful for me....as is the word "meaningful". My classmates and Dr. Gose regularly challenged me to think harder and encouraged me to think about my words before I said them.

It is safe to say my standards are higher, my faith is deeper, and (with risk of sounding vain) I am smarter due to studying the Great Books. In my current work as a therapist, I help others to understand and deepen their values, and I think I was led to my career because of how much Great Books influenced me in my undergraduate education. I am so thankful I took the risk and enrolled in the course as that naïve 18-year-old... If I knew now how much it would challenge me, mold me, and force me to grow out of my comfort zone, I probably would have avoided it.

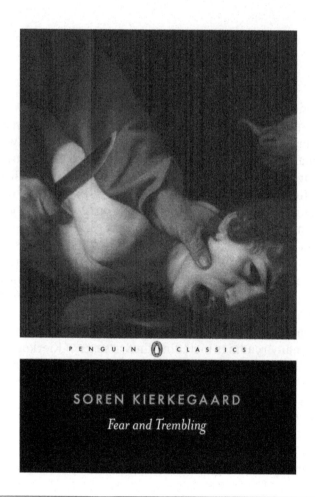

PENGUIN CLASSICS

SOREN KIERKEGAARD

Fear and Trembling

"For faith is just this paradox, that the single individual is higher than the universal, though in such a way that, having been in the universal, the single individual now sets himself apart as the particular above the universal."
-Kierkegaard, *Fear and Trembling*

LXXIV
MARY STUZMAN HINDS

Rethinking Great Books

I dreaded it, I loved it, but Great Books always gave me a headache. No joke, I stopped wearing headbands in college because of the class. For me, a shy student who just wanted to sit and learn without talking or thinking too hard, it was *the* class of college, precisely because I had to do both.

While I don't remember many books or chapters anymore, some moments I do remember include a professor using the word "dismal" to describe a paper and the rewrite that followed, freezing up during a discussion and bursting into tears afterward, and reading all 200-something pages of Paradise Lost in a (very long) day to be ready for class. Sounds not-so-great, but the challenge was good for me; I also remember feeling proud of later papers and grateful for the friendships formed with classmates who learned alongside me and taught me much.

Since then, my life has turned away from academia but many Great Books skills have stuck with me. The class taught me how to discuss important things (to acknowledge even if you disagree), to underline things, to recognize and remember what's most important and write from memory. Most of all though, Great Books taught me to listen to others and rethink for myself.

The ten Great Ideas are engrained in my mind (although I can usually only remember nine at a time) and certain passages emerge often. I've used them in China, trying to teach students to look for more in movies than just English. I've used them in bible classes, after-school programs and relationships, including my marriage. Now as a

251

journalist, these themes influence every interview and article, and change the way I look at the world.

For example, I used one last week, here in rural Kentucky after overhearing a conversation about travel. One person said they would never want go to Turkey or the holy lands, because it's "so just dangerous over there." A second person agreed saying "with all the bombings and shootings, I have no desire to leave the state—it's just a sad world."

This conversation disturbed me for a number of reasons and my thoughts immediately went to Dickens, a line from *Hard Times:* "make the best of us, not the worst." At first, I was frustrated with the speakers assuming the worst of somewhere they had never been and not even wanting to give those places a chance. On rethinking, I realized that I also shouldn't make the worst of these people who spoke thoughtlessly, and turned the challenge on myself.

In college, Great Books looked like students sitting around talking about literature and philosophy in the abstract, but the applications from these stories have stayed with me through the years and become part of my own. This class, more than many, continues to teach and my life is greater for it.

"Communism abolishes eternal truths, it abolishes all religion, and all morality."
-Marx

LXXV
JANE TRAVIS

"There is only one good, namely knowledge, and one only evil namely ignorance."

This quote, with no listed author, is on a big stone close to the ceiling of the majestic Library of Congress, which unbelievably is my local library only one block from my house in Washington, DC. This quote points me back to Great Books and reminds me of the pursuit of "the good" and how I spent much of four semesters trying to define it. Did I ever do it? I don't think so. Does that matter? I don't think so.

Thoughts while taking great books:

-This could either be the best or worst thing I've ever written. I can't even tell anymore.
-To say I wouldn't have liked this book without the Great Books perspective is putting it mildly
-Which philosopher really is Gose's favorite? He must have one. My money is on Kirkegaard. (My favorite too).
-That boy has great thoughts. Wow. I hope he asks me out. (He eventually did, post class).

Thoughts after taking Great Books

-All I want to do is discuss this event from a Great Books perspective and no one gets it.
-So much extraneous noise. I don't want to listen for the loudest voice anymore.

-To quote John Maxwell "you cannot overestimate the unimportance of practically everything."
-Define your terms America! I don't want to be whipped into the mindset of the collective unless I can see what are we talking about when we talk about terms like rights.

Nothing has changed my thinking like Great Books and I can't even define how, I just know it did. I'm not sure if I can pick a word to describe the sense I got while in class. I felt inspired and the opposite of lonely. It felt meaningful. It wasn't quite class and it wasn't quite community but it was definitely bonding. We weren't really sure yet what we were pursuing but it felt meaningful and exciting. We were in it together. This is the essence of college right here, that there isn't quite a word for. *"What Dekalog are you on? Who is the hero!!? Get out of the cave!!"* We had our own dialogue, rhetoric. We were pursuing the good! For what point? I don't think we knew, besides it was electric and receiving a fist bump when you nailed the "defining passage" might have been a better feeling than acing my physics exams.

I have so many conflicting emotions looking back on that experience. I am still impressed that those discussions brought out my best thinking-self. Depressed that my mind has receded in the medical jargon and writing and thinking I use daily now. I'm appreciative of the knowledge I now have of the difference in quality of thought between my peers who have never "gotten there" or even between my college and current self. I'm amused retrospectively at the luxury it was to have the time and space to dwell on such thoughts. I'm concerned I might not continue to "get there" on my own without the support or challenge of that community. We made each other better, it's just inevitable. I'm unsure if my current community is making me better, which is to say asking good questions.

Fear and Trembling by Kirekegaard uprooted my idea of...well everything. Do I even remember the aha! moment that changed my thinking? Not really, sadly. Something about Abraham raising the knife! Leap of faith! I wish I could still grasp it. However, I remember where I was in the room and how things clicked for me. The concept took on a personal meaning I carried with me even though I can't really define it - the intersection between faith and passion and how you can't "learn" passion you have to experience it. That's similar to how I feel about Great Books. I experienced it, and it gave me more passion.

When I sat down to write this reflection on Great Books, all I kept thinking of was questions, but I think they are better questions than I'd have otherwise without Great Books. If there is anything I have a passion for, it is for people and asking better questions helps me experience people at a deeper level. If questions lead to knowledge, and knowledge leads to good, then I think I am getting closer and closer.

"I died for beauty, but was scarce
Adjusted in the tome,
When one who died for truth, was lain
In an adjoining room."
-Emily Dickinson

2008

LXXVI
LAUREN BATTERHAM

In the guise of an unassuming collegiate course, Great books has the uncanny ability to transport you through the ages of Western civilization without skipping a beat. The course enabled me to travel to Ancient Greece, the roaring twenties in America, and to the very depths of hell up to heaven itself. Reading these classics not only improved my critical thinking but allowed me to discover pieces of my moral compass and deepen my belief system. For instance, Buber's *I and Thou* enriched my spirituality, Woolf's *A Room of One's Own* revealed the importance of feminism and being outspoken in a world of men, while Descartes rattled my brain while simultaneously driving me insane (sometimes you just "Kant" even). This is in addition being constantly thankful that I haven't yet woken up as an insect à la Kafka's *The Metamorphosis*.

Great Books also taught me how to write and structure a coherent argument by learning to apply abstract concepts to different factual scenarios, rather than simply stating a bare answer that regurgitated facts. While the learning curve was quite painful as an adolescent, I learned to appreciate and love the curriculum, which ultimately sent me down the path of the law and legal scholarship. It also taught me how to ask an educated question and to express myself in front of my superiors and my peers in a professional setting (the latter of which is an under-appreciated skill). The program also inspires students to ask more profound questions about the meaning of life and the origins of our human experience. In other words, Great Books coaxes students out of the Socratic cave to see the light and truth in their everyday lives.

Further, from an Aristotelian perspective, reaching eudaimonia is the ultimate goal of the human experience—a type of human flourishing that leads to a life of excellence. Great Books sends students on the path to eudaimonia from an early age, developing good character and exercising the rational mind. What I learned in two short years is something that I have and will continue to carry for the rest of my life, hopefully leading to excellence in my personal and professional life and relationships (or at least a good conversant at cocktail parties).

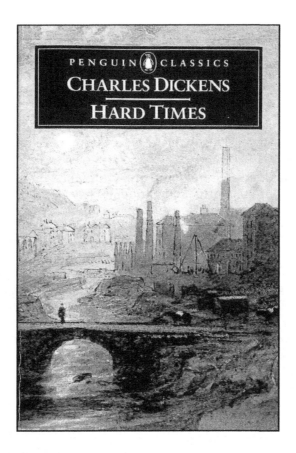

"Cultivate in them, while there is yet time, the utmost graces of fancies and affections to adorn their lives so much in need of ornament; or, in the day of your triumph, when romance is utterly driven out of their souls, and they and a bare existence stand face to face, Reality will take a wolfish turn and make an end of you."

-Dickens

LXXVII
KLAIRE KORVER

I remember you saying that you had former students who said that your class was one of the few (if any) where they actually remembered/applied the curriculum years after graduating college. This comment always stuck with me, and rings far truer now.

I wanted to thank you for having a great influence on my life and how I think about the world. I can honestly say I would have never learned to apply the "lenses" of the great thinkers of the past without your teaching. I find myself frequently referencing Rousseau, Burke, de Beauvoir, Bakunin, Freud, Sartre, and Buber as I try to make sense of the world around me. They have almost become mental commentators or imaginary friends (as weird/creepy as that sounds) as I'm watching Netflix, trying to navigate the workplace, or learning more about what I want (and don't want) in life. What blows my mind is their voices bridge time--their messages so relevant as if written today. I guess that's what makes them great.

Art by Klaire Korver circa 2010

"Some persons hold that there is a wisdom of the Head, and that there is a wisdom of the Heart…I have a misgiving that some change may have been slowly working about me in this house, by mere love and gratitude, that what the Head had left undone and could not do, the Heart may have been doing silently. Can it be so?"
-Mr. Gradgrind, Dickens' *Hard Times*

2009

LXXVIII
ALEXIS ALLISON

Dear Dr. Gose,

I learned as much from Great Books as I do from life experience, and that's the highest praise I can give a class.

In the course of my four semesters in the Colloquium — the latter three with you — I learned to take notes on my notes. I learned to identify key passages, analyze Roland, and that Immanuel Kant was a real pissant. I learned about the enchiridion and the pnyx. I learned a slew of insults I won't repeat here. But mostly I learned to think, and to be human.

For one, you required we fully complete a text before commenting. I remember being slightly annoyed back then (we have to read *The Divine Comedy* in a week??). But the practice stuck with me. I've come to see ingesting an idea whole, before sticking our critical noses in it, as a discipline — one that's humble and open and curious. It made a better person, a better teacher. I learned to withhold judgment on an administrative decision, student's excuse, curriculum change or piece of lunchroom gossip until I knew the whole story. (By the way, I modeled my American literature curriculum after one of the latter Great Books semesters.)

You also required the in-class essay exam (cue the Psycho theme song). Though I might've hated it, I remember boasting to friends and family about the simple audacity of the prompts: they always boiled down to "Analyze so-and-so." (I think "polyfocal conspectus" was thrown in to terrify us.) These taught me to look for and think from perspectives that aren't my own. As I write this, I'm a journalist with a local newspaper in

Columbia, Missouri. I'm not allowed to take a stance, but as I gather stories, I become emotionally involved with my sources and my subject. My Great Books training keeps me level — allowing me to be both deeply personal and critically "objective." I can become immersed in the perspective of an official, expert, or citizen, and know that perspective deeply, and then step out of it and into the next. I'm not always good at it. I wasn't back then, either — took me forever to get an A — but I try, and that has made all the difference.

Finally, you spoke tenderly and often about the Great Books courses as an entrance into the "great conversation" — 3,000 years of Western thought that led us here. Thinking about and studying all those writers, all those ideas, is like the moment when you first, on some black night, recognize the Milky Way. You realize you're one among galaxies. I know that I'm not alone, that the people who came before me and around me carry their own great ideas like stars within them. That they're inherently, incredibly valuable.

So. When you gave us this assignment — to write about Great Books — I struggled. This is my fourth draft. It's difficult to write about something that's become so central to my daily rhythm, almost like breathing. It's even more difficult to separate the subject from the professor. I finally opted for this letter, because yes, Great Books is magic, but you're the maker.

You once told us you wanted to be your students' favorite and best teacher. You were. You are.

Thank you for all of it.

Most sincerely,

Alexis Allison

"The life of the ever-present Spirit is a cycle of morals "utility" or the "greatest happiness principle" holds that actions are right in proportion as they tend to promote happiness; wrong as they tend to produce the reverse of happiness... The utilitarian standard: is not the agent's own greatest happiness, but the greatest amount of happiness altogether."
-John Stuart Mill

2010

LXXIX
LUKE CLARDY

Hope & Doubt

When I think back on my time at Pepperdine University, and life since, I'm often reminded of a line from Todd Snider's "Statistician's Blues" (a great country drinking song that playfully addresses the overwhelming complexities of life). Snider arouses some cheers of agreement with the following line:

"They say 74% of everything you learn in college
is a bunch of bullshit you'll never need."

In my personal experience, I have found this humorous line to be increasingly true – Great Books with Dr. Gose is the other 26%.

Life can be hard. Sometimes it can very hard. And it certainly doesn't get easier once you graduate and advance into the "real world," adopting greater responsibility for yourself and others. Existence is unpredictably chaotic on its own, full of the inevitable struggle and conflict that accompanies a scarce and competitive material world.

Death, decay, and the unknown lurk around the corner for each of us. Regardless of how cushioned life may have been until now, we are all destined for suffering at some point. Those who have lost someone close understand this universal pain that we all must eventually experience. At the time of writing this, I am thinking of my own grandmother who passed away earlier this year. Everyone can relate to this pain, and will have to do so on several occasions in their lifetime. In addition to the physical ailments and very limited duration each of us have here, one will find that the world is a swirling fiasco of emotions and forces seeking to swallow you up and use you without hesitation. Simply put, the world is no place for the faint of heart.

It is a dreadful reality that can drive the unenlightened mind to paralysis. Is it any surprise that we are witnessing an epidemic in mental illness, depression, and in the most tragic of instances – suicide – in the Western world? Revisiting Todd Snider's previously mentioned song (one that makes me grin every time I listen to it, yet like any true comedy gets to the core struggle of the human experience), he describes this feeling of desperation in the chorus:

"(It's) Too much to think about
Too much to figure out
Stuck between hope and doubt
It's too much to think about."

He's not wrong that we have an overbearing, daunting amount to figure out, and that we often find ourselves fluctuating between optimism and pessimism depending on our circumstances. None of us can, with certainty, say where we came from, why we are here, or where we are going. Each one of us is trying to workout for ourselves each of these mysteries, while simultaneously shouldering the suffering described above. To exacerbate the problem, there is a deafening commotion of daily sights and sounds that seek to distract us from solving these great conundrums.

An internal clock ticks desperately inside each of us, an echoing reminder of our limited stay in this world. Vibrant adverts and a never-ending stream of social media feeds call to our impulsive nature demanding our immediate attention. Bosses with selfish agendas demand 110% commitment and sacrifice for the majority of our waking hours. Bright neon lights and deafening rhythms lure us, like Sirens, to immerse ourselves in blinding, deafening and temporal pleasure. The temptation to submit to these forces is powerful, and sometimes we do so with the best of intentions. We want to be successful, so we throw ourselves wholly into our work. But at what cost? This might sound a bit morbid, and evoke emotions of distress and fear.

Good. As Camus wrote in The Plague, "And it was then that fear, and with fear serious reflection, began." I have found myself, in a well-paying and "good" job utterly unsatisfied with the direction and purpose of my life. Jung wrote in great detail about the power of the subconscious, and the effects of suffering: "But when suffering comes... That is when people begin to seek a way out and to reflect about the meaning of life and its bewildering and painful experiences."

I didn't fully understand what he meant until about a year ago when I found myself dissatisfied with the lack of purpose in my occupation. I started to become plagued by restlessness, strange dreams and other internal proddings telling me that I was not on a path towards spiritual satisfaction in life. It was during this time that I fell back on the bedrock of my Christian upbringing and my Great Books education. In a sales environment, I was surrounded by people who would beat their chests, flaunt their material successes and dedicate their identities fully to their work striving to be number one – something that became increasingly hollow to me, as I realized many of my co-workers could not separate their identities from their work. I found a lack of communion in this environment, and despite making good money for my age, kept returning to Jung: "But the meaning of life is not exhaustively explained by one's business life, nor is the deep desire of the human heart answered by a bank account."

After graduating I was one of the people Dr. Gose warned about that quit reading books and learning new things. Although I could feel that something was wrong, I was unable to identify what – looking back now, it is clear to me, in existentialist terms, that I was not happy with the man I was making myself out to be. As Jung wrote, ""WE have obviously been so busy with the question of what we think that we entirely forget to ask what the unconscious psyche thinks about us..." My psyche did not have a high regard for the choices I was making, and the lack of vision that I was demonstrating.

I'm happy to say that this restlessness inspired some serious reflection. Around this time, I watched a documentary about Tony Robbins. One scene stood out to me in which Robbins spoke about being a poor, skinny and timid child. He said, through sheer will power he was able to transform who he was by visualizing the character that he wanted to become, and then making the necessary life changes. He explained, "Tony Robbins didn't exist. I constructed Tony Robbins. I created this [motherforker] standing here." My mind shot back to Sartre: "Man is nothing else but what he makes of himself... That man first of all is the being who hurls himself toward a future and who is conscious of imagining himself as being in the future." That idea that we can create and accomplish anything that we are capable of imagining took hold. I also retrieved the memory of what Descartes had said: "Conquer yourself rather than the world."

In this spirit, I've come to think of the world in terms of inputs and outputs. I've become obsessed with the food I consume, working out regularly, and reading/learning new things every day. More than for health reasons, I've become transfixed with "conquering myself" by having complete control over the inputs I allow into my life (this is not to say I have achieved complete control, but I certainly have greater vision of what I am striving for with each day I look in the mirror).

My good friend, Mason Malpass, introduced me to the audio-lecture "The Strangest Secret" written and narrated by Earl Nightingale in 1957. In it, Mr. Nightingale cautions: "Every one of us is the sum total of our own thoughts. We are where we are because that's exactly where we really want or feel we deserve to be — whether we'll admit that or not. Each of us must live off the fruit of our thoughts in the future, because what you think today and tomorrow — next month and next year — will mold your life and determine your future. You're guided by your mind."

Reverting back one last time to the words of Todd Snider, I believe we are poised with two paths, and two choices. One is the path of "doubt", and the other is the path of "hope." You can choose either the "double shot of something 90 proof" as Todd Snider self-prescribes: a mind-numbing, empty kind of aimlessness which will ultimately lead to uncertainty, anxiety and doubt. Or – like the video my friend Mason and I made for our senior Great Books project – you can get "intoxicated on the Great Ideas." The latter will help you live acutely aware of your existence, and find meaning in a very complex world. As the psychologist Jordan Peterson describes it, this path is "the antidote to chaos." It allows us to visualize and become stronger, more responsible versions of ourselves, so that when the hard times come we are able to maintain the course of hope, and be a source of comfort for others. As Voltaire would say, "but let us cultivate our Garden... it is the only way to render life bearable."

I am eternally grateful for the education I received from Dr. Gose, and the wisdom that has been passed on for centuries through the Great Books curriculum. Although we can never eradicate the uncertainty lurking in this world, through Faith and the Great Ideas that have been bestowed upon us – like a torch throughout the generations from noble men such as Dr. Gose – we can pursue a life of purpose, enlightenment and hope.

"The mass of humans live disheartened lives of earthly sorrow and joy, these are the sitters-out who will not join in the dance. The knights of infinity are dancers too, and they have elevation." – Kierkegaard, Fear and Trembling

Will you join the dance?

"If all mankind minus one were of one opinion, and only one person were of the contrary opinion, mankind would be no more justified in silencing that one person than he, if he had the power, would be justified in silencing mankind."
-John Stuart Mill

LXXX
MARK TRAVIS

George Pepperdine and Justice

As I reflected upon my four semesters with Dr. Gose, I considered which personal anecdote would be worthy to share as my unique contribution to the illustrious Great Books tradition. Fortunately, I didn't have to think long to recall the time when Aristotle helped save me from expulsion.

I was a wide-eyed freshman from Iowa with no prior disciplinary history, and most people would have described me as a pretty straight edged kid. Generally speaking I was a pretty high achiever, so it was pretty jarring to be facing expulsion barely 2 months into college. Without going into all the particulars, essentially, I helped orchestrate arguably the greatest prank/theft/felony (depending on your perspective) in Pepperdine history – stealing the George Pepperdine statue. I later found out that the statue was worth $108,000 and I was soon to be in a lot of hot water.

I'd be happy to recount the full details of the heist if there is interest, but for now I'll keep my reflection centered around the Great Books portion of the story. I vividly remember sitting in Dr. Gose's class the day after the theft, the campus abuzz with theories and rumors of what had happened. We had just finished reading Artistotle's Nicomachean Ethics and the missing statue provided a great opportunity for Dr. Gose and the class to explore various perspectives on Justice. If caught, how should the school punish the culprits? Would it be different if the statue was found? What if it was LMU students? Would the sentence change if the guilty party were generally upstanding and positive contributors to the Pepperdine community? It was immensely entertaining for me to sit quietly (rare for me) and listen to how the class decided my hypothetical fate.

My peers and I were later caught by DPS in the process of returning the statue, and it was only a matter of time before I was brought before the judicial committee. A few weeks later, I was writing a midterm essay for Dr. Gose when I used the principles of corrective vs. distributive justice to defend a point I was making. As I was already caught, I couldn't resist tipping my hand to Dr. Gose and applying my personal situation to help make my point on Justice. The following week, Dr. Gose asked to see me after class. I was a bit apprehensive, but all I saw on Dr. Gose's face in the hallway was a look of bemusement, mixed with concern. He offered to help go to bat for me if needed, which at the time was a huge relief. I let him know that I was getting along as well as could be expected given the uncertainty of my punishment. As I remember I got an "A" on that midterm.

I wrote a preemptive appeal letter to the judicial committee using some concepts I had learned in Great Books, quoting Aristotle and attempting to make my case that justice should not be blind in all circumstances and that context matters. I'm not sure exactly what made the difference – but I ended up avoiding expulsion. I was fined $500 and placed on disciplinary probation, which at the time meant I wasn't eligible to go abroad. While I was definitely happy not to be expelled, the prospect of not being able to go abroad was devastating. By the grace of God my probation ended March 21st and there was still one final slot open in the Buenos Aires program. I went on to have one of the best years of my life there.

The whole incident was kept pretty well under wraps and most of my professors and peers were unaware of my involvement. For the next four semesters of Great Books, Dr. Gose would occasionally drop subtle references in class to the statue theft that only I could pick up on. I later found out that Dr. Gose and I both share an affinity toward The Praise of Folly which probably explains our continued amusement with this story.

As a senior, I was elected to be the President of Interfraternity Council and ended up serving on the same judicial committee that decided my fate freshman year. That bit of irony was amusing to me, especially as I worked alongside a person who attempted to get me expelled three years prior – to my knowledge she never made the connection that I was the same person involved in the statue theft as a freshman. I think my own story gave me a lot of valuable perspective in that role, notably that I should not be too eager to deal out judgement. Justice is a complicated affair, and I'm thankful for the role Great Books played in helping me navigate its complexities during a tumultuous period of my life.

Although I'm sure this will likely illicit in an eyeroll – sincere and special thanks to Dr. Gose for being the Gandalf figure in my (and many others') journey through the Great Books tradition. Your impact in upholding what you believe to be the greatest of the great ideas cannot be overstated.

"The creed which accepts as the foundation of morals "utility" or the "greatest happiness principle" holds that actions are right in proportion as they tend to promote happiness; wrong as they tend to produce the reverse of happiness."
-John Stuart Mill

LXXXI
SCOTT WOODS

It was Friday night, and I was at a party for the first time in a while. Usually, I'm the type to read a book at home or rant about politics or religion with close friends. But tonight, a friend asked me to join him, and I decided to tag along.

Within twenty minutes, I was already regretting my decision. I had forgotten how boring these things could be. My new acquaintances were talking about celebrity gossip, March Madness, and all sorts of things outside my interest. When the subject turned to TV shows, I was ready to scout for the nearest exit. But then I heard it. "Yeah, I just finished the new season of Bojack. It's great!"

Bojack Horseman is a darkly-comedic animated Netflix series about a washed-up Hollywood actor trying to get his life together. It probes the depths of moral improvement, self-worth and loathing, addiction, love, and weakness of will. Also, several of its characters, while speaking and acting like human characters, are animals. The writers and animators exploit this as an incredible source of puns and witticisms. As absurdly as it presents itself, I happen to think that *Bojack* is one of the best shows on television.

"Yeah, I love that show, too!" Heads turned to look at me after I uttered my first words of the evening. I was excited to share my thoughts with a fellow fan. "Did you notice how Aristotelian it is?"

"What...? Uh, no." My blood was pumping. I knew he would appreciate an explanation.

"The writer made it so obvious! At the end of Season One, Diane tells Bojack that a person's moral character is just 'all the things you do' – you know, instead of something 'deep-down' or mystical. And of course, that's practically plagiarized from Aristotle's *Ethics* - virtue is not an act, but a *habit*, and a good person is whoever habitually does the right thing. And he just dropped another quote at the end of the new season – I'm *sure* you noticed – with the metaphor of exercising for moral improvement, when the runner tells him, 'It gets easier. But you gotta do it every day.' It ties *everything* in the series together – the necessity of moral education for youth, the difficulty of breaking vicious habits, the painful persistence of *akrasia*. It's all just Aristotle!"

With a satisfied smile, I ended my raving monologue and looked back to my audience, ready to hear their thoughts about this connection I had found. Instead, I was met with blank stares. One guy had already excused himself to use the restroom. Another was barely suppressing a yawn. "Yeah... cool, dude."

I sighed. I had forgotten why Great Books students don't get invited to parties.

"The life of the ever-present Spirit is a cycle of stages...Two elements, therefore, enter into the object of our investigation; the first the Idea, the second the complex of human passions; the one the warp, the other the woof of the vast tapestry of world history."
-Hegel

2012

LXXXII
MAKENZIE TAYLOR

Living hand to mouth would probably be an easier approach to life. Don't think that taking up the dialectical pursuit of a polyfocal conspectus will smooth the path. More likely you will be viewed as the arrogant jerk who doesn't say "sorry" when you arrive late to a meeting and who constantly denies the confines of the question. This path will make it more difficult to date, to deal with inept coworkers and bad bosses, and to have interesting conversations in which you can rigorously debate an issue without hurting feelings and fissuring relationships.

But it's worth it. One of my more (most?) regrettable college decisions was taking Dr. Gose's advice and enrolling in a Great Books course taught by a professor other than himself. A course that shied away from addressing the big ideas and instead asked about literary themes, social milieus, figurative language…the stuff that's supposed to be restricted to English language classes. I wish I had been bold in declining Dr. Gose's suggestion. Bold like he teaches us to be in engaging the Great works head-on. It is an audacious undertaking and at the same time, with so much of the groundwork already laid for us in our 3,000+ years of history, it is accessible. It is like a decadent, incredible secret that we are in on, to interface with these greatest of thinkers and their works.

To be sure, engaging in this rigorous and liberating enterprise brings extra excitement and joy to life. For me, it was a way to engage my intellect at a higher level, to *play* in place of the usual and more conventional academic work.

I mentioned above that it might also increase the difficulty of some aspects of life.

One way this has proved true for me is romantically. Dating has become nearly intolerable in my enlightened state (there's that arrogance again!). I do not appreciate men calling me 'adorable,' or presuming that I do not know what I want simply because I am thoughtful with my speech and am reticent to blurt out the first thought that comes into my head. I do not do well with men who assume that I desire to have kids and fill my time with innocuous 'feminine' hobbies, or who assert they know my values and the choices I will make as a Christian woman. I am equally intolerant of men's presumptions that I *don't* want to be a homemaker based on the fact that I am a strong woman with a career. And I do not appreciate men who assume they know my past or present reality or future hopes because of the small amount of information I have chosen to share.

Yes, I actually do want kids, no I do not want to be a stay-at-home mother, and yes I enjoy the occasional baking of cookies, but I also enjoy a variety of activities. I am a dynamic, often complicated owner of what Simone de Beauvoir refers to as the androgynous human mind. Having come to acknowledge and appreciate this, I will not date a man who does not recognize my common human mind – a mind that has the capacity and functionality equal to that of men. I am not impressed with a 'feminist' man who still functions under the mindset of 'separate but equal.' I will decide what I am capable of, and to what extent I will be involved in 'feminine' or 'masculine' interests and activities. Maybe I do want what they think I want, but that is not the point. The point is acknowledging my ability to choose which path I'll go and that I am capable of either. I am holding out for a man who respects my right to actively participate in my free will.

Another peeve which I may not have picked up on prior to my Great Books education: men who text me, "hey your amazing" (yes, the grammar is this poor amongst the large majority of our peers, sadly) and "your so gorgeous." I do not say, "thank you" and fish for more compliments. I say, "How can you possibly know that? I *am* gorgeous *and* my mind is amazing. But you don't know me from Adam so you do not possess the knowledge to tell me this about myself as if you are doing me a favor. And, for the record, it's 'you're.' Go read a book, I recommend Descartes' *Discourse on Method*."

In business and social environments, you likely will not give the responses in conversation that are expected of you. After studying Great Books, you will be less likely to politely nod in agreement when others share their contentious views, and instead you might prod deeper, asking, "why?" What is the interest beneath the surface, the purpose of what is being said, the innate belief that is informing someone? You will not automatically give the 'right' or morally permissible and expected answer to questions; no, you will likely find more value in the broadening of perspectives and exploring the 'why' behind the answer given to the question.

You will place a high premium on kindness but you will not necessarily value niceness. You will not be afraid to question the validity of others' assertions or claims. You may develop an "indispensible willingness to fight for [your] views and convictions," attributed by John Stuart Mill to an understanding that, "the peculiar evil of silencing the expression of an opinion is that it is robbing the human race [...]; those who dissent from the opinion, still more than those who hold it. If the opinion is right, they are deprived of the opportunity of exchanging error for truth: if wrong, they lose, what is almost as great a benefit, the clearer perception and livelier impression of truth, produced by its collision with error." As a truly great professor and mentor has often reminded me, your responsibility is to do your own interpretive work (of the text, specifically), and to not accept 'truth' from someone just because they are presumably an expert. He tells us that "the bias of great books is that you insist upon your own interpretation until you find reason to change that interpretation."

Based on my experience I can say that in the course of your Great Books undertaking you will be less terrified to make mistakes, maybe worry less about your GPA, and perhaps become acquainted with Erasmus' presentation of Christian humanism as a perspective to inform your personal faith. You may notice with some amount of consternation, as I did, that you are much more the author of your own life's 'journey' than you realized, because in seeking 'objective' advice and guidance for big decisions you will usually go to people who will support the answers you want to hear. We often outplay our own minds and perpetuate our own preferences anyway.

You will wrestle more, question more, expect more of other people. You will not settle for unclear, sloppy thoughts. You will not be satisfied to mindlessly float through life, and so you may occasionally be frustrated when you realize more and more how much you *don't* know. But in this worthwhile pursuit you will also have much more fun and drink more deeply out of life.

Since going through the Great Books program my intellectual curiosity has been magnified, my relationships have become richer, and my everyday tasks have taken on a brighter quality, because the lens through which I see life has changed and is still changing.

ON

THE ORIGIN OF SPECIES

BY MEANS OF NATURAL SELECTION,

OR THE

PRESERVATION OF FAVOURED RACES IN THE STRUGGLE
FOR LIFE.

By CHARLES DARWIN, M.A.,

FELLOW OF THE ROYAL, GEOLOGICAL, LINNÆAN, ETC., SOCIETIES;
AUTHOR OF 'JOURNAL OF RESEARCHES DURING H. M. S. BEAGLE'S VOYAGE
ROUND THE WORLD.'

LONDON:
JOHN MURRAY, ALBEMARLE STREET.
1859.

The right of Translation is reserved.

"And as natural selection works solely by and for the good of each
being, all corporeal and mental endowments will tend to progress
towards perfection."
-Darwin

2013

LXXXIII
DYLAN SHAPIRO

Great Authors Do Great Books

A modest classroom with seats arranged in a circle. Inside sits SOCRATES, dressed in a white tunic. When the clock (hanging on the wall) strikes 10, the door swings open and discussants begin to walk in. They take their seats:

FRIEDRICH NIETZSCHE sits directly across from Socrates, as if ready to oppose him.

PLATO sits furthest from the door and angles himself so he can see the whole classroom.

VIRGINIA WOOLF and G.W.F. HEGEL flank Plato on each side.

ARISTOTLE sits nearest to the door, in opposition to Plato.

FRANCIS BACON takes a seat directly left of Aristotle. Then he gets up and sits down directly right of Aristotle. Then he returns to the left.

ARISTOTLE: Francis, what are you doing?

FRANCIS BACON: Picking my seat.

ARISTOTLE: And you had to sit in both… why?

FRANCIS BACON: To see which one had a better view.

ARISTOTLE: Ah. I would have said take the middle seat, but I'm already in it.

Aristotle chuckles to himself.

FYODOR DOSTOYEVSKY walks in with a scowl, but his eyes glint and scan the room consciously. He then takes a seat next to Virginia Woolf.

JEAN-PAUL SARTRE walks in. He stands in the center of the circle idly, and then chooses to sit next to Friedrich Nietzsche.

EDMUND BURKE routinely walks down to Nietzsche's seat, and then does a double take as he realizes Nietzsche is in it.

EDMUND BURKE: Friedrich?

FRIEDRICH NIETZSCHE: Yes, Edmund?

EDMUND BURKE: You're in my seat.

FRIEDRICH NIETZSCHE: Meaning what?

EDMUND BURKE: I've used this room before. I always sit there.

FRIEDRICH NIETZSCHE: Ah.

Nietzsche does not budge. Burke stands there awkwardly, shrugs to himself, and then sits down sheepishly on the other side of Nietzsche.

Socrates looks up at the clock, which reads 10:05.

SOCRATES: Whom are we missing?

EDMUND BURKE: Rousseau.

SOCRATES: What a shame. How will Rousseau be freed of ignorance?

EDMUND BURKE: Maybe we should punish him.

SOCRATES: There is no need to. He punishes himself.

EDMUND BURKE: Socrates, he disrespects the whole symposium. He should be punished for that alone. He is late.

SOCRATES: And why do you think it is that he is late?

EDMUND BURKE: I don't know.

FRIEDRICH NIETZSCHE: Probably because he can. Because he can he will.

SOCRATES: We all *can* be late. Yet you all came here on time.

FRIEDRICH NIETZSCHE: I'm here of my own free will. He's not because of his.

SOCRATES: Are you not here because you seek knowledge? Does your will not drive you here because you wish to learn?

FRIEDRICH NIETZSCHE: No. It drives me here so I can think among great men. Speaking of which, there are some in this group who are not great men. There are some in this group who are lambs.

EDMUND BURKE: What?

FRIEDRICH NIETZSCHE: Edmund Burke is by no means a great man. He deadens the quality of discourse.

EDMUND BURKE: Your snide comments deaden the quality of this institution.

SOCRATES: But Edmund: is he not providing us with a chance to hone our knowledge?

EDMUND BURKE: I don't see how.

SOCRATES: He is reminding us to define our terms. Let's do so. What is a great man?

FYODOR DOSTOYEVSKY: A great man must experience *adversity*.

FRIEDRICH NIETZSCHE: Yes. That is what makes him conscious. And once conscious, he must channel his will to power: soar above his challenges and enter a realm in which he is victorious.

SOCRATES: And why must a great man be of this definition?

FRIEDRICH NIETZSCHE: Because he has triumphed --

FYODOR DOSTOYEVSKY: -- Because he has suffered.

FRIEDRICH NIETZSCHE: You are right: because he has triumphed over suffering.

FYODOR DOSTOYEVSKY: That is not what I meant.

FRIEDRICH NIETZSCHE: I supposed not. You too are somewhat of a lamb. I recall in one of your books, you wrote, "Without God, everything is permissible." And you wrote this in a tone of lamentation. Don't lament; God is dead and those who follow him are lambs. Everything is permissible and those who lament this have no will to power.

FYODOR DOSTOYEVSKY: So you wish to kick me out along with Edmund?

FRIEDRICH NIETZSCHE: Until you've proven you can join us by triumphing.

FYODOR DOSTOYEVSKY: I suppose if that is your wish, I will learn more from my suffering.

Dostoyevsky gets up, preparing to leave. Hegel looks at him and holds up a halting finger.

SOCRATES: But Friedrich: is that just?

FRIEDRICH NIETZSCHE: Yes. It is just to ensure that great men can be free of lambs.

SOCRATES: So you would agree with Thrasymachus. Justice is in the interest of the stronger.

FRIEDRICH NIETZSCHE: I would.

SOCRATES: Don't leave, Fyodor. Nor you, Edmund. Let us hear some other views.

Dostoyevsky sits back down.

G.W.F. HEGEL: Friedrich. I'm appalled at your exclusionism. Do you not realize that your plan defeats its purpose? Mankind will become great only through a dialectic of ideas that drives him toward his destiny. All ideas must be discussed.

Virginia Woolf grimaces slightly, yet also nods in agreement.

SOCRATES: That's what I try to guide along with my questions.

FRIEDRICH NIETZSCHE: We don't need all ideas. We need good ones.

G.W.F. HEGEL: They don't have to be good. If you see a bad idea, then construct your own ideas and marshal them into battle. And as they battle, they will grow and merge through the dialectic.

FRIEDRICH NIETZSCHE: No, the bad idea will break. Recede into the nothingness from whence it came. There is no reason to waste breath on a putrid idea.

G.W.F. HEGEL: Other than to coax a good idea out of the mind and into the world. Take you, for example. Perhaps had you not suggested to kick people out of the symposium, I would not have risen to defend their right to be here.

FRIEDRICH NIETZSCHE: And the conversation, consequently, would have been boundlessly more productive.

G.W.F. HEGEL: No, only more productive to your tastes. You are but one man: a thread on the tapestry of mankind.

VIRGINIA WOOLF: Humankind.

G.W.F. HEGEL: What is the difference?

VIRGINIA WOOLF: "Mankind" implies that there too is a "womankind," and that the two are distinct, and that "mankind" is more important than "womankind."

G.W.F. HEGEL: And what is the reality?

VIRGINIA WOOLF: That mankind and womankind are split particulars of humankind, and that humans have both male and female in them.

ARISTOTLE: Well, you're a woman. I'm a man. Are our differences not real?

VIRGINIA WOOLF: They are inconsequential. I am wearing cargo shorts and a T-shirt. The important thing is I have a mind and a room of my own.

FRIEDRICH NIETZSCHE: Perhaps Virginia is a lamb as well. She seems fond of the non sequitur.

VIRGINIA WOOLF: This is by no means a non sequitur. The word "humankind" is more descriptive and accurate than the word "mankind."

ARISTOTLE: Again, I beg to differ.

VIRGINIA WOOLF: Plato. Why have you not spoken? I bet you agree with me.

A short pause, as Plato gathers his thoughts.

PLATO: I've been trying to glimpse the Forms behind all your utterances.

Virginia Woolf sighs as Plato returns to silence.

JEAN-PAUL SARTRE: I wish I had invited my friend Simone de Beauvoir. She would, I believe, have been able to answer Aristotle's objections.

ARISTOTLE: Can you summarize her position?

JEAN-PAUL SARTRE: That remains to be seen.

ARISTOTLE: What?

JEAN-PAUL SARTRE: "I" am merely the sum of what I do. I have never attempted to summarize Simone de Beauvoir's worldview, so I cannot say whether I could.

FRANCIS BACON: But Jean-Paul, you've observed and absorbed her positions, right? How else could you have known that she could address Aristotle's concerns?

JEAN-PAUL SARTRE: I *have* observed and absorbed her positions. I have *not* attempted to articulate them. That is the difference.

FRANCIS BACON: Seems like an odd thing to split hairs over.

JEAN-PAUL SARTRE: Well, let's settle this now then. Simone de Beauvoir believes there are differences in equality: that true equality between the sexes is not homogeneity, but differentiated equality based upon the particular needs of the gender.

VIRGINIA WOOLF: How is that different from sexism, then?

JEAN-PAUL SARTRE: Well, put it this way, Virginia: must men have the right to maternity leave? I'd expect De Beauvoir to say no. Although existence precedes essence so who am I to say?

VIRGINIA WOOLF: That maybe works on a practical level, but on an absolute level, it reinforces gender stereotypes and thus obscures the truth about people. That's not just.

SOCRATES: It would help, all, to define justice.

FRIEDRICH NIETZSCHE: I thought we did earlier. Justice is in the interest of the stronger.

SOCRATES: I've made my position on that clear in *The Republic*.

FRIEDRICH NIETZSCHE: Yes, that dystopian collectivistic drivel.

SOCRATES: It helps to analyze, not judge, Friedrich. Let us hear other views on justice.

FYODOR DOSTOYEVSKY: It doesn't concern me, justice; I only know that I suffer.

The door swings open. In walks JEAN-JACQUES ROUSSEAU.

EDMUND BURKE: Justice is in the interest of the institution.

JEAN-JACQUES ROUSSEAU: What? That is laughable.

EDMUND BURKE: You finally showed up.

SOCRATES: Welcome.

FRANCIS BACON: Have a seat.

Rousseau sits down next to Socrates.

EDMUND BURKE: Why were you late?

JEAN-JACQUES ROUSSEAU: Because I wanted to stay human.

EDMUND BURKE: Stay human? What does that even mean?

JEAN-JACQUES ROUSSEAU: Well, Edmund, humankind is naturally good but we have been corrupted by structures, systems, and rules imposed by the institution. I wish to remain human and not turn into a mindless drone.

EDMUND BURKE: And yet you came.

FRIEDRICH NIETZSCHE: This is the great joke of Rousseau's character. He wants to be free yet cannot will himself to be free forever, cause he is a lamb.

JEAN-JACQUES ROUSSEAU: That's not true.

FRIEDRICH NIETZSCHE: You know it to be.

JEAN-JACQUES ROUSSEAU: It's the rules and systems I oppose, not the meeting itself. How else could I convince you all to be freer of spirit?

EDMUND BURKE: You don't need to. Institutions are sacred; they prevent radical change and uphold traditions, which in turn preserve our values.

JEAN-JACQUES ROUSSEAU: Have you not seen what the evil institutions have done?

EDMUND BURKE: That's the fault of man, not the institutions.

ARISTOTLE: Let's get back on track. We were originally discussing justice.

SOCRATES: Let us continue then. What is justice?

ARISTOTLE: A complicated question. There are both distributive and corrective forms of justice. Like with all things, true justice consists of the balance between the two.

FRIEDRICH NIETZSCHE: Your propensity for moderation is infuriating.

ARISTOTLE: Moderate your anger, then.

VIRGINIA WOOLF: I disagree with all viewpoints so far. Justice is valuing people for their absolute potential and then asserting their equal rights.

FRIEDRICH NIETZSCHE: It is not just to force the strong to stoop down to help the weak.

VIRGINIA WOOLF: Who are you to say men are the strong and women are the weak?

FRIEDRICH NIETZSCHE: I didn't. I only am opposed to stooping down to pet the lambs.

VIRGINIA WOOLF: The context of my view of justice, Friedrich, is that for far too long men have held the power and withheld justice from equally capable women.

FRIEDRICH NIETZSCHE: Then why, if you are so strong, do you women not assert your wills to power?

VIRGINIA WOOLF: So you *are* saying women are weaker than men.

FRIEDRICH NIETZSCHE: No. I'm helping you. Forget your gender. Fight!

Woolf lets out an exasperated sigh, as does Socrates for a different reason.

SOCRATES: There does not need to be so much conflict. We're striving to discover truth.

FRANCIS BACON: Clearly, there *does* need to be conflict. Haven't you observed how this symposium has gone?

SOCRATES: I have. But conflict slows down the process of dialogue.

EDMUND BURKE: I agree with Socrates. By meeting, we have formed an institution. We must be respectful of it.

JEAN-JACQUES ROUSSEAU: How wrong you are.

EDMUND BURKE: Since we can't be respectful, we should cancel future symposiums.

G.W.F. HEGEL: Why? Conflict is natural. It guides us toward the end of time.

EDMUND BURKE: Why does that matter?

JEAN-PAUL SARTRE: There is no "natural."

FRIEDRICH NIETZSCHE: Conflict may not be natural. But it is necessary.

EDMUND BURKE: Too much conflict and we all suffer.

FYODOR DOSTOYEVSKY: Then perhaps the symposiums are indeed worth our time.

FRANCIS BACON: What irony. We can't even agree on *this*.

ARISTOTLE: The problem is you all are too extreme. Have some moderation.

G.W.F. HEGEL: I disagree. We need to flesh out our unfiltered ideas.

SOCRATES: Let's do so on the topic of cancellation. We know Edmund thinks we should cancel future symposiums. What are other views?

Words fly from the discussants' mouths, forming an unintelligible cacophony of opinions. After a few moments, Socrates's voice breaks through:

SOCRATES: Quiet! I cannot hear!

The room goes silent. For the first time, Plato leans forward as if to project his voice and speak. He clears his throat. Surprised, all eyes turn to him.

SOCRATES: Plato. Speak.

PLATO: We have been approaching this symposium entirely wrong. We have been judging our views—often by way of temper or gut. We have to stop that. We have to *reason*.

SOCRATES: I agree with that.

PLATO: But that is no reason to cancel future symposiums. It's a reason to keep them.

SOCRATES: Go on.

PLATO: You once told me that the unexamined life is not worth living. And to cancel the symposiums would be to leave our lives unexamined.

SOCRATES: Maybe so.

PLATO: To stay chained to the cave. And see nothing but shadows.

SOCRATES: To remain ignorant?

PLATO: Yes. For none of us know the Truth in full. We are imitations.

SOCRATES: Yes.

PLATO: But we can reason. We can analyze our utterances calmly and broaden our view of the world. And if we all act according to reason rather than temper or appetite, we can come closer to leaving our chains and glimpsing the Forms that lie beyond the cave.

Hegel, Woolf, and Socrates nod in agreement.

FRIEDRICH NIETZSCHE: I disagree.

Plato frowns as he turns to Nietzsche. Woolf sighs and Hegel groans.

FRIEDRICH NIETZSCHE: I would like a chance to explain.

The aim of this society is the triumph of the principle of revolution in the world, and consequently the radical overthrow of all presently existing religious, political, economic and social organizations and institutions and the reconstitution first of European and subsequently of world society on the basis of liberty, reason, justice and work...equality does not mean the leveling down of individual differences, nor intellectual, moral and physical uniformity among individuals. This diversity of ability and strength, and these differences of race, nation, sex, age and character, far from being a social evil, constitute the treasurehouse of mankind. Nor do economic and social equality mean the leveling down of individual fortunes, in so far as these are products of the ability, productive energy and thrift of an individual."
-Bakunin

LXXXIV
HANNAH ZIEGLER

Great Books: A Continuing Experience

Let me be forthright: I did not come into Great Books with "great" expectations. It was certainly not a choice of reason, because it was not a choice at all. Being a Regents' Scholar at Pepperdine implied a compromise of choice--the choice to be or not be in Great Books. Like Medea, I was distressed by the lack of choice reflected in my obligation to four semesters of Great Books. To me, it entailed rigorous coursework, a seemingly intimidating professor, the lack of a traditional class structure, and overpowering centuries of greatness that I was not sure I would be able to grasp. Looking back, however, I regret not having fully immersed myself in the compelling exchanges among peers and our leader in these great inquiries.

Great Books offers a formal curriculum of exploring classical texts and groundbreaking philosophies, but there's more to it. It entails a "hidden curriculum," which explains how a mere semester's worth of Great Books will teach you that no simple solution exists for a problem as complex as human life. Once you've completed the entire colloquium, you will encounter a sense of pride knowing perfectly well that you've intellectually collected and absorbed thousands of years of history and human experience. These books, along with the discoveries and understanding gained through informed discourse will henceforth act as a constant guide in appreciating humanity's existence.

I am more than grateful for the colloquium cultivating knowledge across all disciplines, whether it be philosophy, literature, religion, politics, humanities, or science. Before the term "interdisciplinary" became common currency in academia, Great Books used a variety of enduring works to help guide the intellectual development of Pepperdine students. The intellect and creativity upheld by arguably the greatest thinkers of all time, certainly shape human thinking beyond time and place. Unlike any other course, it is not the *answer*, but rather, the *question*, that will set you apart from your classmates. Undeniably, Great Books will get you thinking, but over-thinking won't get you ahead--it's the right *kind* of thinking that determines your success in the colloquium.

Needless to say, the challenges presented by this course nurture one's reasoning and judgment skills. You will even find that Great Books functions as an algorithm for solving nearly any decisive problem in life. Thus I challenge myself and my cohorts to continue to engage in the dialectic and live life from a Great Books perspective. Even if I can't quite recall famous quotes from Plato or Aristotle anymore, the ideologies and values, the ways in which I understand the complexities of life and education in America, will be long impacted by Great Books, to say the least. Consequently, Great Books has left me wanting to "cultivate my garden" and aspire to "be good"--concepts that I will continue to contemplate and appreciate throughout life.

"Every man has reminiscences which he would not tell to everyone, but only to his friends. He has other matters in his mind which he would not reveal even to his friends, but only to himself, and that in secret. But there are other things which a man is afraid to tell even to himself, and every decent man has a number of such things stored away in his mind...and so hurrah for underground!... anyway the underground life is more advantageous."
-Dostoevsky

2014

LXXXV
SCOT BOMMARITO

What is good? What is evil? Does it have its own material, or is it rather the absence of good? What is justice? Do merely the strong decide? What is truth? Is it approached through reasoned exercise of the dialectic or through strict empiricism? Does Alcibiades really want to have sex with Socrates? And, most importantly, why does Alcibiades want to share in such an intimate physical act with the gadfly on Athens' rump? These are the questions that the Great Books Colloquium seeks to answer. Peeling back the fabric of our daily reality and gazing up into the blinding light of intellectual enlightenment, armed with the sword of reason, the shield of epistemology, and the helmet of the polyfocal conspectus, we abet an exodus from the cave of shadows.

Perhaps that is a slightly verbose presentation of the Great Books Colloquium, but if after four semesters of reading and discussing the greatest works ever written Great Books students are unable to make themselves sound pompous and pedantic, is the Colloquium really working? The people really must be amused. The truth of the matter (if you will allow me to use such a charged word) is that the Great Books Colloquium does address all of those questions listed. We read, we discuss, we argue, we read some more. We strive to understand the authors on their own terms. How can one properly utilize Kant's categorical imperative to manipulate a roommate into telling the truth about whether or not he ate your leftovers if one does not yet understand Kant? By all accounts (or at least by those that succeed), the cruel means of long readings, precisely defined terms, and careful logic justify this noble end.

In addition to the meaningful academic growth Great Books provided for me, the Colloquium also armed me with powerful practical tools. The tool that I have personally found most useful is the ability to argue any case from any angle, throwing in some daunting names like "Plato," "Descartes," and "Kierkegaard" to support my case. These names themselves are nearly instant argument winners, and their ideas, when properly applied, are even more powerful. Let us follow in the footsteps of our dear friend Aristotle and examine a few tangible examples.

Imagine that I make a joke at someone else's expense. Now for the sake of this exercise, it is imperative that this joke be simply hilarious. Truly tear-inducing. Now let us imagine that the party at whose expense I told this riotous joke, inspiring laughter in all those present, protests. I can quite easily justify myself:

"Listen here, old chap. John Stuart Mill wrote some lovely stuff about this situation in his book *Utilitarianism*. Set aside your perceived inconvenience for a moment, and look at how happy everyone else is now that I have made this joke. They would not have been nearly this joyful without the joke. I have achieved the greatest good for the greatest number, and is that not a truly noble cause, one worth celebrating?"

Consider another social example. Imagine you are spending your weekend with three friends, and you all want to play a board game. However, you must collectively decide which game to play. All three of your friends want to play Sorry. But you hate Sorry. It is childish and foolish, a game for simpletons. You have taken Great Books. You want to revel in the luster of your superior intellect through a stimulating game of Scrabble. But your three friends all hate Scrabble. How do you decide what to play? You have read Nietzsche, so you have the perfect answer. You pick up the Sorry board, rip it to shreds, and light all the cards on fire. You are, after all, beyond good and evil. With a genuine smile on our face you set up the Scrabble board and say to your astonished friends, "behold my will to power! Let's play Scrabble!"

Great Books-inspired conversations like these are great for building lasting friendships. And note the subtle beauty in this particular situation. Had you been of the majority opinion, opposing a strong minority, you could have easily cited John Locke or Jean-Jacques Rousseau to enlighten the staunch minority of the implications of his/her having agreed to enter into a social contract with the rest of the group. If you have your three-thousand years of history to back yourself up, there is no argument you cannot undertake!

These are obviously trivial and intentionally exaggerated examples. They nevertheless exemplify what is, in all seriousness, the greatest tool that Great Books has given me: independent, critical thinking. The skills of reason and dialogue that the Great Books Colloquium fosters allow us all to elevate our conversations and debates to a higher level. Through methodical analysis and detailed inquiry, we practice the invaluable art of sorting out the competing assumptions and values in any given scenario. Through such an exercise we invariably find differences in our underlying worldview, but we at least achieve a better understanding of those differences. Great Books gave me the place to take on this challenge of examining the world around me from different perspectives. I saw new angles and heard new arguments as we sought to disentangle some of the most lasting questions of history. We disagreed frequently. But not even the greatest thinkers and writers to have ever walked this earth could agree on the answers to these questions. Why should we?

"All truly noble morality grows out of triumphant self-affirmation. "

-Nietzsche

LXXXVI
GEORGIANA GIBSON

Reluctant to Glad

Choosing to participate in Great Books Colloquium was the best decision I made in my college career. Ten-thousand years of history now linger in my mind, and connections between the past and present constantly present themselves. My critical thinking and writing abilities flourished, and I support my analysis of texts with textual evidence. Perhaps I have also grown a little prideful, but whether that is "good" or "bad" depends on how you define the words. Either way, I have no regrets after completing the Great Books Sequence. As I said, it was the best decision I made in college.

Of course, it didn't seem that way at first. It all began when I had to select which Freshman Seminar to take. As a student who felt burned out from a rough senior year, I wanted to choose the Film Seminar because watching movies sounded fun and easy. My mother disagreed with my choice. She went on a spiel asking me if I wanted to excel and grow academically or choose the "easy" route. Her lecture quickly expanded to include my whole future, as if this was a decision that would determine whether or not I chose the "easy" way throughout life or challenged myself to be the best that I could be. It ended with something like: "Who do you want your future self to be?" So, begrudgingly, I told her "I don't want to be the person who always takes the easy way out." Thus, I enrolled myself in Great Books.

Promptly moving on with life, I didn't think about my decision again until New Student Orientation week. During that first week, we were all gathered and introduced to our Great Books professor. I expected a gentle introduction to what Great Books was, maybe even some advice about what to expect from college and how to adjust. Boy was I surprised! We sat down and our professor passed around an excerpt from Aristotle. After reading, the discussion began. Someone started: "I feel..." They were immediately shot down by the professor: "I don't care what you feel, what does the text say?" Someone else braved the waters and began explaining their thoughts. They too, were quickly interrupted as the professor asked from where in the text they based their analysis. Thus, the session continued for an hour and all I could think was: "Oh boy, what did I get myself into?" By the end, nobody wanted to risk speaking. Later that afternoon, I met up with my mom and she extolled the praises of my Great Books professor. As she spoke of how intelligent and nice he was (the parents had a separate session), I couldn't help but wonder if we had met the same person.

It turns out we had. Of course, since then, I've been firmly indoctrinated into the Socratic method. Now I too grow frustrated when people begin: "I feel the text is about..." and never back up their analysis with any textual evidence. I utilize my polyfocal conspectus and say things like "polyfocal conspectus". I debate by bringing in writers like Aristotle, Kant, and Rousseau. When I sit in a Humanities class I mentally correct the professor when they mistakenly interpret philosophers like Locke, because I have read those works and I know what they say. Maybe I have grown slightly proud, but I am not sorry. If I define "bad" as taking pride in the expansion of my knowledge then I am bad and will strive to be the bad-est I can be, because I am always learning and will always take pride in learning more. Yes, Great Books was difficult but I have no regrets because all of the work was worth it.

"The world viewed from inside, the world defined and determined according to its 'intelligible character' — it would be 'will to power' and nothing else."
-Nietzsche

LXXXVII
GATHENJI NJOROGE

Reflections on a Good Series of Classes

When I started my Great Books journey, I didn't know what I was getting into. The class was mandatory for me, one of the requirements of a scholarship that I had been awarded. If I am being completely honest, I was certain that Great Books would be a waste of time. Why did I need more reading on top of an already-busy course load?
I was wrong.

The first unofficial Great Books session of that year was held during Pepperdine's New Student Orientation week in a small classroom with far too few chairs. Some students (perhaps those who had arrived early) were seated in chairs and others (perhaps those who felt guilty or arrived later) sat on the floor. I happened to arrive after all the chairs had been taken, so I sat on the floor.

Without warning, the professor, a tall man wearing a full suit, loudly (and somewhat antagonistically) asked us how we decided who would sit in the chairs and who would take less-dignified positions on the floor. Were the seats taken by the stronger students? Were they primarily reserved for the female students out of a traditional (and possibly sexist) sense of justice? Did the students in chairs feel superior to those on the ground? Did the students on the ground feel inferior to those in chairs?

A few nervous laughs skittered through the air. Some brave students offered explanations of why they chose the seats they did. The professor easily rebutted the students' arguments, pointing out contradictions in the reasoning provided. He offered equally rational actions that we could have taken to eliminate the appearance of injustice or inequity. "Why didn't we move the chairs out of the way to make more room and all sit on the ground?" the professor asked.

After this introduction, my curiosity was piqued. I was beginning to look forward to being in Great Books.

I have completed all four classes in the main Great Books series, opting each time for the section taught by the tall, somewhat-antagonistic professor. The goal of these courses is to provide students with an opportunity to survey and join the "great conversation" that authors spanning from those of the ancient Greek era to those of contemporary times have engaged in. This conversation is an interplay of some of the ideas and worldviews that have had a lasting impact on the world. Ideas mold and are molded by cultural shifts as new voices lend themselves to the great conversation and new patterns of thought propagate.

Since that first experience in the under-equipped classroom, I have wrestled with themes of honor, justice, love, hatred, good, evil, free will, destiny, anguish, joy, guilt, empiricism, naturalism, power, and obedience. I have seen through the eyes of long-departed intellectuals and marveled at the fact that despite the passage of millennia, the issues of old are still analyzed and reanalyzed today.

I have spent countless hours reading, and rereading, writing and rewriting in preparation for the Great Books courses. Friends of mine who did not take Great Books courses have asked me why I bothered to take such rigorous classes with such high expectations set by the professor. The answer is fairly simple: I want to explore what people think, how they came to think it, and how these thoughts affect various choices and experiences in the real world.

The Great Books classes taught by my professor were classes in which ideas were not just something found within the pages of dusty books, and analyzed in a vacuum. Rather, ideas are the driving force for individual decision-making and organizational or political policy. The ideas we develop from our families, culture, and experiences affect our lives and our worldviews. Prototypical versions of these ideas are often detailed in literature and examination of this literature can often provide a more nuanced understanding of some of the fundamental assumptions that we make under our worldviews.

Great Books is not an ideological factory, in which students are forced to conform to a certain set of values or ideas. Rather, it is a large, multinational symposium in which students are equipped with the tools to better understand the historical source of various viewpoints as well as examine the assumptions made under these worldviews in their various Forms.

The next 100 years will bring many more stories and perspectives as well as new applications of established ideas. The great conversation will continue to change and grow as new voices join in. Older conceptions may lose favor and be replaced by newer conceptions. It is likely that the next generation of students will have very different ideas about sitting in chairs versus sitting on the floor. The journey will continue. And so it Gose.

"It gives me a sense of liberation to know that an act of deliberate courage is still possible in this world--an act of spontaneous beauty."
-Hedda in Ibsen's Hedda Gabler

LXXXVIII
MARCEL RODRIGUEZ

When I first began the Great Books program, I assumed that everything I learned up to that point would be forged into one method of application to apply to everything academic.

This is not what Great Books is. The program, if I am to borrow my earlier reference to metalworking, scraps everything you have done incorrectly and makes you start rethinking your perception of knowledge. Much like ore, the books do not impart anything beyond material for you to use. The books, stripped of their historical contexts, are not simply handing you instructions or even the tools to understand what lies within. It falls to you to take the raw material and work it into something useful. You must continually hammer away at the ideas within. Each author gives you a different tool, from understanding the worth of the individual, to merits of duty to your country, to a return to the individual and the value of free will. The end result is not a tool, or even anything you can recite or memorize. Beyond anything else, Great Books teaches how to think critically and analyze what you have been given. These skills are indispensable in today's world. As ideas continually get reduced down further and further, to the fifteen minutes of YouTube videos to fifteen second Instagram stories to 140 characters in a Tweet, it falls to us to discern the message that people are trying to send. 'Fake News' is seeding a cloud of misinformation and doubt over even the most basic facts. Great Books is the antidote: a universally applicable method of discovering truth and wrestling with the ideas our society has grappled with since the ancient days of heroes.

When I first started Great Books, I was told that there would be a method that each student had to follow. We were to buy the books, write in them, wrestle with an idea, and prove that we understood how to think critically. While I was happy to buy the books and even more thrilled to be grappling with God, Freedom, the Individual vs Society, and more, I was adamantly opposed to writing in a book. I believed a book was the physical incarnation of the author. Books were a way to not only codify thought, but to immortalize yourself and your achievements for time eternal. It did not matter to me that others claimed it was easier to see their notes. I entrenched myself in my belief and took on additional burdens to make sure that I would keep up with the rest of the class. I began to read every book with the most intense focus. I pulled out quotes that I thought were important and wrote them all in a separate notebook, complete with page number. I memorized the length down the page that each quote was. I went to class, determined to never write in a book. My patience paid off, and my memorization began to demonstrate its utility. I had complete mastery over the text, often able to recall the quote without opening the book at all. My notebook was a codex full of items that only I was able to interpret; thoughts that I had consigned to the page.

When I finished the Great Books program, I had a codex of ideas, a head full of quotes, and a stack of books. I wish I could say it was only after the ordeal that I realized what I had learned, but sometime in the middle, I had found that my very perception of ideas had changed. I no longer read any literature, watched any movies, or saw any plays without apply a devastating barrage of analysis and criticism to which nothing could withstand. Great Books changes the way you interface with the world, but it creates a lens that pulls away the curtain and shows you the truth.

"...it made me ask whether there are two sexes in the mind
corresponding to the two sexes in the body, and whether they
also require to be united in order to get complete satisfaction
and happiness..."
-Woolf

LXXXIX
CASSIE STEPHENSON

If you are an over-thinker, Great Books will not "fix" that. In fact, it will only make it worse. You'll find yourself holding back in conversations only to finally interject pithy comments about reason and choice ("Have you ever read *Paradise Lost*?") and learning to bask in however pretentious that may sound. But you will realize that you wouldn't trade it for anything — being outside of "the cave" makes everything more meaningful. Sure, you won't be able to just skim the surface anymore, but it beats living "hand to mouth."

Great Books gives you a way to make sense of the world, a way to ask better questions. How could you not when you are backed by 3000 years of history? Texts that once seemed intimidating are now old friends. My collection of books from all four semesters offers a physical reminder of the perspectives I carry with me all the time.

I'm a journalist by trade, and I think about *I and Thou* almost every day. I've found myself giving the distilled version of Buber's idea of mutual giving to high school and middle school students when I teach them about journalism and how to interact with sources. Milton's view of "Truth" in Areopagitica — "let her and Falsehood grapple; who ever knew Truth put to the worse, in a free and open encounter?" — has become foundational for my understanding of the role of free speech.

I often recall the power structures in the *Iliad*, the topic of my very first essay exam in Great Books. The seemingly ridiculous "rules" of the funeral games in which only kings can win have helped me understand why seemingly nonsensical power structures (in institutions, the workplace, etc.) sometimes prevail.

Countless songs are ruined for me; I can't listen to lyrics that seem to profess love without considering for at least a moment how their definitions of love are addressed in Plato's *Symposium*. Anything that is purportedly feminist warrants an examination via Woolf or de Beauvoir.

But despite this, Great Books and the weighty ideas it deals in aren't stuffy. They are meant to challenge and be challenged, to be part of something lively and sometimes just plain funny. There are many things I didn't expect to pick up from my Great Books experience. I think I accidentally learned a little bit of Polish while analyzing episodes of Kieslowski's *Decalogue*. I learned more about baseball than I expected to, thanks to one avid fan and professor with a unique talent for using baseball references to somehow make centuries-old ideas suddenly more clear.

For most of my life, I've been a chronic overthinker prone to needless apology. I now find myself biting my tongue a lot more when I'm tempted to say I'm sorry, remembering Kant. But I've learned not to hold back all the time. After all, the goal of Great Books is to continue the Great Conversation, inside and outside of the classroom. When something is important enough to say, you should say it. And don't dare raise your hand.

"I am satisfied with the mystery of the eternity of life and with the awareness and a glimpse of the marvelous structure of the existing world, together with the devoted striving to comprehend a portion, be it ever so tiny, of the Reason that manifests itself in nature...(man) wants to experience the universe as a single significant whole."
-Einstein

XC
ANNA WALKER

In Great Books, one learns that the most imperative rule is to trust the text. Students are invited together to "sharpen their intellectual teeth by gnawing on the classics."
In a conventional literature class, one might approach the discussion of a novel by first understanding the context in which it was written; the time period, political and socioeconomic climate, and life of the author.
Instead of taking this valuable context and deriving meaning from this additional information, the Great Books curriculum urges students to discard all else and simply focus on the writings presented.
In keeping with this theme of discovering the Great Ideas from words rather than the context which they are given, I urge you, the reader, to do the same in order to further understand what takes place in a Great Books classroom.
Below are quotes from a real professor which may shed light on the major themes instilled in the Great Books program:

(On truth) "Honesty has no place in sports."
(On the meaning of life) "As long as I'm well-fed, who cares?"
(On justice) "And I didn't like that, so I went back and torched the place."
(On authority) "Okay, shut up, we only have five minutes."
(On freedom) "He was content... but not content like a cow."
(On the individual in society) "Who the frick cares about what society is telling you to do or not to do!"
(On human nature) "We all deserve to be shot, don't we?"
(On religion) "I don't care if he IS the son of God."

(On good vs. evil) "Kindness is a good thing, but niceness sucks."
(On heroes) "So I thought, 'If this asshole can get all these credentials, then I can too.' And I did."
(On love) "I'm not even sure I have emotions."
(On resilience) "I know I seem older than dirt, but I'm still alive."
(On justifying one's own vices) "Iced animal cookies are very rational."
(On scholarly reading) "How do you read a book? You READ the BOOK. And if you like it, you talk about it."
(And finally, on moving on) "And so it Gose."

"We must not be too hasty in introducing ethical judgments of good and evil. Neither of these instincts is any less essential than the other."
-Freud (letter to Einstein)

XCI
ELIZABETH WATERS

As a first-semester freshman in Great Books One at Pepperdine University in 2014, Dr. Michael Gose gave me one of the greatest compliments I have ever received, masked as an insult.

We were discussing Medea. Dr. Gose went around the room and looked to see if everyone had the definitive passage marked. "I can do no other thing," on page twenty-seven. Medea is about freedom. I stayed relatively quiet during this discussion. I didn't have the confidence and didn't really know what was going on quite yet. I was employing one of the strategies that marked my early years as a learner; stay quiet and wait until someone says something that sounds right, and then agree with them. Wait until the truth is exposed, then write it down in a notebook, and memorize it for the test. It worked before, why couldn't work now? (Little did I know that Great Books was about something entirely different, and frankly much better, than "tests"). Near the end of the class, Room 304 in the Cultural Arts Center was silent. And then, Dr. Gose spoke, and these were the words that came out of his mouth:

"Elizabeth is my greatest disappointment."

My heart dropped. Me? A professor's GREATEST disappointment? But I am usually the teacher's pet! I smile and get my work done! All through high school, I was praised for this. But in this moment, I was a disappointment, and I was horrified. How could this be?

But then Dr. Gose explained. He said that when he checked annotations, I was the only one who starred the definitive passage. When I had entered the classroom, I was on top. However, I didn't bring up the quote in class; I didn't contribute it to the dialectic, and that made me a disappointment. The insult veiled a success, the success of having marked the definitive passage in my reading, which I consider a compliment, but ultimately, I didn't follow through.

Great Books has been a series of these successes paired with the challenge to succeed even further. The challenge to think deeper, to ask bigger questions, to push for knowledge and not sit idly by as the definitive passages wait to be unveiled, analyzed, understood. That moment, that insult/compliment, sparked my confidence to speak when I had an idea, to declare it to the class even if it turned out to be wrong, to put myself out there and work for knowledge, because that is the way to learn.

As I advanced through further semesters of Great Books, I became louder, occasionally boisterous, and likely annoying in my vehement pursuit of "the ideas at stake". I would boldly throw a passage into the air, lobbing it up for consideration, and watch it get shot down, time and time again. And soon enough, with the guide of my peers, we would land on the winner. At the beginning of my time as a Great Books student, I entered the room confused and afraid of that confusion. By the end, I entered the room often still confused, but determined. Rarely did I enter the classroom with the perfect passage starred, or the golden quote underlined. But I made sure that it was marked before I left, and I made sure that I was an active contributor in its recognition and analysis. The days of sitting idly by, waiting for someone else to do my work for me, were gone.

In Great Books, I've learned to not accept the confines of the question, to use the polyfocal conspectus, to not apologize unnecessarily, to not be tardy, and to "be good" (I use quotes because as all Great Books students know, we could spend hours talking through all the things this could mean). These lessons will endure longer than most of the academic knowledge I've acquired throughout my time at Pepperdine, because for me, this is the stuff that matters. It's the underlying assumptions of humans as they fight and struggle toward meaning and understanding in the world. It's the clarifying of terms that allows me to get to the root of an issue with a friend, colleague, or relative. It's not living hand to mouth; rather, it's using the great ideas to examine my own underlying assumptions and to understand the assumptions of others. If I know why someone thinks the way they do, and which ideas they subscribe to, then instead of hating or disdaining them, I can sit down and have a chat instead. It's analytic thinking with the goal of compassionate understanding.

Dr. Gose, thanks for teaching me things that matter through the Great Books Colloquium. Thanks for challenging me with Medea and with every Great Book since. I am honored to have been the greatest disappointment that day in class, and I am happy to know that now, years later, I am still bringing up passages (starred, or otherwise) and asking better questions.

"Man feels himself isolated in the cosmos, because he is no longer involved in nature and has lost his emotional unconscious identity with natural phenomena."

-Jung

2015

XCII
BEN HOWARD

A Eulogy

Friends, family, acquaintance: we gather here today to remember our lives before the Great Books program. Today we remember a life that was marked by pure blissful ignorance, foolish questions, and an inability to handle deep questions beyond "which came first, the chicken or the egg?".

We remember the times before Great Books, where we could hear the words, "I'm sorry", without immediately and emphatically rebuking them with, "No you aren't, you've read Kant.". All empathetic and loving relationships have ceased, as our instinctual battle cry drives out all those who are "sick and tired of these arrogant Great Books students".

We remember the times before Great Books, where we could hear the sentence, "That was a good movie", and not foam and the mouth and scream "DEFINE YOUR TERMS!". Words now carry the weight of

3000 years of history, forcing our minds to actively rebel against such trivial and uninformed speech. Good or bad no longer means, "that which helps me or which harms me" or "that which pleases me or displeases me", but rather carries many different interpretations with which to understand the world. Aristotle's declaration that happiness is the highest form of the good now clarifies many situations in which a person's hedonism influences their every decision. Milton's notion that good and evil come into the world intertwined, and that it is the war faring Christian's responsibility to discern between the two has changed the way that we may encounter different works of art and thought that deviate from our worldviews. Woe to us Great Books students! How we long for the simpler days where aesthetics and our own personal worldview influenced the way we viewed every event!

We remember the times before Great Books, where notes alone were sufficient. Now, anything less than notes on our notes is an abomination. Key ideas must be gleaned from our notes on the key ideas. Because that's where the truly *great* ideas live.

We remember the times before we had ever heard of the polyfocal conspectus and mourn the fact that life will never be as blissfully ignorant as it once was. We bear the punishing weight of millennia's worth of thought and ideas, engaging now with the Great Conversation in every situation. No longer is Romeo and Juliet just a love story–it's nothing more than a political piece. Such is the cost of such enlightenment…

I encourage you each with the truth that it will get better–time will heal these wounds and the memories of your sad life before Great Books will fade. Regardless, may you always keep these words at the forefront of your soul.

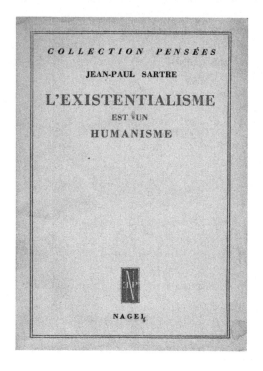

"Existence precedes essence…Man is nothing else but what he makes of himself…anguish forlornness, despair…there is no reality except in action…I build the universal in choosing myself."
-Sartre

XCIII
JULIA HOWE

I do not enjoy being the center of attention and I do not like to be wrong. Because of this, taking Great Books with Dr. Gose was an uncomfortable experience from day one.

On the first day of class Dr. Gose handed out an excerpt by Plato and told us to talk about it, leaving us with a TA who recorded our conversation on camera. He began the next class period by making me and another student move to the center of the circle, interrogating us on why we were the only ones who had said something vaguely intelligent. I remember experiencing some high levels of anxiety as this professor somehow made me feel smart and dumb at the same time. He was impressed with certain things I said and tore me apart for my other comments. I left class annoyed and feeling like an idiot even though he had singled me out for doing something right.

These mixed feelings were pretty consistent throughout my Great Books experience. After the first midterm my essay was chosen to be read in class. Dr. Gose said it was the best one, but he ripped it to shreds and gave it a grade "B-ish" (I still don't understand what that even means). I had feared facing criticism in front of other people, but it made me tougher and provoked me to argue. I learned to look for the definitive passages, define my terms, use text to support my argument, and find an academic problem. I was not going to be pushed around but I was also not afraid to be wrong anymore.

I came to love Great Books and how it changed my thought process. I wrestled with ideas, wrote papers, and participated in discussions that altered my perspective. Religious works usually touched me the most, such as Augustine's *Confessions* or Buber's *I and Thou*. But

Great Books also taught me how to approach both religious and secular works with the same pursuit of the great ideas. I could be open-minded and gain new insights even from philosophers that I completely disagreed with, such as Nietzsche or Dante. I discovered ways to apply these perspectives in analyzing all kinds of situations. It trained my mind to think critically, and I loved the ideas I encountered.

I experienced the height of my discomfort in my final semester, when Dr. Gose asked me to lead a class discussion on Dostoevsky's *Notes from the Underground* in his absence. I still did not like attention or the pressure of speaking in front of everyone. Yet the discussion showed that over the semesters my classmates and I had learned to sort through the pages to find the great ideas without our professor. As we talked about how suffering is the sole origin of consciousness, I realized we could analyze the issues on our own.

Even though I don't have a lot of life experience yet, my polyfocal conspectus is influencing my thoughts in small ways. I can't watch movies like *Schindler's List* or *Shawshank Redemption* without hearing the words of Rousseau or Buber. When I read the news and words of prominent politicians I think about Locke, Burke, or Machiavelli. As I read my Bible I consider what justice means both to the prophets and to Plato. The ideas are everywhere and have an impact on my thinking.

Great Books has meant more to me than I thought it would and will continue to influence me in the coming years. I will always be asking hard questions, sorting through the issues, and remembering the works I have read. I am no longer afraid of speaking up and being wrong in my pursuit of the great ideas.

"Now, what peculiarly signalizes the situation of woman is that she — a free and autonomous being like all human creatures — nevertheless finds herself living in a world where men compel her to assume the status of the Other."

-De Beauvoir

XCIV
SYDNEY JONES

The Prince is Selfish (and a Few Other Things I Learned)

Second semester freshman year, I came into Great Books class after reading *The Prince* and disagreed with my professor. Maybe Machiavelli had struck a chord, or maybe I had finally gained the confidence after a semester and half attempting to understand these books, but I could not be convinced the Prince was doing everything for the good of his principality rather than his own self-interest. Throughout the discussion I listened to the opposing viewpoints, compared their textual support to mine, and in the end decided to disagree rather than accept the professor's idea.

Growing up as a female evangelical Christian, I was pressured to avoid strong opinions and shush any conflict. My personality did not naturally fall into this mindset, but that did not stop me from attempting to shove it into the little box of conformity. Great Books helped me unravel the constant need to acquiesce, and provided a toolset to deal with complicated ideas and discussion when needed.

Through the four courses, I learned how to understand authors on their own terms, how to use evidence to support my arguments, what in the world "categorical imperative" meant, and how to be wrong. The curriculum and discussion format gave me the confidence to learn how to wrestle with and defend my own ideas, but also taught me the humility to recognize when another classmate's understanding of a work was better supported than mine.

My favorite days were those with loud voices, stretching across the room with a quote or an idea to understand what the author wanted to communicate. Who is the hero of the Illiad? How are Eve, Medea, and Candide related? What convinced Hedda Gabbler to commit suicide? Why is all this important? Although the class was not the time and place to discuss how the books made us feel, we gained the ability to critically analyze and understand, without twisting something to say what we want. After beginning to learn this skill, I can then go back on my own time, form opinions on the authors, and use those authors to support or contradict the Great Ideas I face in everyday life.

Great Books has been one of the most influential courses in my college career. I hope you will find it as challenging and rewarding as I, and maybe learn that the Prince is most definitely selfish.

"There are more things to admire in men than to despise."
-Camus

XCV
LAVIN LAHIJI

The more I try to think back to the time in which I had believed my Great Books experience had come to an end, the more I simply cannot. I am still thinking about my life and lives around me through the lens of a Great Books student. In fact, I never stopped. The reason why I enrolled in Great Books was because I had promised my mother that I would read the classics as she had when she was younger. She had urged me and said that it is our duty to ourselves to read the classics. I showed up to the first day of class with my books stacked in my hands thinking that this was just another book club. Little did I know, Great Books would become one of the most transformative experiences of my life.

It wasn't transformative because it made me a better reader or a better writer, it was transformative because it allowed me to understand the minds of others. There was pride in getting to admit that you understood Aristotle, Kant, Milton, and many more brilliant minds, but pride in knowing these writers weren't the most important part of this experience.

There is something distinctly unique in knowing that because you place yourself in the sphere of these great writers, you have gained a tool to understand the world around you. The pride is in knowing that you have the power to understand an idea that is beyond the scope of your immediate thought, and everything that is different from what you believe in.

My professor constantly reminded us that one can only write a paper when there is something to say. Great Books is about taking an issue at hand and being about to look at it through multiple lenses, through a fresh set of eyes. It is about having a point to make, and something to prove. I thought to myself, what do I have to prove? The answer to this wasn't simple and the further I moved along with Great Books, the more inspired I was to become someone who has something to say.

I do not remember a time that my reading wasn't important to me. In fact, the more knowledge I acquired, the closer I felt to having something to say. Reading a great book made me want to tell a great story, and the more knowledge that accumulated in my brain, the richer my own stories became. I realized that these aren't just ancient books written by old men. As Cicero said, "For books are more than books, they are the life, the very heart and core of ages past, the reason why men worked and died, the essence and quintessence of their lives." These writings convey messages we continue to pass on today in our own lives and through our own abilities to tell a story.

As my four years of undergraduate journey is coming to a close, I continue to reflect deeply about what this duty my mother had described meant. I have fulfilled the duty of reading the classics and because of it I am not only closer to my mother, but to my true sense of self and the ever-changing world around me. I am astounded that over forty years ago, my mother held the same books I've had the distinct pleasure of holding. She read with the hunger for knowledge, and today I read because I have something to say.

Great Books gave me something that can never be taken away. It propelled me to take whatever comes towards me in this life and make it into something that has true and undeniable value. It pushed me to pursue the relationships I could have never mended, risks I could have never taken, and perspectives I could have never accepted. I read because there is power in the expansion of our minds and thoughts. Perhaps the biggest gift we can give to ourselves is the gift of grasping a book with all our might and making the decision that today is the day that we will have something more to say.

"The aim of relation is relation's own being--where there is no
sharing there is no reality."
-Buber

2017

XCVI
SIBELL AKOYL

"It's a funny thing coming home.
Nothing changes. Everything looks the
same, feels the same, even smells the
same. You realize what's changed is
you."
–F. Scott Fitzgerald

The above quote is the best description that I have for the Great Books program. I am an unusual case for a Great Books student, yet I believe that this gives me a different perspective on the impact of Great Books on each student. Before my first semester of Great Books, I had been living in Turkey on my gap year, which was taken due to a brain injury that I had received in a cycling accident the year before. Great Books was my assimilation back to the intellectual culture of a university, and I was terrified to see whether I could keep up with my peers and my professor. That was a year ago.

Today, as a current student of Great books, I highly recommend the Great Books program to everyone; however, I do strongly believe that the impact of the Great Books program on the student is dependent on the professor teaching the course. Since I had Professor Gose, I find myself developing as an intellectual and a friendship with my professor. My class made me proud to be the most "annoying" person in a room from questioning people to "define their terms" to asking academics to provide textual evidence for their interpretations on Aristotle's Nicomachean Ethics. Though I have had my fair share of frustration with taking this course, I do believe that it is a necessary step in order to cultivate an environment of cultural understanding and the development of one's polyfocal conspectus..

If I was someone who cared about the social scene of Pepperdine, I would not have chosen a Great Books curriculum. To clarify, Great books does not make friends; it makes intellectuals. That is the beauty in it.

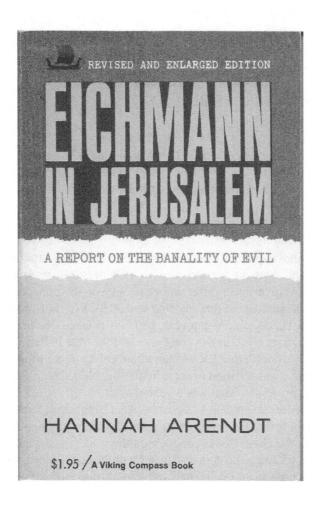

"Of course it is important to the political and social sciences that the essence of totalitarian government, and perhaps the nature of every bureaucracy, is to make functionaries and mere cogs in the administrative machinery out of men, and thus to dehumanize them."
-Arendt

XCVII
MACKENZIE (MACKIE) O'MALLEY

When I think of Great Books, I picture myself sitting in a discussion circle in the Cultural Arts Center (CAC) at Pepperdine University: my book, or books, by my side, fully annotated with the 10 Great Ideas and colorful post-it-notes spilling from its contents. For most people, this doesn't sound like the best way to spend two hours every Monday and Thursday of an already busy week - especially when my Great Books class the second semester was in the afternoon (interfering with prime nap-time). Yet, for me, spending time in this CAC classroom with Dr. Gose and ten of my now closest peers, all with strong personalities like myself, was a time that I looked forward to.

I still remember the day I received an email entitled "Explore the Great Books Colloquium for Your First-Year Seminar" from Pepperdine Seaver College encouraging me to take the Great Books Colloquium since I was "one of [the] top incoming academic students." In high school, I was always fond of reading and writing, as I took two advanced placement English courses over the course of my junior and senior years and loved them. Great Books promised to provide me with a powerful academic, intellectual, and collegial experience. And, by the end of the Colloquium, I would be transformed. Plus, it piqued my interest that, if the Colloquium were to be completed, it would count for five general education requirements (score!). Even though I wasn't a Regent Scholar, I felt that participating in Great Books would give me a competitive edge at not only Pepperdine but in life.

When I first met Dr. Gose, I was slightly intimidated, to say the least. He is a professor with impressive credentials, unbound confidence, and extremely well-spoken. Little did I know that Dr. Gose and his Great Books class would be one of the most formative experiences of my life thus far. Nowadays, my father praises me for my improved writing skills after only several months in the challenging environment fostered by Dr. Gose. My father is a hard person to impress, which just further attests to the excellent teaching style of Dr. Gose. He pushed me so far outside of my comfort zone that I would leave class most days with a headache. Despite the numerous times I promised myself to drop the course, there was always something that kept me coming back. Maybe it was the constant laughing, the freedom to speak my mind, or the comradery of such an eclectic group of individuals. Maybe it was the random tangents our class would go off on, or continually being told by Gose that our class was "unlike any other, he has had in all his years." In the end, I realized that I enjoyed Great Books for its countless memories. One my fondest memories of the class included us writing the Ten Commandments of our Great Books class:

1.

Define your terms

2.

Read "The Enchiridion"

3.

You're not sorry you haven't read Kant

4.

Always be early/on time (except twice)

5.

Always read

6.

Never voice your opinion

7.

Write an academic argument/address an academic problem

8.

Always participate/be attentive because you can't get lower than a B

9.

Have a love for iced animal cookies, Cuban cigars, and the Dodgers

10.

"Be good, mg."

Even though I have not yet finished the Colloquium, I would highly recommend this

class to anyone. If you take this class with Dr. Gose, you will not be disappointed. But rather, be

ready for countless stories about his wild years at Occidental College, the Dodgers, and his

affinity for iced animal cookies. Oh, and did you know he got his Ph.D. from a small college in

Northern California? (*cough* *cough* Stanford University).

My best advice when it comes to Dr. Gose is to be ready for anything.
And, if you are
like me - a bold, intelligent, yet occasionally vulgar mouthed young girl -
then you might just
end up working for him as one of his minions and writing an excerpt for
his next book. As
always, "be good, and don't take any wooden nickels."

"...one of the central moral questions of all time... (is)...the
nature and function of human judgment...What we have
demanded in these trials...is that human beings be capable of
telling right from wrong, even when all they have to guide them
is their own judgment, which, moreover, happens to be
completely at odds with what they must regard as the
unanimous opinion of all those around them. And this question
is all the more serious as we know that the few who were
'arrogant' enough to trust only their own judgment were by no
means identical with those persons who continued to abide by
old values, or who were guided by a religious belief...They had
to decide each instance as it arose..."
-Arendt

XCVIII
COURTNEY PEREIDA

I offer a very different perspective than the rest of the stories in this book. I have only taken two of the four classes in the series that is Great Books. However, in that short amount of time, I have learned a lot about what it means have substance to your essays and your approach to reading.

As a freshman, I remember getting an email about how Great Books was a program where in exchange for reading about eight books a semester, you would have less General Education classes to take. As someone who loves reading and wants to graduate early, I thought what an easy way to get ahead. However, I could not be more wrong.

I knew things would be different from the very first day of class. Gose had us sit around in a circle while he went through the lists we had made about our favorite books, movies, etc. This was a very intimidating process for my first college class. However, I soon learned that this was just how Gose likes to get to know his students and create a community where the people in my Great Books class have became some of my closest friends.

This was one of the lessons that I learned from Great Books. Our Great Books class became a community of friends who are always there for one another. We all knew that you could count on any one in our class to help each other get through any problems or issues that may come up one's first year in college. We also had the advantage of using the Great Books perspective to work through real life problems and find solutions.

This class is where I finally learned to take a chance on my ideas and thoughts. I have always felt like I needed to be a hundred percent certain on my ideas before speaking in class. However, Gose and my classmates taught me that you have to put your ideas out in the world and learn to talk through the ideas to see them through different perspectives. Great Books made me more confident to speak out about my ideas on books, even if I was wrong sometimes, on the chance that I was on to an idea and learn to use that to better understand the works studied in class.

Gose always made it known that he was not just a professor meant to teach us how to solve academic problems, but to teach us to use the polyfocal perspective and great ideas to work through contemporary issues. Great Books is the first class where I have seen how things learned in the classroom can be applied to life in general. In my first semester abroad, I have already had the opportunity to use ideas and perspectives taught in Great Books and believe these are skills I will continue to use in my everyday life.

"During these years in Stamps, I met and fell in love with William Shakespeare."
-Maya Angelou

XCIX
BRANDON ODDO

A Collection—or Conglomeration—of Thoughts, Reflections, and Remarks on Great Books and Associated Topics by Brandon Oddo (the "T, R, and R" Being by Brandon Oddo, not "G.B. and A.T.")

The First Of Many Words of Insight, Guidance, and Constructive Criticism from My Great Books Professor

"ERRRRRR"
-Gose

My Attempt to Decently Reflect in the Book You Are Reading About the Book You Are Reading Or: The Prince of Split Infinitives

I am what fellow classmates of mine—Sibel and Courtney—refer to as one of Gose's minions this semester (meaning I am to basically be working for/with him). Part of my job has been to dutifully help edit and format this book. Thus, I am the only one writing a story after having had read every other one to structurally surround it. That seems to unfortunately (unfatefully? unimportantly?) put me in a peculiar situation. You see, I'd like to uniquely find an idea—lowercase "i" idea—to significantly contribute to this book in a way that hasn't been done in previous stories. I just find it so difficult to ingeniously think of anything else. My fellow Great Books students have done well to virtually cover all I can think to even say. Even throwing in some quote from Ecclesiastes about "nothing new under the sun" wouldn't amount to particularly be anything special (I mean, someone's entire story in here is a "parody" of Ecclesiastes). We've all had the opportunity to incredibly go through similar yet distinctly unique experiences, viz. we're so differently-the-same. I got to repeatedly read

324

about the "B-ish" grades on essays, Kant and saying sorry, class dynamics, and et cetera, such and such, this and that, these and those. This far into the book, I would expect (that could be dangerous) you to probably get the idea. Furthermore, also, in addition, for you to not realize that Gose is a professor who has been a catalyst for the intellectual/spiritual/emotional/physical (i.e. free Chinese food one afternoon) growth, critical thinking, and engagement with ideas of countless (hyperbole) students would strongly suggest to me that you might need a closer reading of the text. I could from here continue to openly discuss how little I know, how lost I find myself amidst seas of ideas, how what I thought was my worldview is slowly evolving into dozens of dozens of different world views at conflict with each other in ways I could not even begin to yet reconcile, how I am considering whether I really believe any one thing or if I just believe many things dependent on the scenario, how I—blablabla—but that has already been done by people who have captured the thoughts well enough that I needn't even attempt (or won't out of laziness). What else is there to then write about?

*I'd like to also recognize my excessive breaking of a specific syntax rule as not accidental but very intentionally a stylistic choice.

An Excerpt from My "Expressive Outcomes" Essay in My First Semester of Great Books (2017) That Was A.) a Means of Reaching a Page Count and B.) For Fun in a Mostly Non-"Academic" Sense

<u>Company in the Colony of Leper</u>
On August 29, 2017, I received a strange invitation to go to the "leper's colony". I decided to go, partly due to intrigue and partly due to having nothing better to do. Well, to be quite honest, there were probably many "better" things I could have done, but none that were compelling enough to motivate me to undertake them at the moment. It also entirely depends on [my] definition of better. I may have to interrupt this story.

<u>Reason for Interrupting this Story</u>
[Omitted. Due to the age of these manuscripts, over one tenth of a decade at the time of this publication, large fragments have gone missing or been lost in the process of translation. Thankfully, the significance of this section in the story you are reading has been deemed negligible.]

Company in the Colony of Leper Continued

I had little idea of what to expect, and the email was certainly lacking in details. I arrived at the "leper's colony", the designated smoking area in the main parking lot on campus. Standing there was Dr. Gose with a cigar in his hand. Two others of his students in grades above mine arrived. They discussed a book titled Infinite Jest for quite some time. I, having had not read the book, was completely confused about their commentary. Furthermore, I, being an avid despiser of [spoilers], was also trying to tune out elements of the plot they described. What I did learn during that discussion was that I admired the manner in which those students spoke and the relationship they seemed to have with their professor. I also noticed that Dr. Gose did not smoke the cigar at all. He just held it in his hand. It was definitely very anticlimactic of him not to smoke after having had scheduled this meeting at the "leper's colony". Now, in hindsight, it is a great misfortune that Dr. Gose did not take advantage of that time to smoke his cigar. Little did he know that a couple of months after that day, Pepperdine would announce their decision to go completely smoke-free by the fall of 2018. This verdict would eventually become a recurrent topic in many Great Books I discussions, but that is another story for another time.

How Great Books Helps Round Out the Sphere (Back to 2018)

Great Books has, at least in the moment, left me feeling as if I know what others think far better than I know what I think. When my opinion is asked of me, there are plenty times when I respond—whether verbally or internally—well Plato/Aristotle/Solomon/Erasmus/Machiavelli/Milton/Locke/Kant/XY &Z thinks... What do I think? Am I to keep picking up the different lenses until I find ones that work out well? Are these various perspectives forming my beliefs, or are they just describing what I am already biasedly predisposed to think? I don't know.
I picked up a golfball yesterday. It's not a perfectly round sphere; there are instead dozens of hexagonal facets that, together, get closer to the shape of a perfect sphere. Maybe that's what these Great Ideas are. They each contribute a facet—a two-dimensional plane through which to view Truth. I paraphrase Gose paraphrasing Adler when I say something along the lines of how a Great Book is not necessarily Truth, but it is just a truth that works as a tool to understand Truth. As each of these truths are added together, their edges intersecting and cutting out the excess, a cohesive ball begins to take shape—it

approaches the form of the ball (Truth). This analogy is a fairly fresh one in my mind, but I already have a strong affinity for it. I would, after all, rather have a ball than be a square.

How round can I get the sphere?

The Heavy, Dense Head

My neck aches. My head has grown heavy. Each idea nestles itself in there, occupying its own nook/cranny. How can my mind be so crammed with thoughts: on the nature of relationships with family/friends, hundreds of anatomical terms, philosophers' viewpoints, childhood memories, movie scenes, introspection, et cetera? I find I not only continue to accumulate thoughts, but they seem to be getting denser (oh dear, how concentrated ideas from Great Books can be). I glance around at certain company at times, thinking to myself, "Oh how wonderfully light it must be to have a head so composed of air. How pleasant helium must feel in the mind. How delightful it must be to allow the brain breath and open space." Of course, these thoughts add to the claustrophobia and suffocation (and arrogance). I strain to hold it all up, yet I couldn't bring myself to empty my thoughts, to give them away, to stop gaining more. Indeed, there are the plenty of thoughts that squeeze out of the cracks—lost and leaving remnants at the most. There are others, though, that are more permanent: the cinder blocks that are the main contributors to the neck pain. I enjoy them. Something in me desires the weight. Maybe I recognize a value—whether that's in the thoughts themselves or the experience of carrying them or both. I want a heavy, dense head.

"One who breaks an unjust law must do so openly, lovingly, and with a willingness to accept the penalty."
-Martin Luther King, Jr.

C
CAROLINE SHARP

The Great Books tradition is a kaleidoscope –
From the earliest philosophies to modern fictions,
Coloured shards of ideas and insight
Affect each other, growing and developing our understanding.
No longer do we see what our biases project;
A turn of perspective and suddenly the light refracts anew to
Reflect and create what we couldn't see before.

With our eye to the glass, we see shapes of religion contort into
sharp edges
As they connect those from the church of old
To those who ring the bell of Enlightenment:
How the tint of Augustine's Christianity pales at the ink that drips
From Voltaire's pen!
Figures of Justice twist into something new when the points of
Rousseau press against the circles of Milton;
We turn the dial and comprehend
How one force influences another.

These images we see, these thoughts like gemstones,
Are excavated through these great works of history.
This beauty continually evolving with the addition
Of each new mind introduced to this tradition:
That is the wonder we see.
Imagine, the wisdom to be purchased by what one can discover in
this
Multicoloured, ever-changing, iridescent landscape
Infinitum

"Polyfocal conspectus is a pretentious name for what may appear at first glance to be a simple procedure. Its unit consists of alternation of mastery of a view-affording doctrine with thorough going involvement in bringing the doctrine to bear as a revealing lens on real, simulated, or reported instances of its subject matter...It is concerned with imparting to students a measure of inclination toward and competence for examining educational situations and problems in more than one set of terms...(It will) convey an ability (and its accompanying habit) to choose different instruments on different occasions, instruments appropriate to the practical situation they confront."
-Joseph Schwab

A POST NOTE ON GREAT BOOKS

I am confident my experience reading the 100 stories was not what Emerson had in mind when he opined, "he cannot be happy and strong until he too lives with nature in the present, above time." But it has to be at least a simile? I had tried not to read the stories as they came in. I wanted mostly to read the entirety at once. Try to take in the mosaic in one reading. I carved out most of a day to read them in one sitting. In a soft chair. Uninterrupted.

I started late morning. My first awareness of passing time was my slight puzzlement about why it was becoming more difficult to read. Why had the room become so much darker. My eyes adjusted and I didn't realize until I stopped that it had not suddenly become a cloudy day. Night had fallen. I was both befuddled and bemused. It had been like all 100 students were on campus in the same time frame. For at least a moment the past had become the present.

Kant warns us that our motives are not likely ever pure. Nothing is praiseworthy about undertaking this effort since I undertook this project for me, but hopefully also for the others who have shared this great conversation. I was most fortunate to have shared the dialectic with students such as those who tell the stories within these pages.

The Charge of the Great Books Brigade
With no apology to: Alfred, Lord Tennyson

I

Half a tome, half a tome,
Half a tome onward,
All in the valley of Death
Rode the one hundred.
"Forward, the Great Books Brigade!
Charge for the end of the thing!"
Into the valley of Death
Rode the one hundred.

II

"Forward, the Great Books Brigade!"
Was there a man (or woman) dismayed?
Not though the student knew
Someone had blundered.
Theirs was to make reply,
Theirs was to reason why,
Theirs was to do or die.
Into the valley of Death
Rode the one hundred.

III

Great Book to right of them,
Great Books to left of them,
Great Books well behind them
Volleyed and thundered;
Stormed at with shot and shell (metaphorically speaking),
Boldly they wrote and well,
Into the jaws of Death,
Into the mouth of hell
Rode the one hundred.

IV

Flashed all their sharpies bare,
Flashed as they turned in air
Checking their underlines there,
Charging another, presumably intentionally, ambiguous assignment,
while
All the world wondered.
Plunged in the mind's foggy-smoke
Write, write, go for broke;
Plato and Aristotle
Reeled from the arduous yoke
Shattered and sundered.
Then they wrote back,
The glorious one hundred.

V

Great Books to right of them,
Great Books to left of them,
Great Books behind them
Volleyed and thundered;
Stormed at with shot and shell,
While heroine and hero fell.
They that had fought so well
Came through the jaws of Death,
Back from the mouth of hell,
All that was left of them,
The mighty one hundred.

VI

When can their glory fade?
O the wild charge they made!
All the world wondered.
Honour the charge they made!
Honour the Great Books Brigade,
Noble one hundred!

APPENDIX/RESOURCES

"Pepperdine Great Books Program"
Jennifer Smodish

After a decade of defining the term "great books", Pepperdine can conclude that its Great Books Colloquium, a discussion-based series of courses, is a success.

The program was developed eleven years ago when four professors, Dr. Michael Gose, Dr. Victoria Myers, Dr. Royce Clark, and Dr. Norman Hughes, designed and implemented an experimental seminar program to expand the minds of eighty incoming Seaver College students.

Currently, the Great Books Colloquium, now taught by a rotating staff of ten faculty members, involves approximately 140 students, ranging from freshmen to seniors.

This success has a been a bit of a surprise to some of the Great Books founders. As Dr. Gose put it, "The colloquium has surpassed my own expectations. We originally thought of it only as an experiment; now it has become my primary teaching load."

One reason for the success of Great Books may be the Seaver College general education requirements that it fulfills. The colloquium fulfills students' education requirements in freshman seminar, English 101 and 102, and Religion 301. It also satisfies either the Economics 200 or Political Science 200 requirement. But if students drop out of the colloquium before successfully completing all of the four courses, they receive only elective credit for the courses.

From its beginnings, the Great Books Colloquium was to be a four-semester series of courses that would meet twice a week. During the four semesters, students would read a variety of classic works and then meet to discuss those "great books" in classes of about twenty students.

Each semester would parallel an area of the Seaver College liberal arts education, either social science, humanities, religion, or natural science. The original four professors represented each of those areas, Dr. Gose in social science, Dr. Myers in humanities/fine arts, Dr. Clark in religion , and Dr. Hughes in natural science.

These professors designed the Great Books Colloquium with five purposes in mind. According to a past Great Books Program Review, the program was intended to engage students in "close critical reading of selected influential works."

Following these readings, students would participate in discussions led by the professor. These discussions gave students the opportunity to learn to listen and to support their own views with textual evidence. Students would learn to be open to other views and ideas. The ultimate goal of the program was for the students to become independent of the professor, leading and participating in the discussions on their own.

Great Books also allowed students to gain knowledge and understanding of Western writings and heritage. The course series would influence and expand students' writing abilities.

Finally, the colloquium intended to develop a sense of community within the groups of participating students. Because students would be working together in such closely knit groups, they would gain a common interest in discovering the purpose and ideas behind their readings.

According to Gose, these original purposes are still being fulfilled in the Great Books Colloquium today. "I have found the great books approach to be an especially powerful paradigm for helping students to improve their critical and analytic thinking," Gose explains. "Our recent survey of graduates tends to confirm this thought. On a five point scale, alumni gave 'improved critical thinking' a 4.82 mark," he says.

However, there have been some changes to the four-semester program since its inception. For example, the program initially intended to have each Great Books section studying the same literature at the same time. But courses have not developed that way.

Today, each section studies literature that the individual professor has chosen from a common list of recommended Great Books reading. This list, which includes works by Homer, Plato, Shakespeare, Milton, was adapted from a Great Books program from St. John's College. But because professors are allowed to choose which works they want to study, there are differences in syllabi between classes.

Students have mixed feelings about these course differences. According to one freshman enrollee, "The work we read in Great Books is fascinating.

But why do the professors choose different works to read? It really divides us into our groups because we are not always able to talk about what we read with students in other sections."

But, as Great Books professor Dr. Darrel Colson explains, "The Great Books Colloquium Reading List is compiled of works that all draw on the same themes. Part of the individuality of the colloquium is the literature that each section reads and the way that the students choose to discuss it," he says.

Colson came to Seaver College to be a part of the Great Books program a year and a half ago. He was drawn to the program because "it offers tremendous opportunities for students to think and grow along with their professors," as he puts it.

Pepperdine's Great Books Colloquium has lived up to his expectations so far, he also mentions. According to Colson, who instructed a similar program at a school in Louisiana before coming here, "The students are diligent both in their outside homework and in their thoughts and discussion within the class."

Freshman English major Mylei Basich feels she has profited from enrolling in the program. "I chose it because I thought it would be interesting and challenging. It has definitely been challenging, probably ten times harder than any of my other courses," Basich said. "But it has been interesting, too, reading stuff writtern over a thousand years ago. The ideas, questions and problems they encounter we still face today."

Another difference that has become apparent over the time that the colloquium has existed is the amount of outside experience that comes with the class. Eleven years ago, in a Graphic article, Gose mentioned that in a typical week, students and teachers would "participate in a related activity, such as a concert, a film or a field trip and work on personal expressions of culture."

But this is not entirely the case today. Generally, due to time constraints on both students and the professors, outside activities are not always possible. In many cases, students think it is enough work simple to get the assigned reading done.

A lack of time does not mean that students would not like to see more outside trips and activities incorporated into the Great Books Colloquium.

One sophomore explains, "My freshman class of Great Books visited the J. Paul Getty museum last year to view the ancient Greek and Roman antiquities after we completed Homer's The Iliad. It was amazing to see those pieces come alive after reading the book." But he adds, "I have not been on a trip like that for Great Books since."

Despite these minor changes, though, Pepperdine's Great Books professors are quite satisfied with the curriculum. In fact, when asked if he would revamp the program in any way after eleven years, Gose responded with a hearty, "no."

He does mention that some changes are considered though. "We, the Great Books discussants, do consider minor changes from time to time. We can never really decide, for example, whether we think Augustine should be taught in Great Books I or II," Gose says.

However, Great Books professors have considered another change.

"We often think about adding more courses," says Gose. "My personal opinion is that most students are fine with the four courses, but that some would profit from a 'great books' or 'great works' emphasis within the existing Humanities Division."

Gose also adds, "I would also like to find an effective way of adding some art and music to the curriculum as 'texts' to be discussed."

Many students, even those not majoring in a humanities-related area, reflect the same satisfaction with the Great Books curriculum. Sophomore Jenette Kyte, an accounting major, explains, "I enjoy the reading we do for Great Books. The books are interesting. Discussing the works and writing papers on them increases my understanding of the literature. Plus, Great Books really is helping me to complete my general education requirements. "

But not every student shares this belief. Sophomore English major Cory Cochrane dropped the colloquium after her freshman year. "I already had the requirements for a couple of the courses Great Books fulfills," she explains. "It would have been redundant to take Great Books, but I do miss reading the books and discussing them."

After 11 years, the Great Books Colloquium is still strong at Seaver College and, with this student and faculty support, will continue to develop students' education and minds.

Adler's 103 Great Ideas
TRANSCENDENTAL
Beauty, Being, Good and Evil, Same and Other, Truth
ETHICS
Beauty, Being, Courage, Desire, Duty, Equality, Good and Evil, Happiness, Honor, Justice, Prudence, Same and Other, Sin, Temperance, Truth, Virtue and Vice, Wealth, Wisdom
POLITICS
Aristocracy, Citizen, Constitution, Custom and Convention, Democracy, Equality, Family, Government, Justice, Labor, Liberty, Monarchy, Oligarchy, Progress, Punishment, Revolution, Slavery, State, Tyranny and Despotism, War and Peace
LIBERAL ARTS
Definition, Dialectic, Hypothesis, Idea, Induction, Language, Logic, Mathematics, Reasoning, Rhetoric
METAPHYSICS
Angel, Being, Cause, Chance, Change, Equality, Eternity, Fate, Form, God, Infinity, Matter, Metaphysics, Nature, Necessity and Contingency, One and Many, Opposition, Principle, Quality, Quantity, Relation, Same and Other, Space, Time, Universal and Particular, World
ANTHROPOLOGY AND PSYCHOLOGY
Animal, Desire, Emotion, Experience, Habit, Immortality, Judgment, Knowledge, Life and Death, Love, Man, Memory and Imagination, Mind, Opinion, Pleasure and Pain, Prophecy, Sense, Sign and Symbol, Soul, Will

PHYSICS
Astronomy and Cosmology, Cause, Chance, Element, Infinity,
Mathematics, Matter, Mechanics, Nature, Quality, Quantity,
Relation, Space, Time, World
SUBJECTS
Art, Education, Evolution, History, Language, Law, Logic,
Mathematics, Mechanics, Medicine, Metaphysics, Philosophy,
Physics, Poetry, Religion, Rhetoric, Science, Theology

Gose's List of Ten Ideas/Ten Issues that come up repeatedly in class.
(Note that they have much in common with Adler's emphasis of the six ideas listed above and below.)

Knowledge/Epistemology/Truth How do we know what we know? Is truth absolute or relative? Objective or subjective?
Who are the heroes? What is the image of man?
Justice. Is the emphasis on "differentiation" or "equality"?
What is the relationship of the particular and the universal?
Good and evil
Human nature. Is it basically good or evil? What is the relationship of emotion and reason? Body and mind/soul?
God
Government/power/authority Conservative or liberal? Hierarchical or egalitarian?
Liberty/Freedom. What is the relationship of freedom and responsibility?
What are the assumptions about the relationship of the individual and society?

BILL MOYERS: **Six great ideas** -- truth, goodness, beauty, liberty, equality, justice. Why these six?

MORTIMER J. ADLER: One answer, Bill, is the Declaration of Independence -- the document that every American should understand -- and five of those six ideas are in the first four lines of the second paragraph. Let me recite those four lines:

"We hold these truths to be self-evident, that all men are created equal, that they're endowed by their Creator with certain unalienable rights. Among these are life, liberty and the pursuit of happiness" -- which is the ultimate good -- "That to secure these rights governments are instituted among men, deriving their just powers from the consent of the governed."

An abbreviated time line placing some of the Great Books and Great Ideas in an historical perspective. Works well with a "memory palace".

1. Homer (one of two with two dates, the first associated with a possible time for the Trojan War and the second with a time of the poem's creation) 1240 BC and 850 BC
2. Sophocles (Antigone) 441 BC
3. Plato (The Republic) 380 BC
4. Aristotle (Ethics) 350 BC
5. Cicero (de Legibus) 50 BC
6. Virgil (Aeneid) 19 BC
7. The Bible (1445 BC to 100 AD)
8. Augustine (City of God) 426 and Aquinas (Summa Theologica) 1274
9. Dante 1321
10. Luther (95 Theses) 1517
11. Machiavelli (The Prince) 1532
12. Shakespeare (Hamlet) 1600
13. Bacon (Novum Organum) 1620

14.Des Cartes (Meditations on First Philosophy) 1641

15.Milton (Paradise Lost) 1667

16.Locke (Two Treatises of Government) 1689

17.Voltaire (Candide) 1759

18.Rousseau (Emile) 1762

19.Smith (Wealth of Nations) 1776 and Kant (Metaphysics of Morals) 1797

20.Burke (On the French Revolution) 1790

21.Emerson (Self Reliance) 1841

22.Kierkegaard (Fear and Trembling) 1843

23.Marx (Communist Manifesto) 1848

24.Dickens (Hard Times) 1854

25.Mill (Utilitarianism) 1863

26.Dostoevsky (Notes from the Underground) 1864

27.Nietzsche (Genealogy of Morals) 1887

28.Buber (I and Thou) 1923

29.Sartre (Existentialism) 1946

30.Woolf (Room of One's Own) 1929 and De Beauvoir (Second Sex) 1949

How to Mark a Book
Mortimer Adler

You know you have to read "between the lines" to get the most out of anything. I want to persuade you to do something equally important in the course of your reading. I want to persuade you to "write between the lines." Unless you do, you are not likely to do the most efficient kind of reading.

I contend. quite bluntly, that marking up a book is not an act of mutilation but of love.

You shouldn't mark up a book which isn't yours. Librarians (or your friends) who lend you books expect you to keep them clean, and you should. If you decide that I am right about the usefulness of marking books, you will have to buy them. Most of the world's great books are available today, in reprint editions. There are two ways in which one can own a book. The first is the property right you establish by paving for it, just as you pay for clothes and furniture. But this act of purchase is only the prelude to possession. Full ownership comes only when you have made it a part of yourself, and the best way to make yourself a part of it is by writing in it. An illustration may make the point clear. You buy a beefsteak and transfer it from the butcher's icebox to your own. But you do not own the beefsteak in the most important sense until you consume it and get it into your bloodstream. I am arguing that books, too, must be absorbed in your bloodstream to do you any good.

Confusion about what it means to own a book leads people to a false reverence for paper, binding, and type - a respect for the physical thing - the craft of the printer rather than the genius of the author. They forget that it is possible for a man to acquire the idea, to possess the beauty, which a great book contains, without staking his claim by pasting his bookplate inside the cover. Having a fine library doesn't prove that its owner has a mind enriched by books; it proves nothing more than that he, his father, or his wife, was rich enough to buy them.

There are three kinds of book owners. The first has all the standard sets and best-sellers-unread, untouched. (This deluded individual owns wood pulp and ink, not books.) The second has a great many books-a few of them read through, most of them clipped into but all of them as clean and shiny as the day they were bought. (This person would probably like to make books his own, but is restrained by a false respect for their physical appearance.) The third has a few books or many-every one of them dog-eared and dilapidated, shaken and loosened by continual use, marked and scribbled in from front to back. (This man owns books.)

Is it false respect, you may ask, to preserve intact and unblemished a beautifully printed book, an elegantly bound edition? Of course not. I'd no more scribble all over a first edition of "Paradise Lost" than I'd give my baby a set of crayons and an original Rembrandt! I wouldn't mark up a painting or a statue. Its soul, so to speak, is inseparable from its body. And the beauty of a rare edition or of a richly manufactured volume is like that of a painting or a statue . .

Why is marking up a book indispensable to reading? First, it keeps you awake. (And I don't mean merely conscious; I mean wide awake.) In the second place, reading, if it is active, is thinking, and thinking tends to express itself in words, spoken or written. The marked book is usually the thought through book. Finally, writing helps you remember the thoughts you had, or the thoughts the author expressed. Let me develop these three points.

If reading is to accomplish anything more than passing time, it must be active. You can't let your eyes glide across the lines of a book and come up with an understanding of what you have read. Now an ordinary piece of light fiction . . . doesn't require the most active kind of reading. The books you read for pleasure can be read in a state of relaxation, and nothing is lost. But a great book, rich in ideas and beauty, a book that raises and tries to answer great fundamental questions, demands the most active reading of which you are capable . . .

But, you may ask, why is writing necessary? Well, the physical act of writing, with your own hand, brings words and sentences more sharply before your mind and preserves them better in your memory. To set down your reaction to important words and sentences you have read, and the questions they have raised in your mind, is to preserve those reactions and sharpen those questions.

Even if you wrote on a swatch pad, and threw the paper away when you had finished writing, your grasp of the book would be surer. But you don't have to throw the paper away. The margins (top and bottom, as well as side), the end-papers, the very space between the lines, are all available. They aren't sacred. And, best of all, your marks and notes become an integral part of the book and stay there forever. You can pick up the book the following week or year, and there are all your points of agreement, disagreement, doubt, and inquiry. It's like resuming an interrupted conversation with the advantage of being able to pick up where you left off.

And that is exactly what reading a book should be: a conversation between you and the author. Presumably he knows more abut the subject than you do; naturally, you'll have the proper humility as you approach him. But don't let anybody tell you that a reader is supposed to be solely on the receiving end. Understanding is a two-way operation; learning doesn't consist in being an empty receptacle. The learner has to question himself and question the teacher. He even has to argue with the teacher, once he understands what the teacher is saying. And marking a book is literally an expression of your differences, or agreements of opinion, with the author.

There are all kinds of devices for marking a book intelligently and fruitfully. Here's the way to do it:

1. Underlining: of major points, of important or forceful statements.

2. Vertical tines at the margin: to emphasize a statement already under lined.

3. Star, asterisk, or other doodad at the margin: to be used sparingly, to emphasize the ten or twenty most important statements in the book. (You may want to fold the bottom corner of each page on which you use such marks. It won't hurt the sturdy paper on which most modern books are printed, and you will be able to take the book off the shelf at any time and, by opening it at the folded-comer page, refresh your recollection of the book.)

4. Numbers in the margin: to indicate the sequence of points the author makes in developing a single argument.

5. Numbers of other pages in the margin: to indicate where else in the book the author made points relevant to the point marked; to tie up the ideas in a book, which, though they may be separated by many pages, belong together.

6. Circling of key words or phrases.

7. Writing in the margin, or at the top or bottom of the page, for the sake of: recording questions (and perhaps answers) which a passage raised in your mind: reducing a complicated discussion to a simple statement; recording the sequence of major points right through the books. I use the end-papers at the back of the book to make a personal index of the author's points in the order of their appearance.

The front end-papers are, to me, the most important. Some people reserve them for a fancy bookplate. I reserve them for fancy thinking. After I have finished reading the book and making my personal index on the back end papers, I turn to the front and try to outline the book, not page by page, or point by point (I've already done that at the back), but as an integrated structure, with a basic unity and an order of parts. This outline is, to me, the measure of my understanding of the work . . .

You may say that this business of marking books is going to slow up your reading. It probably will. That's one of the reasons for doing it. Most of us have been taken in by the notion that speed of reading is a measure of our intelligence. There is no such thing as the right speed for intelligent reading. Some things should be read quickly and effortlessly, and some should be read slowly and even laboriously. The sign of intelligence in reading is the ability to read different things differently according to their worth. In the case of good books, the point is not to see how many of them you can get through, but rather how many can get through you - how many you can make your own. A few friends are better than a thousand acquaintances. If this be your aim, as it should be, you will not be impatient if it takes more time and effort to read a great book than it does a newspaper.

You may have one final objection to marking books. You can't lend them to your friends because nobody else can read them without being distracted by your notes. Furthermore, you won't want to lend them because a marked copy is a kind of intellectual diary, and lending it is almost like giving your mind away.

If your friend wishes to read your "Plutarch's Lives," "Shakespeare," or "The Federalist Papers," tell him gently but firmly, to buy a copy. You will lend him your car or your coat - but your books are as much a part of you as your head or your heart.

How to Read a Difficult Book

A student wrote a professor:

Dear Dr. Adler,
To tell you the truth, I find the so-called great books very difficult to read. I am willing to take your word for it that they are great. But how am I to appreciate them if they are too hard for me to read? Can you give me some helpful hints on how to read a hard book?

and his response:

THE MOST IMPORTANT RULE about reading is one that I have told my great books seminars again and again: In reading a difficult book for the first time, read the book through without stopping. Pay attention to what you can understand, and don't be stopped by what you can't immediately grasp on this way. Read the book through undeterred by the paragraphs, footnotes, arguments, and references that escape you. If you stop at any of these stumbling blocks, if you let yourself get stalled, you are lost. In most cases you won't be able to puzzle the thing out by sticking to it. You have better chance of understanding it on a second reading, but that requires you to read the book through for the first time.

This is the most practical method I know to break the crust of a book, to get the feel and general sense of it, and to come to terms with its structure as quickly and as easily as possible. The longer you delay in getting some sense of the over-all plan of a book, the longer you are in understanding it. You simply must have some grasp of the whole before you can see the parts in their true perspective -- or often in any perspective at all.

Shakespeare was spoiled for generations of high-school students who were forced to go through Julius Caesar, Hamlet, or Macbeth scene by scene, to look up all the words that were new to them, and to study all the scholarly footnotes. As a result, they never actually read the play. Instead they were dragged through it, bit by bit, over a period of many weeks. By the time they got to the end of the play, they had surely forgotten the beginning. They should have been encouraged to read the play in one sitting. Only then would they have understood enough of it to make it possible for them to understand more.

What you understand by reading a book through to the end -- even if it is only fifty per cent or less will help you later in making the additional effort to go back to places you passed by on your first reading. Actually you will be proceeding like any traveler in unknown parts. Having been over the terrain once, you will be able to explore it again from points you could not have known about before. You will be less likely to mistake the side roads for the main highway. You won't be deceived by the shadows at high noon because you will remember how they looked at sunset. And the mental map you have fashioned will show better how the valleys and mountains are all part of one landscape.

There is nothing magical about a first quick reading. It cannot work wonders and should certainly never be thought of as a substitute for the careful reading that a good book deserves. But a first quick reading makes the careful study much easier.

This practice helps you to keep alert in going at a book. How many times have you daydreamed your way through pages and pages only to wake up with no idea of the ground you have been over? That can't help happening if you let yourself drift passively through a book. No one even understands much that way. You must have a way of getting a general thread to hold onto.

A good reader is active in his efforts to understand. Any book is a problem, a puzzle. The reader's attitude is that of a detective looking for clues to its basic ideas and alert for anything that will make them clearer. The rule about a first quick reading helps to sustain this attitude. If you follow it, you will be surprised how much time you will save, how much more you will grasp, and how much easier it will be.

Hutchins and Adler

Why Read Great Books?

Dear Dr. Adler,

Why should we read great books that deal with the problems
and concerns of bygone eras? Our social and political problems
are so urgent that they demand practically all the time and energy
we can devote to serious contemporary reading. Is there any
value, besides mere historical interest, in reading books written in
the simple obsolete cultures of former times?

People who question or even scorn the study of the past and
its works usually assume that the past is entirely different from
the present, and that hence we can learn nothing worthwhile from
the past. But it is not true that the past is entirely different from
the present. We can learn much of value from its similarity and its
difference.

A tremendous change in the conditions of human life and in
our knowledge and control of the natural world has taken place
since ancient times. The ancients had no prevision of our present-
day technical and social environment, and hence have no counsel
to offer us about the particular problems we confront. But,
although social and economic arrangements vary with time and
place, man remains man. We and the ancients share a common
human nature and hence certain common human experiences and
problems.

The poets bear witness that ancient man, too, saw the sun rise
and set, felt the wind on his cheek, was possessed by love and
desire, experienced ecstasy and elation as well as frustration and
disillusion, and knew good and evil. The ancient poets speak
across the centuries to us, sometimes more directly and vividly
than our contemporary writers. And the ancient prophets and
philosophers, in dealing with the basic problems of men living
together in society, still have some thing to say to us.

I have elsewhere pointed out that the ancients did not face our
problem of providing fulfillment for a large group of elderly
citizens. But the passages from Sophocles and Aristophanes show
that the ancients, too, were aware of the woes and disabilities of
old age. Also, the ancient view that elderly persons have highly
developed capacities for practical judgment and philosophical
meditation indicate possibilities that might not occur to us if we

just looked at the present-day picture.

No former age has faced the possibility that life on earth might be totally exterminated through atomic warfare. But past ages, too, knew war and the extermination and enslavement of whole peoples. Thinkers of the past meditated on the problems of war and peace and make suggestions that are worth listening to. Cicero and Locke show that the human way to settle disputes is by discussion and law, while Dante and Kant propose world government as the way to world peace.

Former ages did not experience particular forms of dictatorship that we have known in this century. But they had firsthand experience of absolute tyranny and the suppression of political liberty. Aristotle's treatise on politics includes a penetrating and systematic analysis of dictatorships, as well as a recommendation of measures to be taken to avoid the extremes of tyranny and anarchy.

We also learn from the past by considering the respects in which it differs from the present. We can discover where we are today and what we have become by knowing what the people of the past did and thought. And part of the past -- our personal past and that of the race -- always lives in us.

Exclusive preference for either the past or the present is a foolish and wasteful form of snobbishness and provinciality. We must seek what is most worthy in the works of both the past and the present. When we do that, we find that ancient poets, prophets, and philosophers are as much our contemporaries in the world of the mind as the most discerning of present-day writers. In fact, many of the ancient writings speak more directly to our experience and condition than the latest best sellers.

Columbia University Great Books

Homer, *Iliad*
Homer, *Odyssey*
Herodotus, *The Histories. Books I, III, VI, VII*
Aeschylus, *The Oresteia*
Sophocles, *Sophocles I: Antigone and Oedipus the King*
Thucydides, *Peloponnesian Wars. Books I-III, V-VIII*
Euripides, *Euripides V: The Bacchae*
Plato, *Republic, Parts 1, 3, 5, 7, 10, 11*
Plato, *The Trial and Death of Socrates: "The Apology"*
Plato, *Symposium*
Aristotle, *Ethics, Books I, II, X*
Aristotle, *Aristotle on Poetry and Style*
Virgil, *Aeneid of Virgil*
Bible, *King James Version: Genesis, Exodus, Job, Matthew, Romans, Galatians*
Augustine, *Confessions*
Von Strassburg, *Tristan*
Aquinas, *Introduction to Saint Thomas Aquinas*
Dante, *Inferno*
Erasmus and Luther, *Discourse on Free Will*
Machiavelli, *The Prince and The Discourses*
Rabelais, *Gargantua and Pantagruel, Books I and III*
Montaigne, *Essays: "To the Reader," "Of Idleness," "Of Cannibals," "Of Democritus and Heraclitus," "Of Repentance," "Of Experience"*
Shakespeare, *Henry IV, Part One*
Shakespeare, *King Lear*
Cervantes, *Don Quixote*
Hobbes, *Leviathan, Parts I and II*
Locke, *Two Trectises on Government: "Second Treatise on Government"*
Galileo, *The Discoveries and Opinions of Galileo: "Letter to the Grand Duchess Christina" and "Letter on Sunspots"*
Descartes, *Discourse on Method and Meditations on First Philosophy*
Rousseau, *The Social Contract*
Kant, *Foundations of the Metaphysics of Morals*
Hume, *Inquiry Concerning Principles of Morals*
Smith, *The Wealth of Nations*
Mill, *Selection of His Works: "On Liberty," "Utilitarianism," "On Bentham," "On Bentham's Principles"*
Dostoyevsky, *Crime and Punishment*
Marx, *The Marx-Engels Reader: Selections from "The German Ideology," "The Communist Manifesto," "Capital," "Two Theories of Socialism"*
Darwin, *Autobiography of Charles Darwin, Chapters 3-6 and summary*
Nietzsche, *On the Genealogy of Morals and Ecce Homo*

Freud, *An Outline of Psycho-Analysis*
Freud, *Three Essays on the Theory of Sexuality*
Freud, *Civilization and Its Discontents*

Pepperdine University List of Great Books
(circa 1986)

Great Books I:
Homer, *The Iliad*
Homer, *The Odyssey*
Sophocles, *Antigone*
Sophocles, *The Three Theban Plays*
Sophocles, *Medea*
Sophocles, *Medea and Other Plays*
Plato, *The Republic*
Aristotle, *The Nicomachaean Ethics*
Aristotle, *Introduction to Aristotle*
Virgil, *The Aeneid*
St. Augustine, *City of God*
The Holy Bible

Great Books II:
Dante, *The Inferno*
Dante, *The Purgatorio*
Dante, *The Paradiso*
Shakespeare, *Volpone*
Shakespeare, *Hamlet*
Shakespeare, *Richard III*
Shakespeare, *King Lear*
Shakespeare, *As You Like It*
Machiavelli, *The Prince*
Luther, *Martin Luther: Selections From His Writings*
Aquinas, *Summa Theologica*

Great Books III:
Milton, *Paradise Lost*
Descartes, *Meditations on First Philosophy*
Locke, *The Reasonableness of Christianity*
Rousseau, *The Creed of a Priest of Savoy*

Kant, *Religion within the Limits of Reason Alone*
Swift, *Gulliver's Travels*
Voltaire, *Candide*
Jane Austen, *Emma*
Jane Austen, *Pride and Prejudice*
Wordsworth, *The Prelude*
Goethe, *Faust*

Great Books IV:
Dostoyevsky, *Crime and Punishment*
Dostoyevsky, *The Brothers Karamazov*
Kierkegaard, *Fear and Trembling*
Tillich, *Dynamics of Faith*
Buber, *I and Thou*
WM James, *The Varieties of Religious Experience*
Darwin, *The Origin of Species*
Marx, *The Portable Karl Marx*
Freud, *The Interpretation of Dreams*

St. John's List

Freshman Year:
Homer: *Iliad, Odyssey*
Aeschylus: *Agamemnon, Choephoroe, Eumenides, Prometheus Bound*
Sophocles: *Oedipus Rex, Oedipus at Colonus, Antigone, Philoctetes*
Thucydides: *Peloponnesian War*
Euripides: *Hippolytus, Bacchae*
Herodotus: *Histories*
Aristophanes: *Clouds*
Plato: *Meno, Gorgias, Republic Apology, Crito, Phaedo, Symposium, Parmenides, Theaetetus, Sophist, Timaeus, Phaedrus*
Aristotle: *Poetics, Physics, Metaphysics, Nicomachean Ethics, On Generation and Corruption, The Politics, Parts of Animals, Generation of Animals*
Euclid: *Elements*
Lucretius: *On the Nature of Things*
Plutarch: *Pericles, Alcibiades, Lycurgus, Solon*
Nicomachus: *Arithmetic*
Lavoisier: *Elements of Chemistry*
Essays by: *Archimedes, Torricelli, Pascal, Fahrenheit, Black, Avogadro, Cannizzaro*

Harvey: *Motion of the Heart and Blood*

Sophomore Year:
The Bible
Aristotle: *De Anima, On Interpretation, Prior Analytics, Categories*
Apollonius: *Conics*
Virgil: *Aeneid*
Plutarch: *Lives*
Epictetus: *Discourses, Manuel*
Tacitus: *Annals*
Ptolemy: *Almagest*
Plotinus: *The Enneads*
Augustine: *Confessions*
Anselm: *Proslogium*
Aquinas: *Summa Theologica*
Dante: *Divine Comedy*
Chaucer: *Canterbury Tales*
Des Prez: *Mass*
Machiavelli: *The Prince, Discourses*
Copernicus: *On the Revolutions of the Spheres*
Luther: *The Freedom of a Christian, Secular Authority, Commentary on Galatians, Sincere Admonition*
Rabelais: *Gargantua*
Palestrina: *Missa Papae Marcelli*
Montaigne: *Essays*
Viete: *Introduction to the Analytical Art*
Bacon: *Novum Organum*
Shakespeare: *Richard II, Henry IV, The Tempest, As You Like It, Twelfth Night, Hamlet, Othello, Macbeth, King Lear, Sonnets*
Poems by: *Marvell, Donne, and other 16th and 17th century poets*
Descartes: *Rules for the Direction of the Mind, Geometry*
Pascal: *Generation of Conic Sections*
Bach: *St. Matthew Passion, Inventions*
Haydn: *Selected works*
Mozart: *Selected operas*
Beethoven: *Selected sonatas*
Schubert: *Selected songs*
Stravinsky: *Symphony of Psalms*
Webern: *Selected works*

Junior Year:
Cervantes: *Don Quixote*
Galileo: *Two New Sciences*
Hobbes: *Leviathan*

353

Descartes: *Doscourse on Method, Mediations, Rules for the Direction of the Mind, The World*
Milton: *Paradise Lost*
La Rochefoucauld: *Maximes*
La Fontaine: *Fables*
Pascal: *Pensees*
Huygens: *Treatise on Light, On the Movement of Bodies by Impact*
Spinoza: *Theologico-Political Treatise*
Locke: *Second Treatise of Government*
Racine: *Phedre*
Newton: *Principia Mathematica*
Kepler: *Epitome IV*
Leibnitz: *Monadology, Discourse on Metaphysics, What is Nature?, Essay on Dynamics*
Swift: *Gulliver's Travels*
Berkeley: *Principles of Himan Knowledge*
Hume: *Treatise of Human Nature*
Rousseau: *Social Contract, The Origin of Inequality*
Adam Smith: *Wealth of Nations*
Kant: *Critique of Pure Reason, Fundmental Principles of Metaphysics of Morals, Critique of Judgement*
Mozart: *Don Giovanni*
Jane Austen: *Pride and Prejudice, Emma*
Hamilton, Jay and Madison: *The Federalist*
Melville: *Billy Budd, Benito Cereno*
Fielding: *Tom Jones*
Tocqueville: *Democracy in America*
Essays by: *Young, Maxwell, S. Carnot, L. Carnot, Mayer, Kelvin, Taylor, Euler, D. Bernoulli*

Senior Year:
Articles of Confederation
"Declaration of Independence"
Constitution of the United States of America
Supreme Court Opinions
Moliere: *The Misanthrope, Tartuffe*
Goethe: *Faust*
Mendel: *Experiments in Plant Hybridization*
Darwin: *Origin of Species*
Hegel: *Phenomenology, Logic (from the Encyclopedia), Philosophy of History*
Lobackevsky: *Theory of Parallels*
Tocqueville: *Democracy in America*
Lincoln: *Selected Speeches*
Kiekegaard: *Philosophical Fragments, Fear and Trembling*

Wagner: *Tristan and Isolde*
Marx: *Communist Manifesto, Capital, Political and Economic Manuscripts of 1844*
Dostoevski: *Brothers Karamazov*
Tolstoy: *War and Peace*
Mark Twain: *The Adventures of Huckleberry Finn*
William James: *Psychology, Briefer Course*
Nietzsche: *Birth of Tragedy, Thus Spake Zarathustra, Beyone Good and Evil*
Freud: *General Introduction to Psychoanalysis*
Valery: *Selected Poems*
Kafka: *The Metamorphosis, The Penal Colony*
Einstein: *Selected Papers*
Millikan: *The Electron*
Conrad: *Heart of Darkness*
Joyce: *The Dead*
Poems by: *Yeats, T. S. Eliot, Wallace Stevens, Baudelaire, Rimbaud, and others*
Essays by: Faraday, Lorenz, J.J. Thomson, Whitehead, Minkowski, Rutherford, Einstein, Davisson, Bohr, Schrodinger, Maxwell, Bernard, Weismann, Millikan, de Broglie, Heisenberg, John Maynard Smith, Dreisch, Boveri, Mendel, Teilhard de Chardin

Great Books Colloquium X Commandments

I.   Thou shalt define thy terms.

II.   Thou shalt read all the text before discussing it.

III.   Thou shalt not judge the book (at least before understanding it on its own terms).

IV.   Thou shalt not be nice (kind and candid can work though).

V.   Thou shalt not say "I feel, or "I think" (understanding and stating what the author had to say is the place to start).

VI.   Thou shalt analyze (not judge or sermonize). (i.e. understand a work on its own terms first)

VII. Thou shalt appreciate thy 3000 years of history and not live hand to mouth (Goethe)/

VIII. Thou shalt not say "I'm sorry" when it is clearly a statement of "prudence" (Kant).

IX.   Thou shalt distinguish between liberty (responsible use of freedom) and license (irresponsible use).

X.   Thou shalt marketh thy tome, and take notes on thy notes.

XI.   Thou shalt not raise thy hand.

XII. Thou shalt assert, give evidence, provide commentary .

XIII. Like Baseball's Ted Williams, think you are the smartest person in the room.

XIV. A great, Great Books student does not accept the dictates of the question. Nor stops at a predesignated number.

Great Books Colloquium Objectives

The student will

1. Write critical essays which consistently: introduce, support, conclude; assert, give evidence, offer commentary; define key terms; answer the question; have a clear line of argument; and support a thesis with well-selected specifics.

2. Read not only for "comprehension" but for major themes and inter-relationships of ideas amongst all the readings. Improve skills at finding "proof texts," asking quality questions, identifying significant "problems".

3. Push thinking beyond "comprehension" and "application" to "analysis" in which course concepts are neither under nor over interpreted.

4. Appreciate everyone's rights to the classics, but eschew the tendency toward elitism.

5. Appreciate the special qualities of the maieutic seminar while recognizing its relationship to other conceptions of curriculum and its implications for social class.

6. Participate in the "great conversation" about the classic issues: good/evil; freedom/responsibility; ends/means; justice; happiness; destiny; life/death; nature of God; being/becoming; reason/emotion; body/mind; etc. and enjoy the camaraderie of this worthy pursuit.

7. Actively engage in the questioning/answering process of the socratic method.

8. Evidence an improved 'tolerance of ambiguity' and enjoy a 'polyfocal conspectus.'

9. Cultivate an "acquired taste" for the great books, recognizing that "even Homer nods," and that the joy of recognition may surpass the joy of surprise.

10. Install a bullet proof, shock resistant, waterproof, crap detector.

"But though this be a state of liberty, yet it is not a state of license[1]"
-John Locke, *Of Civil Government*
[1]abuse of liberty

For Jason Cavnar was it liberty or license to submit his story after our book was virtually wrapped? For Michael Gose was it liberty or license in putting Jason's story, not only after the other 100 stories, but also after everything else?

GREAT BOOKS: 101 YEARS, 101 STORIES

CI
JASON CAVNAR

Great Books was a catalytic experience for me.

Of course, there are the simple and fond memories I have. I will always cherish late night conversations with new friends from class talking about what we loved and hated about the books we were reading. The banter in the classroom. Moments when someone would express something that would shift a whole conversation in an exciting direction.

An athlete in college at the time, I distinctly remember my efforts to get through the books as a more exhausting physical challenge than the grueling practices and training sessions! I fought my way through a two year effort to strike a balance between an environment in which I could focus on reading and one in which I could stay awake. Library reading nooks inevitably gave way to fighting off and eventually succumbing to long unplanned naps and subsequent late night cramming. Attempts to read in the lively cafeteria so as to stay awake inevitable led to being interrupted by friends (some welcome) who clearly had no empathy for the amount of reading we were up to. I also credit my lifelong coffee affair (addiction) to Great Books.

Beyond the mundane, Great Books taught me how to truly think. It was the first time I felt like I could see things "from above". How the dialectic of history and current events layer up to a higher set of great ideas. How these ideas are infused into culture that lead to movements that shape history. I found both frameworks really powerful.

Great Books also expanded my understanding of how to express my thinking. The discourse in the classroom and the writing of exams challenged me to work with text as subtext in support of examining higher points. To this day, I am grateful for that.

CII
TO BE CONTINUED

13120422R00203

Made in the
USA
Monee, IL